The Most Instructive
Games of Chess Ever Played:
62 Masterpieces of
Chess Strategy

The Most Instructive Games of Chess Ever Played: 62 Masterpieces of Chess Strategy

IRVING CHERNEV

DOVER PUBLICATIONS, INC.
NEW YORK

Published in Canada by General Publishing Company, Ltd., 30
Lesmill Road, Don Mills, Toronto, Ontario.
Published in the United Kingdom by Constable and Company, Ltd.,
3 The Lanchesters, 162–164 Fulham Palace Road, London W6 9ER.

This Dover edition, first published in 1992, is an unabridged and
unaltered republication of the work first published by Simon &
Schuster, New York, in 1965.

Manufactured in the United States of America
Dover Publications, Inc., 31 East 2nd Street, Mineola, N.Y. 11501

Library of Congress Cataloging-in-Publication Data

Chernev, Irving, 1900–1981
    The most instructive games of chess ever played : 62 masterpieces
of chess strategy / Irving Chernev.
        p.   cm.
    Originally published: New York : Simon and Schuster, 1965.
    Includes index.
    ISBN 0-486-27302-4
    1. Chess—Collections of games. I. Title.
GV1452.C49 1992
794.1′5—dc20   92-25679
                                                          CIP

To My Dear Wife

Chess, like love, is infectious at any age—Flohr

Table of Contents

Introduction

Chess masters play to win. In doing so they would like to create master-pieces. They would like to conjure up brilliant combinations that leave everybody gasping with wonder and admiration—but first and foremost, they play to win, and win quickly and easily.

The chess master knows which positions are favorable, and tries to bring these positions about. He knows that his pieces must be placed where they exert the utmost influence, and where they prevent the opponent's pieces from moving about freely. He knows that Rooks must seize the open files, with a view to gaining control of the seventh rank. He knows that Bishops must either command long diagonals, or else pin down and paralyze the opponent's Knights. He knows the squares on which his Knights must be posted to get a powerful grip on the position. He realizes the essential truth in Tartakover's epigram, "Seize the outpost K5 with your Knight, and you can go to sleep. Checkmate will come by itself." The chess master knows how to obtain a slight advantage, and then exploit it to the fullest. In short, he knows the strategy of winning.

The games in this book are to my mind the most instructive examples in the whole literature of the game, of position play—the strategy of winning chess. Who, for example, will doubt the tremendous power exerted by a Rook posted on the seventh rank, after seeing Capablanca's delightfully clear-cut demonstration in Game No. 1 against Tartakover? And who will not learn a great deal about the art of handling Rook and Pawn endings (the most important endings in chess) after playing through Tarrasch's game against Thorold? And can there be a more convincing illustration of the paralyzing effect on the opponent's position that comes from control of the black squares, than in the Bernstein–Mieses game? Or are there more enlightening and entertaining Bishop and Pawn endings than feature the two games between Blackburne and Weiss?

These games, as well as all the others, are masterly demonstrations of the basic strategy of winning. So much so that I thought an appropriate title for a book of these games should be **The Most Instructive Games of Chess Ever Played.**

But I might just as well have called this collection **The Most Beautiful Games of Chess Ever Played.**

Paris 1965
New York 1965   —Irving Chernev

Rook on the Seventh Rank

J. R. Capablanca · S. Tartakover

New York 1924, DUTCH DEFENSE

José Raoul Capablanca

Capablanca's play in the game that follows provides us with a magic formula for conducting Rook and Pawn endings: seize the seventh rank with your Rook, and advance your King to the sixth!

Capablanca gives up a couple of valuable Pawns to get his King and Rook onto the key squares. Once there, they keep the adverse King busy warding off threats of mate, and leave him no time to defend his Pawns. Four of these pawns fall victims in half-a-dozen moves, after which resistance is of course hopeless.

Capa's clear-cut, methodical play is so easy to understand that the whole ending is a marvellous piece of instruction, and a thing of beauty as well.

1 P—Q4	P—KB4
2 Kt—KB3	P—K3
3 P—B4	Kt—KB3
4 B—Kt5	B—K2
5 Kt—B3	O—O
6 P—K3	P—QKt3
7 B—Q3	B—Kt2
8 O—O	Q—K1

Black evidently intends to attack on the King side by *9* ... Q—R4 and *10* ... Kt—Kt5—customary strategy in the Dutch Defense.

9 Q—K2!

This move makes Tartakover change his mind, since *9* ... Q—R4 is met by *10* P—K4, and White's center is imposing.

9 ...	Kt—K5
10 B × B	Kt × Kt
11 P × Kt	Q × B

The exchanges have left White with a doubled Bishop Pawn. In compensation for this weakness, the Knight file has been opened and is available to his Rooks.

12 P—QR4!

A clever preventive move! It stops an unwelcome intrusion by *12* ... Q—R6, and also prepares to meet *12* ... Kt—B3 with *13* KR—Kt1, and if then *13* ... Kt—R4 *14* P—B5 undoubles the Pawns by force, since the continuation *14* ... P × P *15* R—Kt5 is to White's advantage.

12 ...	B × Kt
13 Q × B	Kt—B3
14 KR—Kt1	QR—K1
15 Q—R3	

Another preventive move. Black cannot free himself by *15* ... P—K4 as *16* B × P would follow. The Queen's move also makes it possible for White to play *16* P—B4, giving him a grip on the square K5.

15 ...	R—B3
16 P—B4!	Kt—R4
17 Q—B3	

The Queen returns to B3, to dominate the long diagonal.

17 ...	P—Q3
18 R—K1	

Having done its work on the Knight file, the Rook moves to the center, to support a break by *19* P—K4.

18 ...	Q—Q2

19 P—K4!

White opens up the position to give his pieces more scope.

19 ...	P × P
20 Q × P	P—Kt3
21 P—Kt3	

White stabilizes his position with this move and the next, before starting an attack on the King-side by P—R4 and P—R5.

21 ...	K—B1
22 K—Kt2	R—B2
23 P—R4	P—Q4

This leads to an exchange of Queens, leaving White with a tiny advantage—but all Capablanca needs is a microscopic advantage!

24 P × P	P × P
25 Q × Rch!	Q × Q
26 R × Qch	K × R
27 P—R5!	

All according to plan! If Black plays 27 ... P × P, there follows 28 R—R1, K—B1 29 R × P, and White wins the Rook Pawn or the Queen Pawn.

27 ...	R—B3
28 P × P	P × P
29 R—R1	

Good players always seem to hold the high cards. Capablanca's Rook controls an open file and will seize the seventh rank next move. Should Tartakover's Rook become ambitious and try to counter-attack by 29 ... R—B3, the reply 30 B—Kt5 would come like a flash and pin the unfortunate piece.

29 ...	K—B1
30 R—R7	

Rook to the seventh—the magic move in Rook and Pawn endings. What is the secret in the strength of this move? It is this:

(*a*) The Rook is in perfect position to attack any Pawns that have not yet moved—those still standing on the second rank.

(*b*) The Rook is prepared to attack any Pawns that have moved, by getting behind them *without loss of time.* The Pawns would be under constant threat of capture, no matter how many squares they advanced on the file.

(*c*) The Rook's domination of the seventh rank confines the opposing King to the last rank, preventing him from taking any part in the fighting.

30 ...	R—B3
31 P—Kt4	Kt—B5

The Knight hastens to get into active play. Black naturally avoids 31 ... R × P, as the reply 32 B × P allows his opponent to have two connected passed Pawns.

32 P—Kt5

Threatens to win by 33 R—R6, K—Kt2 34 P—B5.

32 ...	Kt—K6ch
33 K—B3	Kt—B4
34 B × Kt	P × B

This is the position, with White to move:

Now comes a brilliant continuation, which Capablanca must have planned many moves before. In a simplified ending where Pawns are worth their weight in gold, he gives away two Pawns! Moreover he lets Black capture them with check!

35 K—Kt3!

The King is headed for B6, a square from which he can assist the Rook in mating threats, and also help the passed Pawn take those last three steps.

| 35 ... | R × Pch |
| 36 K—R4 | R—B6 |

Instead of this, if Black tries to exchange Rooks, this follows: *36 ... R—B8 37 K—R5, R—R8ch 38 K—Kt6, R × R 39 K × R, P—B4 40 P—Kt6,* and the Pawn crashes through.

| 37 P—Kt6 | R × Pch |
| 38 K—Kt5 | R—K5 |

Capturing the Queen Pawn would be fatal: *38 ... R × P 39 K—B6, K—Kt1* (on *39 ... K—K1 40 R—R8ch, K—Q2 41 P—Kt7,* and Black must give up his Rook for the Pawn) *40 R—Q7,* and White mates next move.

39 K—B6!

Excellent! The King is beautifully placed to support the passed Pawn, and incidentally to frighten Black with threats of mate.

Notice that White disdained capturing Black's Pawn. Now it acts as a buffer against annoying checks by the Rook.

39 ...	K—Kt1
40 R—Kt7ch	K—R1
41 R × P	R—K1
42 K × P	R—K5
43 K—B6	R—B5ch
44 K—K5	

White goes after the Queen-side Pawns. Contrasting the activity of the two Kings, White is practically a piece ahead!

| 44 ... | R—Kt5 |
| 45 P—Kt7ch | K—Kt1 |

Black doesn't dare take the Pawn. If *45 ... R × P 46 R × R, K × R 47 K × P, K—B2 48 K—Q6, K—K1 49 K—B7, K—K2 50 P—Q5,* and the Pawn cannot be stopped.

46 R × P	R—Kt8
47 K × P	R—QB8
48 K—Q6	R—B7
49 P—Q5	R—B8
50 R—QB7	R—QR8
51 K—B6	R × P
52 P—Q6	Resigns

The continuation (for anyone still skeptical) would be *52 ... R—Q5 53 P—Q7, R—B5ch* (if *53 ... K × P 54 P—Q8 (Q) dis ch wins) 54 K—Kt7, R—Q5 55 K—B8,* and the Pawn becomes a Queen next move.

"No one has ever played these endgames with such elegant ease as Capablanca," says Réti.

The King Is a Strong Piece

M. Tal · G. Lissitzin

Leningrad 1956, SICILIAN DEFENSE

Mikhail Tal

To those of us who worry about the safety of the King, Tal's play in this game is a joy and a revelation. Tal realizes that the power of the King increases as the game progresses and as the pieces come flying off the board. By the time the ending has been reached, the King is truly a formidable fighting piece.

Watch Tal's King stroll nonchalantly into the heart of the enemy camp, gather up a couple of Pawns, and then prepare to escort one of his own Pawns to the Queening square. It is a treat to watch, an absorbing lesson in endgame procedure.

1 P—K4	P—QB4
2 Kt—KB3	P—Q3
3 P—Q4	P×P
4 Kt×P	Kt—KB3
5 Kt—QB3	P—KKt3
6 P—B4	Kt—B3

Black avoids a trap with this move, indicating that one must not play mechanically even at this early stage. If *6* ... B—Kt2 (the natural follow-up to *5* ... P—KKt3) the continuation is *7* P—K5, P×P *8* P×P, Kt—Kt5 *9* B—Kt5ch, K—B1 (on *9* ... B—Q2 or *9* ... Kt—Q2 *10* Q×Kt wins a piece) *10* Kt—K6ch, and White wins the Queen.

7 Kt×Kt	P×Kt
8 P—K5	Kt—Q2
9 P×P	P×P
10 B—K3	

Other lines of play look more aggressive, but lead to no more than equality. For example: *10* Q—Q4, Kt—B3 *11* B—K3, B—K2 *12* B—K2, O—O *13* O—O, P—B4. Or *10* Q—K2ch, B—K2 *11* B—K3, O—O.

10 ...	B—K2
11 Q—B3	P—Q4
12 O—O—O	B—B3
13 B—Q4	

Proper development does not concern itself merely with placing the pieces where they are effective for attack. It is equally important to interfere with the range of influence of the opponent's pieces. You must dispute control, as Tal does here, of every file, rank and diagonal.

13 ...	O—O
14 P—KR4	

Indicating his intention of opening up the Rook file by *15* P—R5.

14 ...	R—Kt1

Black seizes an open file. Capturing the Rook Pawn instead would be dangerous, as after *14* ... B×P *15* Q—R3, P—Kt4 *16* P—KKt3, Kt—B3 *17* P—B5, and the Bishop is trapped.

15 Q—B2	

Guards against the threat *15* ... B×B *16* R×B, Q—Kt3, and Black attacks the Rook as well as the Queen Knight Pawn.

15 ...	R—Kt5
16 B×B	

Tal is not tempted by the offer of a Pawn. It is easy to yield and then fall into something like this: *16* B×P, Q—R4 *17* B—K3, R×KtP! *18* K×R, B×Ktch *19* K—B1, Q—R6ch *20* K—Kt1, Q—Kt7 mate.

16 ...	Kt×B
17 P—R3	

Here too Tal resists temptation. If *17* Q×P, Q—Q3 *18* P—KKt3, R×KtP *19* K×R, Q—Kt5ch *20* K—B1, Q×Kt, and Black has a strong attack, one threat for example being *21* ... Q—R8ch *22* K—Q2, Kt—K5ch *23* K—K1, Q—B6ch *24* K—K2, B—Kt5 mate.

17 ...	Q—Kt3
18 Q×Q	R×Q

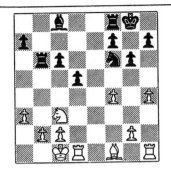

19 Kt—R4!

A powerful move, even though the Knight moves to the side of the board. Tal has two objects in mind: To fix Black's center Pawns so that they may not advance, and to dominate his opponent's weakened black squares.

19 ...	R—Kt2
20 B—Q3	Kt—R4
21 KR—B1	R—K2
22 P—B5!	

A fine positional sacrifice. At the cost of a Pawn Tal disrupts his opponent's Pawn structure on the King side. In addition to this, the acceptance of the sacrifice leaves Black's Bishop hemmed in by Pawns occupying white squares.

22 ...   P×P

Black is hypnotized into taking the Pawn, and that leads to his ruin.

23 R(B1)—K1!

Another fine positional move. Tal is a Pawn behind, but does not hesitate to exchange pieces. The point is that he must dispute control of the open King file, or else Black will double Rooks and gain complete possession of it.

| *23* ... | R(B1)—K1 |
| *24* R×R | R×R |

This is the position with Tal to play:

25 K—Q2!

The beginning of a remarkable tour. The King is headed for the Queen side where it will terrorize all the Pawns in sight.

| *25* ... | Kt—Kt6 |
| *26* K—B3 | P—B5 |

Clears the way for the Bishop to come into the game.

27 K—Q4

The King continues his journey along the black squares.

27 ...   B—B4

Not only does Black want to exchange Bishops (being a Pawn ahead) but he has this idea in mind: *28* ... B×B *29* K×B, R—K6ch *30*

K—Q4, R—K7, and his Rook controls the seventh rank.

| 28 R—Q2 | R—K3 |

Obviously, to go after the Rook Pawn.

29 Kt—B5	R—R3
30 K—K5!	B×B
31 P×B	R×P
32 K—Q6	

The King goes merrily on his way.

| 32 ... | R—R3ch |
| 33 K—B7 | |

Despite the fact that he is two Pawns down, White's chances are better in the ending. His King is so wonderfully active, and Black's so woefully passive, that he is in effect a King ahead!

| 33 ... | Kt—B4 |
| 34 K—Kt7 | Kt—Q5 |

The Knight guards the Queen Bishop Pawn, freeing the Rook for active duty. Black threatens now 35 ... R—R7 followed by 36 ... P—B6, winning another Pawn.

35 R—KB2	P—R4
36 R×P	Kt—K3
37 R—Kt4ch	K—B1

Instead of this, if Black tried to exchange Rooks (being a Pawn ahead), this would teach him the error of his ways: 37 ... R—Kt3 38 R×Rch, RP×R 39 Kt×Kt, P×Kt 40 K×P, K—B2 41 P—QKt4, and White will have a new Queen in a few moves.

| 38 K×P! |

The King fears nothing—not even discovered check.

38 ...	Kt×Ktch
39 K×Kt	R—K3
40 K×P	

(One must resolutely avoid the impulse to say, "The Pawns fall like ripe apples.")

40 ...	R—QKt3
41 P—Kt4	P×P
42 P×P	K—K2
43 K—B5	R—KB3
44 R—Q4	

This cuts off Black's King from the Queen side, and the possibility of blocking the passed Pawn.

| 44 ... | R—B4ch |
| 45 K—Kt6 | |

Better than 45 R—Q5 when 45 ... R—B5 (threatening 46 ... R—Kt5) allows Black counter-play.

45 ...	R—B3ch
46 K—B7	R—B4
47 R—K4ch	

Drives the King still farther away from the Queen side.

47 ...	K—B3
48 K—B6	R—B7
49 P—Kt4	P—R4

Black sacrifices one Pawn to make a passed Pawn of the other. There was nothing in 49 ... R—B7ch, as after the reply 50 R—B4, Black has simply wasted a move.

50	P×P	K—Kt4
51	P—Kt5	P—B4
52	R—QKt4	P—B5
53	P—Kt6	P—B6
54	P—Kt7	Resigns

The finish, had Lissitzin played on, would have been *54* ... R—B7ch *55* K—Q5, P—B7 *56* P—Kt8(Q), P—B8(Q) *57* Q—Kt3ch, K—B3 (or *57* ... K—B4 *58* Q—Kt6 mate) *58* Q—Kt6ch, K—K2 *59* R—Kt7ch and quick mate.

Knight Outpost at Q5

I. Boleslavsky · G. Lissitzin

Moscow 1956, SICILIAN DEFENSE

Boleslavsky knows that a good grip on the center almost always guarantees the success of a King-side attack. He therefore plans to anchor a Knight at Q5—so firmly that it can *never* be driven away. To accomplish this he must do away with two enemy pieces that bear down on that square, a Bishop and a Knight. He lures the Bishop off by a gift of a Pawn, and disposes of the Knight by pinning it and forcing its exchange.

Once Boleslavsky's Knight reaches the magic square Q5, combinations appear out of the air as a reward, and the King-side attack seems to play itself.

1 P—K4	P—QB4
2 Kt—KB3	P—Q3
3 P—Q4	P×P
4 Kt×P	Kt—KB3
5 Kt—QB3	P—KKt3
6 B—K3	B—Kt2
7 P—B3	

This move does many things: it strengthens the center, prevents an attack on the Bishop (and its subsequent exchange) by 7 ... Kt—Kt5, and prepares for a later Pawn storm by P—KKt4 and P—KR4.

7 ...	O—O
8 Q—Q2	Kt—B3
9 O—O—O	Kt×Kt

An attempt by Black to free himself by 9 ... P—Q4 could lead to this interesting combination: *10* Kt×Kt, P×Kt *11* P×P, P×P *12* Kt×P, Kt×Kt *13* Q×Kt, Q—B2 *14* Q×R, B—B4 (threatens mate) *15* Q×Rch, K×Q *16* R—Q2, and White has the better prospects.

10 B×Kt	Q—R4
11 K—Kt1	

Threatens *12* Kt—Q5, Q—Q1 (if *12* ... Q×Q *13* Kt×Pch wins a Pawn) *13* Kt×Ktch, and White will win the Queen Pawn.

11 ...	P—K4
12 B—K3	B—K3
13 P—QR3	KR—Q1

Prepares for an eventual ... P—Q4, which would free his game.

14 Kt—Kt5

This powerful move interferes with Black's plans. If Black replies to it with *14* ... Q×Q, then *15* R×Q follows and White threatens *16* R×P as well as *16* Kt—B7, QR—B1 *18* Kt×B, and he has the advantage of two Bishops against Knight and Bishop.

14 ...	Q—R5

The Queen Pawn is attacked three times, but if White took it this would be the consequence: *15* Kt×QP, Kt—K1 *16* B—B5, Kt×Kt *17* B×Kt, B—B1 *18* Q—Kt4, R×B! *19* R×R (on *19* Q×Q, R×R is checkmate) Q×Q *20* P×Q, B×R, and Black has won a piece.

This is the position, with White to play:

At this point Boleslavsky has two objects in mind:

(1) Prevent Black from freeing himself by ... P—Q4.

(2) Establish his Knight firmly at the outpost station Q5.

To bring the latter about it is necessary to rid the board of the two black pieces that guard the square Q5, the Bishop at K3 and the Knight.

> *15* P—QB4!

A brilliant sacrifice which must be accepted. Refusing the Pawn means that Black could never free himself by ... P—Q4. It would also enable White to play *16* Kt—B3 next move (attacking the Queen) and thus gain time for *17* Kt—Q5, establishing a strongly-supported outpost.

15 ...	B×P
16 Kt—B3	Q—Kt6
17 B×B	Q×B

One black piece has been disposed of. Now to get rid of the other!

> *18* B—Kt5!

White pins the Knight to keep it from running away. Now he is assured of being able to remove it from the board.

18 ...	Q—K3
19 B×Kt	Q×B
20 Kt—Q5	

Now we shall see whether Boleslavsky's imaginative strategy is justified. He has given up a solid, valuable Pawn for something that is intangible—the unassailable position of his Knight. The Knight, it is true, dominates the board and cannot be driven off, but is that worth a Pawn?

| *20* ... | Q—R5 |

Black tries to prevent the advance of the adverse King-side Pawns. He intends to meet *21* P—KKt3 with *21* ... Q—R6, while the reply to *21* P—R3 would be *21* ... B—R3 followed by *22* ... B—B5.

| *21* Q—K2 | B—B1 |
| *22* Q—B1! | |

A subtle preparatory move. If at once *22* P—KKt3, Q—R6 blockades the Rook Pawn.

| *22* ... | QR—B1 |

This is how things look:

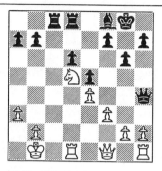

23 P—KKt3

The Pawns begin their advance to break up Black's King-side.

23 ...	Q—Kt4
24 P—KR4	Q—R3

If *24 ... Q×KtP 25 R—Q2* leaves Black curiously helpless against the threat of *26 R—Kt2* winning the Queen.

25 P—KKt4

Now White intends *26 P—Kt5, Q—Kt2* (if *26 ... Q—R4 27 Kt—B6ch wins the Queen) 27 Kt—B6ch, K—R1 28 P—R5* (threatens to win the Queen by *29 P—R6) P×P 29 R×RP*, and the attack on the Rook Pawn will force Black to give up his Queen.

25 ...	P—KKt4
26 P×P	Q×P
27 R—R5	Q—Kt3
28 P—Kt5!	

Threatens annihilation by *29 Kt—B6ch* followed by *30 R×Pch*.

Black has no defense in *28 ... Q×R*, as *29 Kt—B6ch* wins the Queen, nor in *28 ... B—Kt2* when *29 Kt—K7ch* does likewise.

28 ...	P—KR3
29 R×P!	Q×KtP

Here too *29 ... B×R* is penalized by *30 Kt—K7ch* and loss of the Queen.

30 R—R5!   Resigns

On *30 ... Q—Kt3*, the continuation is *31 Q—R1* (threatens *32 R—Kt1* winning the Queen) Q—K3 *32 R—R8ch, K—Kt2 33 Q—R7* mate.

The King-side Pawns did an amazing job of opening up files for the benefit of the heavy pieces.

Aggressive Rook in the Ending

S. Tarrasch · E. Thorold

Manchester 1890, FRENCH DEFENSE

Tarrasch plays the following game as though he were giving a good friend a lesson in the art of winning an ending. "In a Rook and Pawn ending," Tarrasch used to say, "the Rook must be used aggressively. It must either attack enemy Pawns, or give active support to the advance of one its own Pawns to the Queening square."

Here, with the help of an active Rook that keeps the opponent under unremitting pressure, Tarrasch's King and passed Pawn march methodically up the chessboard. As they move forward step by step, the opponent's pieces are driven further and further back until they reach the very edge of the board. There, they can put up little resistance to the inexorable advance of the passed Pawn.

The classic simplicity of Tarrasch's technique in the conduct of this ending is so impressive as to make it in my opinion:

The most Instructive Rook and Pawn Ending Ever Played.

1 P—K4	P—K3
2 P—Q4	P—Q4
3 Kt—Q2	

Tarrasch prefers this to the usual *3* Kt—QB3, since the Knight is developed without blocking the Queen Bishop Pawn.

3 ...	P—QB4
4 KP×P	Q×P

This is better than *4* ... BP×P *5* B—Kt5ch, B—Q2 *6* P×P, B×B *7* Q—R5, (threatens *8* Q×P mate) Q—K2 *8* Q×Bch, and White enjoys a pleasant initiative.

5 KKt—B3

A temporary Pawn sacrifice, to gain time for quick development of the pieces.

5 ...	P×P
6 B—B4	Q—KR4
7 O—O	Kt—QB3

It would be a mistake to protect the Queen Pawn by *7* ... P—K4 as the continuation *8* Kt×KP, Q×Q (if *8* ... Q×Kt *9* R—K1 wins) *9* B×Pch, K—K2 *10* R×Q would cost Black a couple of Pawns.

8 Kt—Kt3

With a triple attack on the Queen Pawn.

8 ...	P—K4
9 Kt×KP!	Q×Q

Other captures lose instantly: 9 ... Kt×Kt by the brusque 10 Q×Q, and 9 Q×Kt by the equally ungallant pin of the Queen, 10 R—K1.

10 R×Q	Kt×Kt
11 R—K1	

This pin, followed by 12 P—B4, will regain the piece given up by White.

11 ...	P—B3
12 P—B4	

The threat is now 13 P×Kt, P×P 14 R×Pch followed by 15 Kt×P, and White is a pawn ahead.

12 ...	B—QKt5

Not merely a developing move, this attack on the Rook must be met carefully, if White is to avoid being forced into a draw.

13 B—Q2

Tarrasch sidesteps the plausible 13 R—K2, after which 13 ... B—Kt5 14 R—K4, B—KB4 15 R—K2, B—Kt5 allows Black to draw by his perpetual attack on the Rook.

13 ...	B×B
14 Kt×B	B—B4
15 P×Kt	O—O—O

Best, since the King reaches comparative safety while the Queen Rook comes into play.

16 B—Q3	B×B
17 P×B	

White benefits in two ways by the exchange of pieces: he is rid of Black's active Bishop, and he has an open file for his Queen Rook.

17 ...	P×P
18 QR—B1ch!	

This prevents the King from moving toward the center for the ending. If he does so by 18 ... K—Q2, there follows 19 R×P, K—Q3 20 R—K4, K—Q4 21 R—B4, and White wins the Queen Pawn.

18 ...	K—Kt1
19 R×P	Kt—B3
20 R(B1)—K1	KR—K1

Preferable to this is 20 ... R—Q2, to dispute possession of the seventh rank. If then 21 R—K7, KR—Q1 gives Black a fair chance to hold the game.

21 R×R	Kt×R

If 21 ... R×R instead, 22 R×Rch, Kt×R 24 Kt—Kt3 follows, and White wins a Pawn.

Rook on the Seventh Rank.

22 R—K7

A paralyzing move! Black must submit to the loss of a Pawn.

22 ...	P—QR3
23 Kt—Kt3	P—QKt3

To prevent the Knight from coming in at R5. If instead 23 ... K—R2, to get the King into play, then 24 Kt—R5, R—Kt1 25 Kt—B6ch wins a whole Rook.

24 Kt×P	R×Kt
25 R×Ktch	K—B2

This is the position on the board:

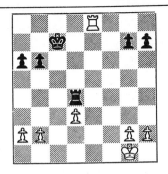

White is a Pawn ahead, and that should be sufficient to win. If he is greedy though, and wants to pick up another Pawn or two (just to make sure) this is what might happen: *26* R—K7ch, K—Q3 *27* R×P, R×P *28* R×P, R—Q8ch *29* K—B2, R—Q7ch *30* K—B3, R×QKtP, and Black has good drawing chances, his Rook being so active.

26 R—K3!

A star move! White protects the important passed Pawn, while keeping the adverse Rook out.

26 ...	K—Q2
27 K—B2	P—Kt3
28 R—R3!	

This forces the Rook Pawn to advance, thus weakening the Knight Pawn.

| *28* ... | P—KR4 |

Changing of the Guard.

29 K—K3!

This move accomplishes a great deal:
(1) The King protects the Pawn, freeing the Rook for active duty.
(2) The King is brought closer to the center.

(3) Black's Rook, blockader of the Pawn, is forced to retreat.
(4) The passed Pawn will be able to advance.

29 ...	R—Q3
30 P—Q4	R—K3ch
31 K—Q3	R—K8

An attempt to get behind White's Pawns.

| *32* R—Kt3 | R—K3 |

The Rook must return to defend the Knight Pawn. On *32* ... R—QKt8 instead, *33* K—B2 wins a Pawn for White.

33 R—K3

An offer to exchange Rooks, which Black dares not accept. The ensuing Pawn ending would be an easy win for White.

| *33* ... | R—Q3 |
| *34* R—K5 | R—KB3 |

Once more the Rook tries to get at the Pawns.

35 P—QR4

Mindful of the safety of his Queen side Pawns, Tarrasch moves them away from the second rank and possible attack by the Rook.

| *35* ... | R—B7 |
| *36* R—K2 | |

The hostile Rook must be evicted—and at once!

36 ...	R—B3
37 P—QKt4	R—B8
38 R—K5	R—B7

The Rook persists in trying to settle down on the seventh rank. An attack on the Queen side Pawns would be futile, 38 ... R—QR8 being met by 39 P—R5, and 38 ... R—QKt8 by 39 P—Kt5.

39 R—KKt5

Combines attack (on Black's Knight Pawn) with defense (of his own). Black's Rook will have to scurry back.

39 ...   R—B3

Clearly, this is better than *39 ... R—QKt7*, which loses a Pawn at once after *40 K—B3* in reply.

40 P—R3!

An effective waiting move. If at once *40 P—Q5, R—B5* is annoying, while *40 K—K4* is met by *40 ... R—K3ch 41 R—K5, R—QB3*, and Black has some counter-play.

40 ...   K—Q3
41 K—K4   R—K3ch
42 R—K5   R—B3
43 P—Q5!

Cuts down the choice of reply. For example, if *43 ... R—B7 44 R—K6ch* wins a Pawn. Or if *43 ... P—QR4 44 P×P, P×P 45 R—K6ch, R×R 46 P×R, K×P 47 K—Q4, K—Q3 48 K—B4, K—B3 49 P—R4, K—Kt3 50 K—Q5, K—Kt2 51 K—B5, K—R3 52 K—B6*, and Black has run out of moves.

43 ...   K—Q2
44 R—Kt5!

Clears the square K5 for the King, and also arranges to bring the Rook

to Kt3 and then to KB3, where the threat of exchange will drive the opposing Rook off the open file.

44 ...   K—Q3
45 R—Kt3   K—K2
46 R—KB3   R—Q3

The Rook must leave the only available open file, since an exchange would be ruinous.

Advance of King and Pawn.

47 K—K5

White threatens a quick win by *48 R—B7ch, K×R 49 K×R, K—K1 50 K—B7*, and the Pawn marches through.

47 ...   R—Q1

This is the position, with White to play:

48 P—Q6ch!

Very pretty! If Black captures by *48 ... R×P*, the continuation is *49 R—B7ch, K×R 50 K×R*, and White picks off the Queen side Pawns, winning easily.

48 ...   K—Q2

No better is *48 ... K—K1 49*

K—K6, P—KKt4 *50* P—Q7ch, R × P
51 R—B8ch, and it's all over.

| *49* R—B7ch | K—B1 |

A humiliating retreat, but *49* ...
K—B3 *50* R—B7 mate is even more
embarrassing.

| *50* R—B7ch | K—Kt1 |

Forcing the Exchange of Rooks.

51 R—B2	R—K1ch
52 K—B6	P—QKt4
53 P—Q7	R—R1
54 K—K7	R—R2ch
55 K—Q6	R—R1
56 R—K2	

Indicating that he will check at
K8, and Queen the Pawn. The
threat is decisive, so ...

| *56* ... | Resigns |

The Passed Pawn

A. Rubinstein · O. Duras

Vienna 1908, QUEEN'S PAWN GAME

I don't know which you will enjoy more—Rubinstein's explosive combination early in the game to win a Pawn, or his skillful play thereafter to exploit his advantage.

The combination, involving a Queen sacrifice, is brilliant and clear-cut. The subsequent strategy of winning with an extra Pawn may be summed up as follows:

(1) Rubinstein simplifies the position by exchanging as many pieces as possible.

(2) He returns the extra Pawn on one wing to create a passed Pawn on the other.

(3) He rushes the passed Pawn to the Queening square.

1 P—Q4	P—Q4
2 Kt—KB3	P—QB4
3 P—K3	Kt—KB3
4 P×P	Q—R4ch

The Queen should not come into play so soon. A safer way to regain the Pawn is by the simple *4 ...* P—K3. White could not then hold on to the Pawn, for if *5* P—QKt4, P—QR4 *6* P—B3, P×P *7* P×P, P—QKt3, and if White continues stubbornly by *8* B—R3, then *8 ...* P×P *9* P×P, R×B *10* Kt×R, Q—R4ch, and Black wins two

pieces for a Rook.

5 QKt—Q2	Q×BP
6 P—QR3	Q—B2
7 P—B4	P×P

This move not only surrenders the center, but helps White develop his pieces. A preferable move is *7 ...* P—K3.

8 Kt×P	B—Kt5

"Knights before Bishops!" advised Lasker, 'way back in 1895, but some people just won't listen.

9 P—Kt4	Kt—B3
10 B—Kt2	P—QKt4

A nervous attempt to force the Knight to retreat, but Rubinstein has other plans for the piece. Its next move initiates a spectacular combination.

11 Kt(B4)—K5!   Kt×Kt
12 Kt×Kt!   B×Q
13 B×Pch   Kt—Q2

The alternative *13 ... K—Q1* leads to this sparkling finish: *14* R×Bch, K—B1 *15* B—R6ch, K—Kt1 *16* Kt—B6ch, Q×Kt *17* B—K5ch, Q—Q3 *18* R—QB1, and mate follows next move.

14 B×Ktch   Q×B

Practically forced, as after *14 ... K—Q1*, *15* R×B leaves Black helpless to ward off the many threats.

15 Kt×Q   B—R4
16 Kt—K5   R—B1
17 P—Kt4   B—Kt3
18 Kt×B

The two Bishops might enable Black to put up a good deal of resistance, so Rubinstein removes one of them. In return, Black gets an open file for his King Rook.

18 ...   RP×Kt
19 B—Q4   P—QR3
20 K—Q2

The King moves toward the center, to take an active part in the endgame.

20 ...   P—B3

Preparing to evict the Bishop by *21 ... P—K4*, from its strong position in the middle of the board.

21 QR—QB1!

Puts the question to Black. He must either exchange Rooks or abandon control of the open file.

21 ...   R×R
22 R×R!

Much better than capturing with the King. *The Rook must attack in the endgame, not stay inert at R1 protecting a Pawn.*

22 ...   P—K4

If *22 ... R×P 23* R—B8ch, K—B2 *24* K—K2, P—K4 *25* B—B5, B×B *26* R×B, R—R1 *27* R—B7ch, K—K3 *28* R—R7, and White will soon have two connected passed Pawns.

23 B—B5   R×P

Or *23 ... B×B 24* R×B, K—Q2 *25* R—R5, R—R1 *26* P—QKt5, and White wins.

24 B×B   K×B
25 K—K2   P—K5
26 R—B6   R—Kt7
27 R×RP   R×KtP

Material is even, but Rubinstein has a great positional advantage in his two connected passed Pawns—either of them a potential Queen.

28 R—R7

Almost instinctively the Rook hastens to seize control of the seventh rank.

28 ...   R—Kt8
29 P—Kt5!   R—Kt8
30 P—R4   P—Kt4
31 R—Kt7   R—QR8

This is the position, with White to play:

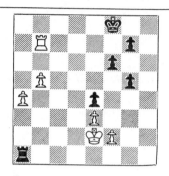

32 P—Kt6!

Rubinstein doesn't waste time saving both Pawns. One Pawn (in the right hands) is enough to win.

32 ...	R × P
33 R—R7	

Offers an exchange of Rooks (which Black dares not accept) and clears the way for the Pawn's advance.

33 ...	R—Kt5
34 P—Kt7	

With the threat of winning by *35 R—R8ch* followed by Queening the Pawn.

34 ...	P—Kt5

Nothing else is any better, *34 ... K—K2* losing instantly by *35 P—Kt8(Q) dis ch.*

35 R—R8ch	K—B2
36 P—Kt8(Q)	R × Q
37 R × R	K—K3
38 R—K8ch	K—B4
39 K—B1	Resigns

Further resistance is not only useless, but could lead to this humiliating finish: *39 ... P—Kt6 40 P × P, K—Kt5 41 K—Kt2, P—B4 42 R—K7, P—Kt4 43 R—KKt7, P—B5 44 KP × P, P—K6 45 R × P* mate.

Weak Pawns, Weak Squares and Mighty, Mighty Knights

H. Mattison · A. Nimzovich

Carlsbad 1929, Nimzo-Indian Defense

It is amazing how much instructive strategy Nimzovich can pack into a mere 23 moves.

His attack on a doubled Pawn leads to a weakening of a key square. On this important square Nimzovich plants a Knight so firmly that it cannot be dislodged. He then forces open a file for the benefit of his Queen Rook. With that sector under control, he switches the King Knight over to the center of the board. The power generated by the centralized Knights is devastating. So great is the effect that Mattison feels compelled to resign, though he hasn't lost so much as a Pawn.

Is chess of this sort an art or a science? In the hands of a craftsman like Nimzovich, it may be either.

1 P—Q4	Kt—KB3
2 P—QB4	P—K3
3 Kt—QB3	B—Kt5
4 Kt—B3	B × Ktch
5 P × B	

An exchange which probably pleases both parties. White, because he has the two Bishops, and an open file for his Queen Rook. Black, because he has created a weakness—a doubled Pawn—in his opponent's position.

5 ...	P—Q3
6 Q—B2	Q—K2

Black is ready to meet *7* P—K4 with *7* ... P—K4, securing a fair share of the center.

7 B—R3

With two objects in mind:
(1) To prevent *7* ... P—K4, after which *8* P × P leaves Black unable to recapture, and
(2) To advance *8* P—B5, with the idea of dissolving the doubled Pawn.

7 ...	P—B4

This fixes White's Pawn at B4, making it a stationary target at which Nimzovich can aim attack.

8 P—KKt3

White prepares to fianchetto the Bishop and control the long diagonal. Ordinarily, this is a commendable development, but here this has the drawback of depriving the weak Pawn (at QB4) of a defender. A better course was probably *8* P—K4 followed by *9* B—Q3.

8 ...	P—QKt3

Black of course intends to dispute control of the diagonal.

9 B—KKt2   B—Kt2
10 O—O   O—O
11 Kt—R4

White is anxious to exchange Bishops, since Nimzovich's has more scope, and bears down (together with the Knight) so strongly on the square K5.

A better way to bring about an exchange though was by 11 Kt—Q2. The Knight would then not only exert more influence on the center, but would be a useful protector of the frail Bishop Pawn.

11 ...   B×B
12 K×B

Much better than this was the recapture by 12 Kt×B, to bring the Knight back into play. If then 12 ... Kt—B3 13 P—K4, Kt—QR4 14 Kt—K3, and White does not stand too badly, his Knight being centralized, and his Bishop Pawn defended.

This is the situation, with Black to play:

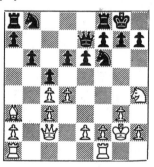

12 ...   Q—Kt2ch
13 K—Kt1

White gets into difficulties after this. The right move was 13 Kt—B3, which gets the Knight back from the sidelines, and gives White a fighting chance.

Interposing by 13 P—B3 would lose a piece after 13 ... P—KKt4 14 Q—Q2, P—KR3, and the Knight has no flight square.

13 ...   Q—R3

Attacks Bishop and Bishop Pawn, forcing White's reply.

14 Q—Kt3   Kt—B3
15 KR—Q1

The alternatives are:

(1) 15 P×P, KtP×P, and Black threatens 16 ... QR—Kt1 winning the Bishop and 16 ... Kt—K4 winning the Bishop Pawn.

(2) 15 Kt—B3, Kt—QR4 16 Q—Kt5, Q×Q 17 P×Q, Kt—B5 18 B—B1, Kt—Q4, and the Bishop Pawn falls.

15 ...   Kt—QR4
16 Q—Kt5   Q×Q
17 P×Q

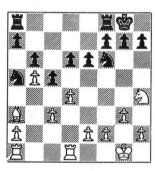

17 ...   Kt—B5!

The doubled Pawn has been dissolved, but the weakness of the square on which it stood remains. Nimzovich anchors his Knight on this vital square, and with that move he secures new advantages:

(1) The Knight is posted aggressively. It attacks the Bishop and drives it back to its original square.

(2) The Knight is posted defensively. It protects the Queen Pawn and the Knight Pawn against possible attack.

(3) The Knight has a great deal of influence on the important central squares.

(4) The Knight cannot be dislodged by Pawns, nor by the Bishop (which operates on black squares only).

18 B—B1   P—QR3!

This forces open the Queen Rook file, since White must capture or lose a Pawn.

19 KtP×P   R×P

Now the Rook has a fine target in the isolated Rook Pawn.

20 P×P   KtP×P
21 Kt—Kt2

The Knight returns, but it's late in the day.

21 ...   Kt—Q4

A comparison of the positions shows the superiority of Black's in that his Knights are strongly centralized, and his Rooks can operate on the two open files. White's minor pieces are widely scattered, and his Rooks out of touch with each other.

22 R—Q3   KR—R1
23 P—K4   Kt—K4!
24 Resigns

Mattison surrenders though he hasn't lost so much as a Pawn! If he chose to play on, this would be the continuation: *24* R—Q1, Kt×P *25* R—B1 (on *25* R—Q2 or *25* R—K1, Kt—B6ch wins the exchange) R×P *26* R×R, Kt—B6ch *27* K—R1, R×R, and White must lose a third Pawn.

Finesse in the Ending

R. Domenech · S. Flohr

Rosas 1935, SICILIAN DEFENSE

Salo Flohr

For a description of Flohr's skill in this game, I commend you to Roget's Thesaurus, where you will find such adjectives as exquisite, elegant, artistic, and enchanting.

Throughout the play there are delightful finesses and touches of originality. Who but Salo Flohr would interrupt a series of exchanges, force an irreparable weakness, and then proceed to complete the exchanges?

To my mind, this quiet little positional game, played with crystalline clarity, outshines all the blazing combinations of a dozen wide-open, slam-bang attacking games.

1 P—K4	P—QB4
2 Kt—KB3	P—K3
3 P—B4	

An attempt to get the Maroczy Bind, which is no improvement on the usual *3* P—Q4. A move has been wasted that should have been devoted to straightforward development, while the Pawn at B4 restricts the scope of White's King Bishop.

3 ...	Kt—QB3
4 P—Q4	P × P
5 Kt × P	Kt—B3
6 Kt × Kt	

Apparently White does not care to play *6* Kt—QB3, when *6* ... B—Kt5 in reply puts him on the defensive. He would have to guard against *7* ... Kt × P (winning a Pawn) as well as *7* ... B × Ktch *8* P × B (saddling him with a doubled Pawn).

6 ...	QP × Kt!

Geniuses do not have to capture toward the center! Black wants the Queen file open so that he can exert pressure on White's Q3 and Q4 squares, both of these squares having been weakened by White's premature third move.

These weaknesses are almost imperceptible, and it is difficult at this early stage to see how Flohr can possibly exploit them, but he does so—and beautifully!

7 Q × Qch	K × Q

Black has lost the privilege of Castling, but it is of no consequence. The King is more useful in the center than hidden away in a corner. With Queens off the board, there is little danger of the King running into a mating attack.

8 P—B3	

This saves the King Pawn, but it limits still more the scope of White's King Bishop. The more of White's Pawns there are on white squares, the less freedom of action the King Bishop has, since it travels on white squares only.

On *8* P—K5 instead, there follows *8* ... Kt—Kt5 *9* B—B4, B—B4 (threatens *10* ... Kt × BP) *10* B—Kt3 (or *10* P—B3, Kt—B7 *11* R—Kt1, Kt—Q6ch, and Black wins the exchange) B—Q5, and Black wins a Pawn.

8 ...	P—K4!

A little move, but it accomplishes a great deal:

(1) It releases the Queen Bishop, which will assume a strong attacking position at K3.

(2) It fixes White's King Pawn at K4, preventing it from advancing to K5.

(3) It exerts pressure on Q5, one of the weak squares in White's position.

9 B—K3	K—B2
10 P—QR3	

White's idea may have been to prevent *10* ... B—Kt5ch (a move his opponent had no intention of making) but time is wasted, and another weakness created—a "hole" at QKt3. This will cause White bitter regret later on.

The simple *10* Kt—B3, developing a piece, would have been better.

10 ...	Kt—Q2!

The point of this is that it will enable Black to play ... B—QB4, and force an exchange of Bishops. This would eliminate White's good Bishop, and leave him with the one that is ineffectual.

11 Kt—Q2   P—QR4!

The Pawn is to advance to R5, where it will have a crippling effect on White's Queen side.

12 B—K2   P—R5!
13 K—B2

This is the position, with Black to move:

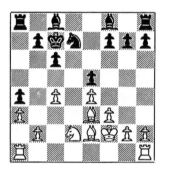

13 ...   B—QB4!

Forces an exchange which will leave Black in control of the black squares.

14 B×B   Kt×B
15 QR—QB1   B—K3

This Bishop is aggressive, White's Bishop is passive.

16 KR—Q1   KR—Q1

Intending to double Rooks on the Queen file. If White tries to dispute

control of the file, this is what might happen: *17 Kt—B1, Kt—Kt6 18 R×R, R×R 19 R—Q1, R×R 20 B×R, B×P*, and White has lost a Pawn.

17 K—K3   R—Q2
19 P—KKt3

The purpose of this move and White's next, is to place some Pawns on black squares, thereby allowing his pieces (notably the Bishop) more freedom of movement.

18 ...   QR—Q1

Black now has a powerful grip on the Queen file. His opponent can do little but sit tight and await developments.

19 P—B4

A perfectly natural move, but it opens the door to a surprising delayed-action combination. It is one that is unique, so far as I know, in the literature of chess.

This is the position, with Black to play and win:

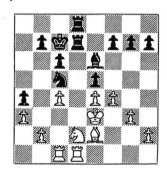

19 ...   P×Pch
20 P×P

Obviously *20 K×P* loses a piece

instantly by *20 ... R × Kt.*

| *20 ...* | **R—Q6ch!** |

At this point, with so little material on the board, this is a startling sacrifice of the exchange.

| *21* B × R | R × Bch |
| *22* K—B2 | |

The alternative is *22 K—K2*, after which the play would go *22 ... B—Kt5ch 23 K—K1, B × R 24 R × B* (if *24 K × B, Kt × P 25 R—B2, R × Ktch,* with an easy win for Black) *Kt × P 25 Kt × Kt, R—K6ch 26 K—B2, R × Kt,* and Black wins another Pawn and the game.

| *22 ...* | **B—Kt5** |

Threatens a quick finish by the simplification: *23 ... B × R 24 R × B, R × Ktch 25 R × R, Kt × Pch* followed by *26 ... Kt × R.*

23 P—K5

White is practically in *zugzwang* (compelled to move, without a playable move left):

(1) If the King Rook moves, *23 ... R × Ktch* wins a piece.

(2) If the Knight moves to B3 to shield the Rook from the Bishop, *23 ... R × Ktch* finishes the Knight's career.

(3) If the Queen Rook moves, Black wins as in the previous note.

Grateful for small favors, White advances the King Pawn to rescue it from immediate danger of capture.

| *23 ...* | **B × R** |
| *24* R × B | |

One would now expect Flohr to continue by *24 ... Kt—Kt6 25 K—K2, R × Ktch 26 R × R, Kt × R,*

leaving him with a slightly superior position. Whether Flohr could squeeze a win out of it is doubtful, skilled though he is in the endgame.

Flohr does bring the Knight to Kt6.

Flohr does clear away all the pieces.

But first his Knight will make two moves that will create irreparable weaknesses in White's Pawn position.

Watch the Knight do some fancy stepping!

| *24 ...* | **Kt—K3!** |

Attacks the Bishop Pawn, and forces its advance.

25 P—B5

Nothing else saves the Pawn, *25 K—K2* being refuted by *25 ... Kt × Pch.*

| *25 ...* | **Kt—Q5!** |
| *26* P—B6 | |

Once again the only move.

| *26 ...* | **P × P** |
| *27* P × P | Kt—Kt6! |

Plants a piece in the "hole" created by White's tenth move.

28 K—K2	R × Ktch
29 R × R	Kt × R
30 K × Kt	K—Q3
31 Resigns	

The rest is a matter of counting moves. In order that White may Queen a Pawn he must capture the Queen Knight and Queen Bishop Pawns (six moves), move his King aside (one move) and advance the Queen Bishop Pawn (four moves). Total—11 moves.

Black meanwhile captures the King Bishop Pawn (two moves), moves his King aside (one move), and advances the King Bishop Pawn (five moves). Total—8 moves.

Resignation for White was clearly in order.

Phalanx of Pawns

T. Petrosian · Kozali

Montevideo 1954, QUEEN'S PAWN GAME

Tigran Petrosian

Petrosian's moves flow along in this game like the words of a well-written short story. Imperceptibly he gets one little advantage, transforms it to another, and then to still another. Thus, an admirable centralization allows Petrosian to start a flank attack with his Pawns.

The invasion of these Pawns opens up files for the pieces behind the Pawns. One of the pieces (a Rook) shoots up a file to the seventh rank, and imprisons the enemy King. The end comes very quickly after that—loss of material, or checkmate in two.

1 P—Q4	Kt—KB3
2 P—QB4	P—K3
3 Kt—QB3	P—Q4
4 P×P	

A favorite move of many modern players, among them Botvinnik, Keres and Reshevsky. It simplifies the position without relieving the pressure Black is under in Queen side openings.

4 ...	P×P
5 B—Kt5	QKt—Q2
6 P—K3	

Naturally, White does not try to win a Pawn, as that would land him in a well-known opening trap: 6 Kt×P, Kt×Kt! 7 B×Q, B—Kt5ch 8 Q—Q2, B×Qch 9 K×B, K×B, and Black has won a piece.

6 ...	B—K2
7 B—Q3	O—O
8 KKt—K2	R—K1
9 Q—B2	P—B3

Protects the Queen Pawn so that he can free himself by 10 ... Kt—K5.

10 P—KR3	Kt—K5
11 B—KB4	

With the mild threat of gaining a Pawn by 12 Kt×Kt, P×Kt 13 B×P, and the vicious threat of winning the Queen by 12 Kt×P, P×Kt 13 B—B7.

11 ...	Kt(Q2)—B3
12 P—B3	

This Knight must be dispossessed!

12 ...	Kt×Kt
13 P×Kt	B—Q3

An attempt to relieve the pressure by exchanging pieces. Strangely enough, this does not lessen Black's troubles.

14 B×B	Q×B
15 P—K4	

Threatens to win a piece by 16 P—K5.

15 ...	Kt—R4

This leads to difficulties for the Knight. A better defense, though not an agreeable one, was 15 ... Kt—Q2 followed by ... Kt—B1 later on.

16 P—K5

Attacks the Queen, and also threatens 17 B×Pch.

16 ...	Q—R3

This is the position, with White to move:

17 Q—Q2!

Brilliant! White's threat of winning the stranded Knight by 18 P—Kt4 forces an exchange of Queens. Though the forces are then greatly diminished, Petrosian can, remarkably enough, really start an attack rolling.

17 ...	Q×Qch
18 K×Q	

The King is now closer to the center for the endgame, and the Rooks are in touch with each other. White still threatens to win the Knight by *19 P—Kt4*.

18 ...	P—KKt3
19 P—Kt4	Kt—Kt2
20 P—KR4	

The stabilized center enables White to set in motion the phalanx of Pawns on the King side, without worrying too much about counter-play.

20 ...	P—KR3

Black prepares to meet *21 P—R5* with *21 ... P—KKt4*.

21 QR—KB1	B—Q2
22 KR—Kt1	

This protects the Knight Pawn, making *23 P—KB4* and *24 P—B5* possible—the next steps in the invasion.

22 ...	P—QKt4
23 P—KB4	P—QR4

Black tries a diversion on the Queen side, a gesture to which his opponent pays no attention.

24 P—B5	

The attack begins! Two immediate threats are: *25 P×P, P×P 26 B×KKtP* winning a Pawn, and *25 P—K6, BP×P 26 P—B6*, stealing the Knight, which has no flight square.

24 ...	P×P

No better is *24 ... K—R2 25 P×Pch, P×P*, when White can attack the doomed Knight Pawn again by *26 P—R5* or *25 R—B6*.

25 P×P	

The last exchange has uncovered an attack on Black's Knight. It it pinned by the Rook, and White threatens to win the beast by *26 P—B6*.

25 ...	K—R1
26 P—K6!	

This of course is the way to break up the position, and not *26 P—B6*, to which Black replies *26 ... Kt—K3*.

26 ...	P×P
27 P—B6	Kt—B4

Forced, the alternative *27 ... Kt—R4* losing a piece by the Bishop fork *28 B—Kt6*.

28 B×Kt	P×B

This is the position before Petrosian administers the *coup de grâce:*

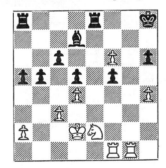

29 R—Kt7!	

Decisive! At one stroke the Bishop is attacked, the King imprisoned, and mate in two threatened by the Knight!

29 ...	Resigns

Black is curiously helpless! After *29 ... QR—Q1, 30 Kt—B4* threatens a mate at Kt6 which cannot possibly be parried.

Passed Pawn's Lust to Expand

R. Fischer · H. Berliner

New York 1960, ALEKHINE DEFENSE

Bobby Fischer

"A passed Pawn increases in strength," says Capablanca, "as the number of pieces on the board diminishes."

In this game Fischer demonstrates in brilliant style the power that is pent-up in a passed Pawn. Note how Fischer drives off the blockaders of the Pawn, and disposes of the pieces that impede its progress. Note also how Fischer's persistent threats against unprotected Pawns and pieces keep his opponent on the run while he gains precious time.

Fischer's restless energy in attack is reminiscent of the fire and dash of that other prodigy who dazzled the chess world with his mastery—

Paul Morphy.

1 P—K4	Kt—KB3

This defense to *1* P—K4 was first played in serious tournament chess in 1921, when Alekhine beat Steiner with it at Budapest. Previous to this no master had ever ventured on *1* ... Kt—KB3. It seemed a sad waste of time to let the Knight be chased around by Pawns, aside from the fact that these Pawns were building up an imposing center for White. Alekhine showed that the Pawn center was not so strong as it looked, and that the advanced Pawns could be vulnerable objects of attack.

2 P—K5	Kt—Q4
3 P—Q4	P—Q3

But not *3 ... Kt—QB3*, when *4 P—QB4, Kt—Kt3 5 P—Q5, Kt×KP* (if *5 ... Kt—Kt5 6 P—B5, Kt(Kt3)×P 7 P—QR3*, and Black loses a Knight) *6 P—B5, Kt(Kt3)—B5 7 P—B4* wins a Knight, as Borochow did from Reuben Fine.

4 P—QB4	Kt—Kt3
5 P×P	BP×P
6 Kt—QB3	P—Kt2
7 B—Q3	B—Kt2
8 KKt—K2	

Preferable to *8 Kt—B3*, which allows an annoying pin by *8 ... B—Kt5.*

8 ...	Kt—B3
9 B—K3	O—O
10 O—O	P—K4!

This is the sort of move *which must be made, win or lose.* Black must assert his right to a fair share of the center.

11 P—Q5	Kt—K2
12 P—QKt3	

Protects the Bishop Pawn, relieving the King Bishop of that task. It is important not to tie pieces down to menial duties.

12 ...	Kt—Q2

This is the position, with White to play:

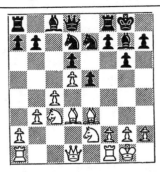

13 Kt—K4	Kt—KB4
14 B—Kt5	P—B3
15 B—Q2	

Now there is a threat of *16 P—KKt4*, dislodging the protector of the Queen Pawn.

The best way to meet the threat is probably by *15 ... Q—B2*. Then if *16 P—QKt4, P—Kt3* leaves Black with a cramped but tenable position.

15 ...	Kt—B4

This remedy though, proves worse than the disease. White simply exchanges Knights, thereby creating a passed Pawn.

16 Kt×Kt	P×Kt
17 B×Kt	

It may hurt a bit to let Black have the two Bishops, but otherwise the Knight (ideal blockader of a passed Pawn) settles down on Q3, and stops the Queen Pawn dead in its tracks.

17 ...	B×B
18 P—B4!	P×P

It is true that *18 ... P—K5* is not promising, as White can win a Pawn by *19 Kt—Kt3, B—Q2 20*

Kt × P,   P—B4   *21* Kt—B3, but giving up the center without being compelled to do so, has no justification. Black should batten down the hatches with *18* ... Q—Q3, and prepare for the storm that will assail his K4 square.

| *19* Kt × P | Q—Q3 |
| *20* Kt—R5! | |

An alert move that kills off one of the Bishops.

| *20* ... | QR—K1 |

Clearly, *20* ... P × Kt *21* R × B leaves Black's Pawn position on the King side in ruins, but if Black tries to keep both his Bishops by *20* ... B—R1, then *21* Kt—Kt3, B—Q2 *22* B—B4, Q—K2 *23* R—K1, Q—Kt2 *24* B—Q6, P—B4 *25* B × R, Q × R *26* Q × Q, B × Q *27* B × P gives White the advantage, as Leonard Barden points out.

| *21* Kt × B | K × Kt |

This is the situation:

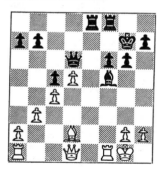

22 B—B4

White's pieces spring to life, with this and the next few moves. The Bishop comes into active play by the attack on the Queen, and a blockader of the passed Pawn will be driven away. The Pawn, with its lust to expand, is anxious to press on.

| *22* ... | Q—Q2 |
| *23* Q—Q2 | |

Threatens to win the exchange by *24* B—R6ch, and at the same time clears the way for the Queen Rook to come into the game.

23 ...	R—B2
24 B—R6ch	K—Kt1
25 QR—K1	R(B2)—K2
26 R × R	Q × R
27 P—KR3!	

Believe it or not, this is a strong attacking move!

| *27* ... | Q—K5 |

The tempting *27* ... Q—K7 would be fatal after *28* Q × Q, R × Q *29* P—KKt4, B—K5 *30* R × P, and Black is faced with unavoidable mate.

28 Q—KB2

White does not play *28* P—KKt4 at once, as after *28* ... B × P *29* P × B, Q × Pch, Black has an easy draw by perpetual check. In fact, there are a number of amusing ways in which White could lose if he tried to avoid the draw. For example:

(1) *30* K—R2, R—K7ch winning the Queen.

(2) *30* K—R1, R—K7, and White must give up the Queen or be mated.

(3) *30* Q—Kt2, Q—Q5ch *31* K—R2, Q—R5ch *32* Q—R3, R—B7ch and Black wins the Queen.

(4) *30* Q—Kt2, Q—Q5ch *31* R—B2, R—K8ch *32* K—R2, Q—R5ch

33 Q—R3, R—R8ch *34* K×R, Q×Qch *35* R—R2 (to save the Bishop) Q—B8 mate.

(5) *30* Q—Kt2, Q—Q5ch *31* K—R1, Q—R5ch *32* Q—R2, Q—K5ch *33* K—Kt1, Q—Kt5ch *34* K—B2, R—K7 mate.

The move White does play attacks the Queen Bishop Pawn, and also threatens *29* P—KKt4, B×P *30* Q×KBP, and Black must give up a piece by *30* ... Q—Q5ch *31* Q×Q, P×Q *32* P×B, or be mated.

| 28 ... | Q—K2 |
| 29 P—KKt4 | B—Q6 |

Things go at a rapid pace from now on. Every one of Fischer's moves is a hammer blow!

| 30 R—Q1 | B—K5 |
| 31 P—Q6 | |

The Pawn takes a giant step.

31 ...	Q—K4
32 B—B4	Q—B6
33 P—Q7	R—Q1
34 Q—K2	Q—B6

There is no hope in *34* ... Q× KRP *35* Q×B, Q×Pch *36* K—B2, Q×R *37* Q—K6ch, K—Kt2 (or *37* ... K—B1 *38* B—R6 mate) *38* Q—K7ch, and White wins.

| 35 Q×Q | B×Q |
| 36 B—B7! | Resigns |

If *36* ... B×R *37* B×R, K—B2 *38* B×P, and the Pawn becomes a Queen next move.

Rook and Pawn Ending

V. Smyslov · S. Reshevsky

Moscow 1948, RUY LOPEZ

Vassily Smyslov

All chess players (and that includes you and me) must have a sadistic streak or we would not enjoy seeing a fellow chessplayer being methodically and remorselessly crushed.

In this game Smyslov gets an iron grip on the center almost from the start. He tightens the grip move by move in the style made famous by Tarrasch. Something has to give way, and it turns out to be a Pawn that weakens and can not avoid being captured.

Once Smyslov is a Pawn ahead he brings the game quickly to an ending. He brings it in fact to one of those Rook and Pawn endings which are so confounded instructive. His treatment is more than worthy of note, as Smyslov plays it beautifully. His skill in that department is now so evident as to find his name mentioned in the same breath with those of Capablanca and Rubinstein.

There is no higher praise.

1 P—K4	P—K4
2 Kt—KB3	Kt—QB3
3 B—Kt5	P—QR3
4 B—R4	P—Q3
5 P—B3	KKt—K2

This development of the Knight was favored by Steinitz, although he was not particularly successful with it. The idea is to bring the Knight to Kt3, where it exerts pressure on the square K4 and is prepared to seize the outpost B5.

6 P—Q4	B—Q2
7 B—Kt3	

With the transparent threat of *8* Kt—Kt5, attacking the vulnerable Bishop Pawn with two pieces.

7 ...	P—KR3
8 QKt—Q2	

This Knight is headed by way of QB4 and K3 for the outpost Q5, where it can make its presence felt.

8 ...	Kt—Kt3
9 Kt—B4	

Nice timing! A mechanical move, such as *9* O—O would allow the reply *9* ... Kt—B5 followed by *10* ... P—KKt4, and Black has seized the initiative.

9 ...	B—K2
10 O—O	O—O
11 Kt—K3	B—B3
12 Kt—Q5	R—K1

The Rook move turns out to be inferior to *12* ... P×P *13* Kt×QP, R—K1, played in an earlier round

of the tournament by Keres and Euwe.

Here is the position:

13 P×P!

This deserves an exclamation point! White gets the advantage with this capture, no matter how the opponent recaptures the Pawn—and he has five ways of doing so!

13 ...	B×P

If *13* ... P×P *14* Kt×Bch, P×Kt (but not *14* ... Q×Kt as *15* Q×B wins a piece for White) *15* B×RP, and White wins a Pawn.

If *13* ... KKt×P *14* Kt×Kt, Kt×Kt *15* P—KB4, Kt—B3 (on *15* ... Kt—Kt5 *16* P—KR3 wins a Pawn) *16* Q—B3, with a fine position for White.

14 Kt×B	P×Kt
15 Q—B3!	

The Queen comes into play while vacating a good square for the benefit of the Rook.

15 ...	B—K3
16 R—Q1	

Strategically, White's game is superior. His Knight dominates the center, his Rook exerts pressure on the Queen file, and he has two active Bishops.

Tactically, White has threats in *17* Kt—Kt6, winning the exchange by virtue of the discovered attack on the Queen, and in *17* B×P, P×B *18* Kt—B6ch, winning the Queen for Rook and Bishop.

16 ...	B×Kt

Black is understandably anxious to remove the Knight, even at the cost of increasing the power of the Bishops.

17 R×B

Of course not *17* P×B, as the Pawn would shut off the action of the Bishop and the Rook. The capture with the Pawn would also allow Black counter-play by *17* ... P—K5 *18* Q—K2, Kt—R4.

17 ...	Q—K2
18 Q—B5!	

A powerful move! The immediate threat is *19* R—Q7 winning on the spot, as the Rook attacks the Queen and the tender King Bishop Pawn behind the Queen.

18 ...	Kt—B1

Keeps the Rook out. If instead *18* ... QR—Q1 *19* R×R, R×R *20* B×RP (not *20* Q×Kt as *20* ... R—Q8ch *21* B×R, P×Q is a nasty surprise for White) P×B *21* Q× Ktch, and White wins a couple of Pawns.

19 B—K3	Kt—K3

This prevents the Bishop from coming in at B5.

20 QR—Q1	KR—Q1
21 P—Kt3!	

Euwe points out the merits of this quiet little move:

(1) It provides the King with a flight square against threats of mate on the back rank.

(2) It prevents an unwelcome intrusion at B4 by the Knight.

(3) It protects the square R4, the importance of which will be evident later on.

21 ...	R—Q3

A desperate attempt to relieve the pressure on the Queen file by doubling Rooks.

22 R×R

Smyslov doesn't give him time to complete the operation.

22 ...	P×R

This leaves Black with an organic weakness—a backward Pawn on an open file.

23 Q—Kt4

A subtle move. The direct threat is *24* B×P winning a Pawn, the indirect threat is *24* R—Q2 followed by *25* Q—Q1, bearing down on the luckless Queen Pawn.

23 ...	K—R1

Black would have no picnic after *23* ... K—B1, when the reply *24* B—Kt6 threatens to win by *25* B×Kt, P×B *26* Q—B3ch, K—K1 *27* Q—Q3, K—Q2 *28* B—B5, and the Queen Pawn cannot be saved.

24 B—Kt6!

Very strong! It prevents *24* ... R—Q1 protecting the Pawn, and also deprives Black of counter-play beginning with *24 ... Kt—R4.*

White's intention now (if undisturbed) is to win the Queen Pawn by doubling his heavy pieces on that file.

24 ...   Kt—Kt1

An awkward move (since the Rook is shut off) but the Knight wants to get to Q2, to drive the troublesome Bishop away.

Other defenses are no more satisfactory. For instance:

(1) *24 ... Kt—B4 25 B × Kt, P × B 26 R—Q7,* winning a Pawn.

(2) *24 ... Kt(B3)—Q1 25 R—Q2, P—B3* (to protect the Pawn by *26 ... Kt—KB2) 26 B × Kt!, Kt × B 27 Q—Q1,* and the Pawn falls.

(3) *24 ... R—QB1 25 R—Q2, Kt—Kt1 26 Q—Q1, R—B3 27 B—R7, Kt—Q2 28 B—Q5, R—B2 29 B × Kt, Q × B 30 R × P,* and White has won a Pawn.

25 B × Kt   P × B

Capturing with the Queen instead is more expensive, viz: *25 ... Q × B 26 Q × Q, P × Q 27 R × P,* and the King Pawn comes off the board next move.

This is the position, with White to play:

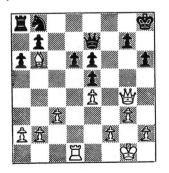

26 Q—R4!

Clever play! The idea is to force an exchange which will rid the board of Black's Queen, the only defender of the Queen Pawn.

Note that this stratagem was made possible by White's triple-threat 21st move P—Kt3.

26 ...   Q—Q2

No better is *26 ... Q × Q 27 P × Q,* and the Pawn is beyond help.

27 Q—Q8ch!

Brutal, but they always say, "Chess is not for the kind-hearted."

27 ...   Q × Q
28 B × Q   Kt—Q2

There is no way to save the Pawn. On *28 ... Kt—B3 29 B—B7* seals its fate.

29 B—B7   Kt—B4
30 R × P

It is easy to go wrong, even in a winning position. For instance, if *30 B × P* (plausible enough) *R—Q1 31 P—B3, P—QKt3,* and Black will attack and win the pinned Bishop next move by *32 ... Kt—Kt2.*

30 ...   R—QB1

There is no comfort in *30 ... Kt × P* when *31 R × KP* wins two King Pawns for one.

31 B—Kt6   Kt—R5
32 R × P   Kt × KtP
33 R × P   Kt—B5

If *33 ... R × P 34 B—Q4!, R—B8ch 35 K—Kt2, Kt—Q6 36 R—K7,* and the rest is easy for White.

34	R—K6	Kt×B
35	R×Kt	R×P
36	R×KtP	R—B7
37	P—KR4	

The Queen Rook Pawn could not be saved, but White can put his trust in the Pawn majority on the King-side.

| 37 ... | R×RP |
| | |

This is how things stand:

We now have a position of the sort Capablanca had in mind when he said, "Endings of one Rook and Pawns are about the most common sort of endings arising on the chess board. Yet though they do occur so often, few have mastered them thoroughly. They are often of a very difficult nature, and sometimes while apparently very simple they are in reality extremely intricate."

We can appreciate this particular ending if we have an outline of Smyslov's general plan.

White's Rook will assume its best position—at QR7, where it dominates the all-important seventh rank, and at the same time keeps the adverse passed Rook Pawn under constant attack, *no matter how far it advances on the file.*

White's King will advance under a Pawn shelter to KKt6, where it is in position, assisted by the Rook, to remove Black's King side Pawns. The Pawn shelter is necessary to prevent Black from checking and then Queening his Pawn, this Pawn having reached QR7, with the Rook defending it at QR8.

38	K—Kt2	P—QR4
39	P—R5	P—R5
40	R—R7!	

The Rook not only keeps the dangerous Pawn under surveillance, but ties down the adverse Rook to its defense.

| 40 ... | K—Kt1 |
| 41 P—Kt4 | P—R6 |

On *41 ... R—R6* (to keep the King from advancing), White builds a shelter by *42 P—B3*, and then continues by *43 K—Kt3* and *44 K—B4*.

42	K—Kt3	R—K7
43	K—B3	R—R7
44	K—K3	K—B1
45	P—B3	R—R8
46	K—B4	

Intending (if let alone) to follow with *47 K—B5* and *48 P—B4*.

| 46 ... | P—R7 |
| 47 P—K5 | |

Care is needed every step of the way. The hasty *47 K—K5* would lead to *47 ... R—KB8 48 R×RP* (the Pawn was threatening to become a Queen) R×P, and White will have trouble winning.

| 47 ... | K—Kt1 |

A King move is about all that

Black has left. If he plays *47* ...
K—K1, then *48* K—B5, R—KB8 *49*
R×P, R×Pch *50* K—K6 (threatens
mate) K—Q1 *51* R—R8ch, K—B2
52 R—R7ch, and White wins.

48 K—B5!	R—KB8
49 R×P	R×Pch
50 K—Kt6	K—B1

Or *50* ... R—B2 *51* R—R8ch
(definitely not *51* P—K6, R—B3

mate!) R—B1 *52* R×Rch, K×R *53*
P—K6, K—K2 (if *53* ... K—Kt1 *54*
P—K7 and mate next) *54* K×P and
wins.

51 R—R8ch	K—K2
52 R—R7ch	Resigns

Black loses the King-side Pawns.
After *52* ... K—B1 *53* R×P, R—B5
54 K×P, White's Pawns can not be
stopped.

King in the Center

S. Tartakover · M. Frentz

Paris 1933, ENGLISH OPENING

If once a man delays Castling and his King remains in the center, files will open up against him, Bishops sweep the board, Rooks will dominate the seventh rank, and Pawns turn into Queens. Irving Chernev.

The moment I wrote this I recalled another piece of advice, moral in nature:

If once a man indulges himself in murder, very soon he comes to think little of robbing; and from robbing he comes next to drinking and Sabbath-breaking, and from that to incivility and procrastination. Thomas De Quincey.

1 P—QB4	Kt—KB3
2 Kt—QB3	P—K3
3 P—K4	P—Q4
4 BP×P	P×P
5 P—K5	P—Q5

Black has a good line in *5 ...* Kt—K5, sacrificing a Pawn for the sake of the initiative. The continuation could be *6* Kt×Kt, P×Kt *7* Q—R4ch, Kt—B3 *8* Q×KP, B—B3 *9* B—Kt5, B—Q4 *10* Q—KKt4, P—QR3 *11* B×Ktch, B×B.

6 P×Kt	P×Kt
7 P×KtP	P×Pch

It is almost incredible that each player should have at this early stage a passed Pawn on the seventh rank. Naturally, this remarkable position will last only for a fleeting moment.

8 B×P	B×P
9 Q—B2	Kt—B3
10 Kt—B3	B—Kt5

Black is neglecting the safety of his King. The modest *10 ...* B—Q2, with a view to Queen side Castling offered better chances.

11 O—O—O	B×Kt
12 P×B	Kt—Q5

This attacking move is unjustified in view of the dangers facing his exposed King. It is hard to suggest an airtight defense, but Black might have done better with *12 ...* Q—B3 *14* R—K1ch, K—B1, and prepare for a long, hard winter.

13 Q—K4ch	Q—K2

Good moves are getting scarce: *13 ...* K—B1 loses at once by *14* B—Kt4ch, K—Kt1 *15* R—Kt1 (threatens *16* R×Kt), while *13 ...* Kt—K3 fails after *14* B—Kt5ch, P—B3 *15* B×Pch, P×B *16* Q×Pch, K—B1 *17* B—Kt4ch, and White wins the Queen.

14 Q×Qch	K×Q
15 B—Kt4ch	K—K1

Just about the only move. The

alternatives are:

(1) *15* ... K—Q2 *16* B—B5 (not *16* B—B3, P—QB4) winning the pinned Knight.

(2) *15* ... K—K3 *16* B—R3ch, P—B4 *17* KR—K1ch, K—B2 *18* R—K7ch, K—B1 *19* R×B dis ch, and White wins two pieces for a Rook.

(3) *15* ... K—K3 *16* B—R3ch, Kt—B4 *17* KR—K1ch, K—B3 *18* B—B3ch, K—Kt4 (if *18* ... K—Kt3 *19* B×Ktch wins a piece) *19* R—Q5, and White wins a piece.

16 B—Kt5ch!   P—B3

Here if *16* ... Kt×B *17* KR—K1ch and mate next move.

17 KR—K1ch

Every piece is engaged in the attack!

17 ...   Kt—K3
18 B—B4   R—Q1

This is the position, with White to play:

19 B×Kt

White does not hold on to his Bishops. One must know when to give up one advantage for the sake of securing another, and perhaps better one.

19 ...   R×Rch
20 K×R   P×B
21 R×Pch   K—Q1
22 R—K7!

Much better than the meek *22* K—B2, protecting the Knight Pawn. *The Rook must be aggressive in the endgame.*

22 ...   B×P

If *22* ... B—B1 *23* R×KtP (guards the Bishop directly) K—B1 *24* R×QRP (now indirectly by the threat of *25* R—R8ch) K—Kt1 *25* R—R4 (once again directly, having picked up two Pawns in the interval).

23 R×KtP

Attacks the Queen Rook Pawn, and also threatens *24* B—R5ch, discovering an attack on the Bishop.

23 ...   B—Q5

The Bishop now protects the Pawn at one side of the board and the Rook at the other. So White disturbs the Bishop by a problem-move. This is the position:

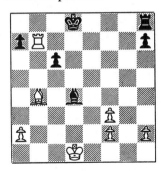

24 B—B5!

A pretty move which renews the threat of winning the Queen Rook Pawn.

24 ...	K—B1

Obviously *24 ... B×B* would lose the Rook by *25 R—Kt8ch.*

25 R×QRP	K—Kt1
26 B×B	R—Q1

Black will win the piece back, but White meanwhile gains time—and Pawns.

27 R×P	R×Bch
28 K—K2	R—QR5
29 P—R4	

"Passed Pawns must be pushed!" as I must have said a thousand times.

29 ...	R×Pch
30 K—K3	K—B1

The King hurries back to head off the Pawn. If Black defends by getting his Rook behind the passed Pawn, this is how the play might run: *30 ... R—R8 31 P—R5, R—R8 32 P—R6, P—B4 33 K—Q3, R—R5 34 P—B4, R×BP 35 R—KKt7, R—KR5 (if 35 ... R—B1 36 P—R7 followed by 37 R—Kt8 wins) 36 P—R7, K—B1 37 R—Kt8ch and White wins.*

31 P—R5	K—Q1
32 P—R6	K—K1
33 R—QKt7	K—B1

Or *33 ... R—R8 34 P—R7, R—R8 35 P—R8(Q)ch, R×Q 36 R—Kt8ch, and White wins.*

34 P—R7	R—R6ch
35 K—B4	Resigns

An easily understood bright little game.

The Shifting Attack

S. Reshevsky · M. Najdorf

Dallas 1957, NIMZO-INDIAN DEFENSE

The attack of a tactician can be troublesome to meet—that of a strategist even more so. Whereas the tactician's threats may be unmistakable, the strategist confuses the issue by keeping things in abeyance. He threatens to threaten!

Take this game for instance: Reshevsky posts a Knight at Q6 to get a grip on the center. Then he establishes a passed Pawn on one wing to occupy his opponent on the Queen side. Finally he stirs up the position on the King-side. What does the poor bewildered opponent do? How can he defend everything at once? Where will the blow fall?

Watch Reshevsky keep Najdorf on the run, as he shifts the attack from side to side!

1	P—Q4	Kt—KB3
2	P—QB4	P—K3
3	Kt—QB3	B—Kt5
4	P—K3	

A quiet-looking but exceedingly strong move.

4	...	P—B4
5	KKt—K2	P×P

This is better than *5* ... P—Q4 *6* P—QR3, P×QP *7* P×B, P×Kt *8* Kt×P, O—O *9* P×P, Kt×P *10* Kt×Kt, Q×Kt *11* Q×Q, P×Q *12* B—Q2, as Najdorf discovered when

he lost with this line to Botvinnik in 1956.

6	P×P	P—Q4
7	P—B5	Kt—K5
8	B—Q2!	

Reshevsky cheerfully allows one of his Bishops to be exchanged for a Knight. The old line of play *8* P—QR3, Kt×Kt *9* Kt×Kt, B×Ktch *10* P×B, P—QKt3 *11* P×P, P×P *12* B—Q3, B—R3, is in Black's favor.

8	...	Kt×B
9	Q×Kt	P—QKt3
10	P—QR3	B×Kt

Forced, since *10* ... B—R4 allows *11* P—QKt4 trapping the Bishop.

11	Kt×B	P×P
12	P×P	P—QR4

This prevents White from supporting his passed Pawn by *13* P—QKt4. It might have been better though to Castle, and get some pieces into active play.

13	B—Kt5ch	B—Q2

Clearly, *13* ... Kt—Q2 is immediately fatal, as after *14* P—B6 the Knight dares not move away.

14 O—O   O—O

If Black tries to prevent *15* P—QKt4 by *14* ... Kt—R3, the advance *15* P—B6 wins a piece, or if *14* ... Kt—B3 (with the same object) *15* Kt × P, (a sacrifice one would make instinctively) P × Kt *16* Q × QP needs no analysis to demonstrate Black's helplessness.

15 P—QKt4

White will now have two connected passed Pawns, whether Black captures or not.

15 ...   B × B

This will enable White to anchor a Knight at Q6, but if *15* ... Kt—B3 instead, *16* B × Kt, B × B *17* P—Kt5 is not particularly pleasant for Black.

16 Kt × B   Kt—R3
17 Kt—Q6

White gets a tremendous positional advantage with this move. The Knight exerts pressure in every direction, and is not easily dislodged from its fine outpost.

The immediate threat is *18* Kt—Kt7, Q—B2 *19* Kt × P, Kt × BP *20* KR—B1!, Kt—K5 *21* R × Q, Kt × Q *22* P—B3 (cuts off the Knight's retreat) KR—B1 *23* QR—QB1, R × R *24* R × R, Kt—Kt8 *25* P—Kt5!, P—R3 *26* P—Kt6, R × Kt *27* P—Kt7, R—Kt4 *28* R—B8ch and White wins.

17 ...   Q—Q2

This is the position, with White to move:

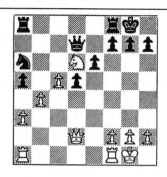

18 P—B4!

The attack shifts to the King side! The threat is *19* P—B5 followed by *20* P—KB6, disrupting the Pawns guarding Black's King. If Black tries to prevent the advance by *18* ... P—Kt3, this might occur: *19* P—B5!, KP × P (if *19* ... KtP × P *20* Q—Kt5ch, K—R1 *21* Q—B6ch, K—Kt1 *22* R—B3, and mate follows soon) *20* R × P, P × R *21* Q—Kt5ch, K—R1 *22* Q—B6ch, K—Kt1 *23* Kt × P(B5), and Black must give up his Queen to prevent mate.

18 ...   QR—Kt1
19 P—B5   KP × P

Here if *19* ... RP × P *20* P—KB6 (threatens *21* Q—Kt5, P—Kt3 *22* Q—R6 and mate next) P × BP *21* Q—R6 and there is no defense, e.g. if *21* ... P—B4 *22* Q—Kt5ch, K—R1 *23* Q—B6ch wins, or if *21* ... Q—K2 *22* R—B3, K—R1 *23* R—R3 is decisive.

20 QR—Kt1   P × P
21 P × P   K—R1

If Black defends the Bishop Pawn by *21* ... P—Kt3, the reply is still *22* Kt × P(B5), after which *22* ... P × Kt *23* Q—Kt5ch, K—R1 *24* Q—B6ch, K—Kt1 allows White the luxury of choosing one of several winning moves—*25* R—B3, or *25* R—Kt3, or *25* R×P—but not *25* Q×Kt, which would be petty, even if it did win.

In this line, if Black refused the Knight and played *22* ... P—B3 to give his King more room, White could force a quick win by *23* Q×Pch, Q×Q (on *23* ... R—B2 *24* Kt—R6ch wins) *24* Kt—K7ch followed by *25* Kt×Q, and the passed Pawns are irresistible.

This is the position on the board:

22 Q—B3!

A master move! The Queen operates on both wings simultaneously! On the King side, the Queen's pin of the Knight Pawn prevents it from moving to Kt3 to protect the Bishop Pawn. On the Queen side, the Queen's defense of the Bishop Pawn makes the advance of the Queen Knight Pawn feasible.

22 ...   Kt—B2

The Knight returns to the theater of action.

23 Kt×P(B5)   Kt—K3
24 Kt—Q6   P—B3
25 Q—KR3!

Threatens to win a piece (or at

least the exchange) by *26* KR—K1.

25 ...   KR—Q1

Protects the Queen, and thereby frees the Knight—but it's getting late!

26 KR—K1   Kt—Q5

This allows White to win the Queen by drawing away the Rook that protects it, but if *26* ... Kt—B1 instead, there follows *27* Q×Q, R×Q (on *27* ... Kt×Q *28* Kt—B7ch wins the exchange) *28* P—Kt5, an advance by the Pawns which will be decisive.

27 R—K8ch!   Q×R

Obviously *27* ... R×R *28* Q×Q does not improve matters.

28 Kt×Q   R×Kt
29 P—Kt5!

Nicely played! Giving up a Pawn to disorganize Black's pieces is the quickest way to break down resistance.

29 ...   Kt×P

Or *29* ... R×P *30* R×R, Kt×R *31* Q—Q7, R—QKt1 *32* P—B6, and White wins easily.

30 Q—Q7   Kt—B6

Attacking the Queen by *30* ... R(K1)—Q1 is useless. White simply plays *31* R×Kt, and Black may not capture either Queen or Rook.

31 R×R   R×R
32 P—B6   Kt—K5

Does Najdorf really think that Reshevsky will fall into *33* P—B7, R—Kt8 mate?

33 P—R4   Resigns

Every Move a Threat!

M. Porges · E. Lasker

Nuremberg 1896, RUY LOPEZ

One of the reasons Lasker was a tough man to beat was that he made use of ideas in his games years before they were discovered by the Hypermoderns. Here for example he demonstrates the Nimzovich concept that a restricted position is not necessarily disadvantageous. What counts is the amount of pent-up energy in the position, and the possibility of this energy exploding.

I think you will enjoy the way Lasker lets loose with ten moves in a row, each of them containing a threat!

1 P—K4	P—K4
2 Kt—KB3	Kt—QB3
3 B—Kt5	Kt—B3

Lasker preferred this move, which develops a piece, to the popular *3 . . . P—QR3.*

| 4 O—O | Kt × P |

Regarding the capture of a Pawn early in the game, Lasker gives this advice: "When you are conscious not to have violated the rules laid down, you should accept the sacrifice of an important Pawn, as the King Pawn, Queen Pawn, or one of the Bishop Pawns. If you do not, as a rule, the Pawn which you have rejected will become very trouble-some to you. Do not accept the sacrifice, however, with the idea of maintaining your material advantage at the expense of development. Such a policy never pays in the end. By far the better plan is to give the Pawn up after your opponent has made some exertions to gain it."

| 5 P—Q4 | B—K2 |
| 6 Q—K2 |

This is stronger than *6 P × P*, which lets Black free his game by *6 . . . P—Q4 7 P × P e.p., Kt × QP.*

6 . . .	Kt—Q3
7 B × Kt	KtP × B
8 P × P	Kt—Kt2

The Knight retreats, but after it makes its way back to K3, by way of B4, it will exert a great deal of influence on the center squares.

| 9 P—QKt3 |

The fianchettoed Bishop is not particularly well placed, as it exerts no pressure on Black's position. The natural *9 Kt—B3* is stronger, or perhaps *9 Kt—Q4* to prevent Black from playing *9 . . . P—Q4.*

| 9 . . . | O—O |
| 10 B—Kt2 | P—Q4! |

Once he gets ... P—Q4 in, Black can equalize in nearly all King Pawn openings.

11 P×P e.p.

This does away with Black's center Pawn, but in return it enables him to dissolve his doubled Pawn.

11 ...	P×P
12 QKt—Q2	R—K1!

With indirect threats against the Queen. It is interesting to see how quickly Black acquires a decisive advantage.

13 KR—K1

Restrains the Bishop for the time being. If instead *13 Q—Q3, Kt—B4* forces the Queen back to the King file, since *14 Q—B4* loses the exchange after *14 ... B—R3*, and *14 Q—B3* is dangerous after *14 ... B—B3 15 Kt—Q4, Q—Kt3*, and Black threatens *16 ... Kt—K3*.

13 ...	B—Q2

Protects the Rook (a necessary step, as we shall see) while developing a piece.

14 Kt—K4

An attempt to be aggressive, but it turns out to be a waste of time. The modest *14 Q—B1* was safer, even though it seems to be an admission of helplessness.

14 ...	P—Q4

Once again Black establishes a Pawn in the center—and with gain of time!

15 QKt—Q2

The Knight is forced to return to the square it came from. If instead *15 Kt—Kt3*, the reply *15 ... B—QKt5* wins the exchange for Black, while *15 Kt—B3* loses a whole piece by *15 ... B—QR6 16 Q—R6, B×B*.

This is the position, with Black to play:

15 ...	B—QR6
16 B—K5	

The only move, since *16 Q—R6* loses a piece by *16 ... B×B 17 QR—Kt1, Kt—B4*.

16 ...	P—B3
17 Q—R6	

This was forced, but is White wriggling out of his troubles? The Queen is now attacking two pieces.

17 ...	P×B
18 Q×B	

This is better than *18 Q×Kt, P—K5 19 Q—R6* (on *19 Kt—Q4, B—Kt7* wins the exchange) *B—Kt7 20 QR—Kt1, B—B3*, and White's unfortunate Knight, having no flight square, is lost.

18 ...	P—K5
19 Kt—Q4	Q—B3!

Black has attained his objective. All his pieces are admirably placed for a King side attack, while White's pieces are disorganized and ineffective.

| 20 P—QB3 | R—KB1 |
| 31 P—B3 | |

If *21* R—KB1 (to protect the Bishop Pawn) Q—Kt4 (attacks the Knight) *22* Q—B1, B—R6, and White must give up the exchange by *23* P—Kt3 to prevent mate.

| 21 ... | Q—Kt4! |

"One attacking move after another! Lasker plays this very strongly," says Tarrasch, who was usually rather chary of praise.

22 Q—B1

The threatened Knight cannot move because of *22* ... P—B4 followed by *23* ... P×P and wins; or if *22* QR—Q1, P—B4 *23* Kt—K2, P×P, and White is overwhelmed with threats, chief of which are *24* ... Q×P mate, *24* ... P—B7ch and *24* ... P×Kt.

| 22 ... | Kt—B4! |

The Knight enters with powerful effect. The first threat is *23* ... Kt—Q6 winning the exchange.

23 Kt—B1	Q—Kt3
24 R—K3	Kt—Q6
25 Q—Q1	

This is the position, with Black to move:

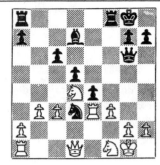

| 25 ... | Kt—B5! |

Threatens mate in one move (*26* ... Q×P mate) and the Queen in two (*26* ... Kt—R6ch *27* K—R1, Kt—B7ch).

| 26 Kt—Kt3 | P—KR4! |

The Knight must be dislodged!

| 27 Kt(Q4)—K2 | Kt×P! |

The sacrifice will bring the King out into the open.

28 K×Kt	P×Pch
29 R×P	B—R6ch!
30 K×B	

Or *30* K—B2, B—Kt5 *31* R×Rch, R×Rch *32* K—K3, P—R5 *33* Kt—KB1, Q—K5ch *34* K—Q2, R—B7, and White is lost.

30 ...	Q—Kt5ch
31 K—Kt2	Q×Rch
32 K—Kt1	

Or *32* K—R3, Q—Kt5ch *33* K—Kt2, P—R5, and the poor Knight is pinned.

| 32 ... | P—R5 |
| 33 Kt—R1 | |

If *33* Kt—KB1, P—R6 forces mate quickly.

| 33 ... | Q—K6ch |
| 34 Resigns | |

For *34* K—Kt2 allows a pretty mate by the Rook Pawn.

A Touch of Jujitsu

T. Petrosian · V. Korchnoi

Leningrad 1946, DUTCH DEFENSE

Petrosian must have the spark of genius! How else could he, with a few mysterious moves, cause the quick collapse of so eminent a player as Korchnoi?

By means of subtle strategy Petrosian brings about a position where his opponent's pieces must depend on each other for support. The Queen defends a Knight which defends a Rook which defends a Pawn. With the skill of a jujitsu expert, Petrosian applies pressure to the critical points, and Korchnoi is forced to resign at once.

1 P—Q4	P—K3
2 Kt—KB3	P—KB4

The Dutch Defense was for a long time a favorite defense of Alekhine and Botvinnik, both of whom won some marvellous games with it. One has only to recall Bogolyubov-Alekhine, Hastings 1922 (in my opinion the most brilliant game ever played), Rabinovich-Botvinnik, Moscow 1927, and Steiner-Botvinnik, Groningen 1946 to realize that the Dutch can be a formidable weapon in the right hands.

3 P—KKt3	Kt—KB3
4 B—Kt2	P—Q4
5 O—O	B—Q3
6 P—B4	P—B3

Black adopts the Stonewall formation. In this type of counterattack, the Knight will occupy the outpost K5, the Queen (after the King has Castled) will move to KR4, by way of K1, the King Knight Pawn will start the attack rolling by advancing to Kt4, and the King Rook will swing over to KR3 by way of KB3 to add weight to the assault.

7 P—Kt3	O—O
8 B—QR3!	

One would expect the fianchetto development of the Bishop after *7* P—QKt3, but Petrosian prefers to remove Black's King Bishop, a potentially dangerous attacking piece. Black's other Bishop is less to be feared, hemmed in as it is by Pawns on white squares.

8 ...	B×B
9 Kt×B	Q—K1
10 Kt—B2	

The Knight must not stay on the sidelines! The great master, you will note, does not waste time at every stage looking for a move or a combination that will suddenly win the game in a burst of brilliancy. What he is concerned with, long before he looks for any combinations, is to see that every piece is placed where it can do some good. Every piece should be centralized (if possible), every piece should have a fair amount of mobility (freedom of movement), and every piece should have some influence on the course of the game.

10 ...	Q—R4
11 Q—B1!	

Only a great master would find this move! Its first effect is to prevent Black from continuing his attack with *11* ... P—KKt4. (*It is as important to prevent the opponent from making good moves as it is to make them yourself.*) Its later effect will be the entrance of the Queen at QB7, with startling consequences.

11 ...	Kt—K5
12 Kt(B2)—K1!	

This is the sort of move Nimzovich would recommend. The Knight is headed for K5, to exploit the weakness created on that square by Black's Pawn position in the center. Nimzovich gave it as a principle that "Strategically important points should be overprotected. If the pieces are so engaged, they get their reward in the fact that they will then find themselves well posted in every respect."

12 ...	P—KKt4
13 Kt—Q3	Kt—Q2
14 Kt(B3)—K5	K—R1

Stealing a Pawn would be disastrous: After *14* ... Q×KP *15* P—B3, Kt(K5)—B3 (or *15* ... Kt—Q7) *16* R—K1 follows, and White wins the Queen.

15 P—B3	Kt—Q3

This is the position, with White to play:

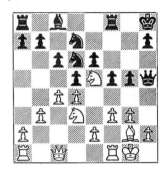

16 P—K4!

An offer of a Pawn which Black does not dare accept. For instance: If *16* ... BP×P *17* Kt×Kt, B×Kt *18* Kt—K5, QR—Q1 *19* P×KP, R×Rch *20* Q×R (the threats now are *21* Q—B6ch winning a Rook, and *21* Kt×B, R×Kt *22* Q—B8 mate) Q—K1 (if *20* ... Q—R3 *21* P—B5 wins the Knight since it must stay put) *21* Q—B6ch, K—Kt1 *22* Q×KtPch, K—R1 *23* R—KB1, and Black is helpless against the threats (*24* P—B5 followed by *25* Kt—B7ch, and *24* Q—B6ch, K—Kt1 *25* R—B4).

16 ...	Kt—B2
17 BP×P	Kt(Q2)×Kt
18 P×Kt	QBP×P
19 P×QP	P×P

Material is even, but White has more freedom of movement. Is that enough to be decisive?

20 P—B4	

Discovers an attack on the Queen Pawn.

20 ...	R—Q1

If *20* ... B—K3 *21* Kt—B5, QR—B1 *22* Q—K3, Q—Kt3 *23* QR—Q1, and White wins a Pawn.

21 Q—B7!

Did Petrosian foresee that he could make this tremendous move when he played Q—B1 ten moves earlier?

21 ...   P—Kt3

Black avoids the temptation to drive the Queen off by *21* ... R—Q2. The reply would be *22* Q—B5, when suddenly White has three threats:

(1) *23* Q—B8 mate.
(2) *23* P—K6, winning a piece.
(3) *23* B×P, winning an important Pawn while bringing the Bishop strongly into the game.

With the move he makes, Black hopes at long last to develop his Queen Bishop, and unite his Rooks.

22 P×P   B—R3

Quite plausible. The Bishop comes into play attacking a piece, and communication is established between the Rooks.

Here too, driving the Queen away by *22* ... R—Q2 is fatal. White meets the attack by *23* Q—B6, after which he can win as he pleases— *23* ... R—Kt2 *24* Q—K8ch, K—Kt2 *25* P—K6 being one possibility. This is the position:

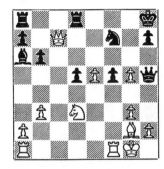

Notice how Black's pieces must depend on each other for protection. His Queen Pawn is defended by the Rook, the Rook by the Knight, and the Knight is defended by the Queen. *Something has to give way if pressure is exerted at the right point.*

23 Kt—B4!   Resigns

The Queen must abandon the Knight, after taking which, White has an easy win.

The King-Side Attack

S. Tarrasch · T. von Scheve

Leipzig 1894, QUEEN'S GAMBIT DECLINED

"A plan is made for a few moves only," says Reuben Fine, "not for the whole game."

This may be so, but here is an instance where Tarrasch maps out a course of play leading practically to mate, from so early a stage as the eighth move in the game!

His attack on a Pawn forces an exchange which pries open the Knight file. On this file, leading straight to von Scheve's King, Tarrasch posts both his Rooks. Then he adds to this concentration of power by swinging the Queen over to that area. The way these heavy pieces then crash through the barriers is in itself an object lesson in the art of conducting an assault against the King.

1 P—Q4	P—Q4
2 P—QB4	P—K3
3 Kt—QB3	Kt—KB3
4 Kt—B3	B—K2
5 B—B4	P—B3

Instead of this meek move, Black should attack the center by 5 ... P—B4.

6 P—K3	QKt—Q2
7 P—KR3	

Prepares a flight square for the Bishop in the event that Black plays 7 ... Kt—R4. Even in his early years Tarrasch knew the value of preserving the two Bishops.

7 ...	Kt—K5

Believe it or not, this might be the losing move! This is Tarrasch's own comment on 7 ... Kt—K5: "The decisive error. After the exchange of Knights, Black's capturing Pawn becomes weak and needs protection by ... P—KB4. It is then attacked by P—B3, forcing Black to exchange and open the Knight file for White. Thereupon there ensues a combined attack of White's Queen, both Rooks and the Queen Bishop against the Knight Pawn (the keystone of the Castled position), an attack which is irresistible. I know of no game in all of chess literature in which it is possible to conceive so detailed a plan, leading almost to mate, and in which the remaining 20 moves lead up to a catastrophe."

This is the position, with White to play:

8	Kt×Kt	P×Kt
9	Kt—Q2	B—Kt5

Of this move Tarrasch says characteristically, "Had Black foreseen the consequences of my plan (which could hardly have been expected of him) he would have retained this Bishop for the protection of the King Knight Pawn."

10	P—R3	B×Ktch
11	Q×B	

Now White has the advantage of the two Bishops.

11	...	O—O

There was no hurry to Castle, and let the opponent know the new address of the King. There was more fight in 11 ... Q—K2 followed by 12 ... P—K4, to get some counter-play in the center.

12	Q—B2	P—KB4

If Black protects the Pawn by 12 ... Kt—B3 instead, then 13 B—K5 followed by 14 B×Kt will win the Pawn.

13 B—Q6!

Gets a grip on the black squares, while preventing 13 ... Q—K2 and

14 ... P—K4.

13	...	R—K1

Better than this was 13 ... R—B2, which defends the vulnerable Knight Pawn. Black would surely have played this move had he visualized the attack contemplated by Tarrasch against this Pawn.

14	O—O—O	Kt—B3
15	B—K5	B—Q2
16	P—B3!	

Threatens to win a Pawn by 17 B×Kt, Q×B 18 P×P, P×P 19 Q×P, and forces Black's reply.

16	...	P×P
17	P×P	

Second step of the plan: the Knight file is now open for business.

17	...	P—QKt4

Black tries to get some sort of counter-play.

18	R—Kt1	R—KB1

Ready to meet 19 Q—Kt2 with 19 ... R—B2. Of course not 18 ... R—K2, with the same object in mind, as White simply snips off a piece by 19 B×Kt.

19 R—Q2!

Much more to the point than mechanically developing a piece. A move such as 19 B—Q3 would be a waste of time, as the Bishop can take no part in the attack against the King Knight Pawn.

19	...	R—B2
20	R(Q2)—Kt2	P—QR4
21	Q—B2!	

The Queen is on her way to R4 and then R6.

21 ...   Kt—K1

This move not only defends the Pawn once more, but prevents White from moving his Queen to R4.

22 R—Kt5!

"Behind the broad back of this Tower, the Queen will manage to get to the square R4," says Tarrasch.

22 ...   Q—K2

If *22 ...* P—Kt3, White breaks through by *23* P—KR4 and *24* P—R5.

Or if *22 ...* P—R3 *23* R—Kt6, K—R2 *24* Q—Kt3, Q—K2 *25* R×RPch!, P×R *26* Q—Kt6 mate. This is the position:

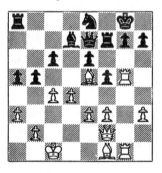

23 Q—R4

Threatens *24* Q—R6 followed by *25* R—R5. If then *25 ...* P—Kt3 *26* R×Pch, Kt—Kt2 (or R—Kt2) *27* Q×Pch, and White wins.

23 ...   Kt—B3
24 Q—R6

Threatens *25* B×Kt, Q×B *26* Q×Q, R×Q *27* R×Pch, K—R1 *28*

R×B, and White wins a piece.

24 ...   R—R2

Other defenses lose quickly:
(1) *24 ...* P—Kt3 *25* R×Pch, P×R *26* R×Pch, R—Kt2 *27* B×Kt.
(2) *24 ...* K—R1 *25* R×P, R×R *26* B×Kt.
(3) *24 ...* B—K1 *25* B×Kt, Q×B *26* Q×Q, R×Q *27* R×Pch, K—B1 *28* R×P, and White wins easily.

25 B—Q6!

In a strategically superior position, the combinations come of themselves!

White sacrifices the Bishop to lure away one of the defenders of the Knight Pawn.

25 ...   Q×B
26 R×Pch   K—B1

Black must walk into a discovered check! If *26 ...* K—R1 instead, *27* Q×Pch, Kt×Q *28* R—Kt8 is checkmate.

27 R×P dis ch

It is necessary to remove this Pawn, as we will see later.

27 ...   K—K2
28 R×Rch   K×R
29 R—Kt7ch   K—K1
30 Q×Kt

The threat is *31* R—Kt8ch and mate next move. If Black defends by *30 ...* Q—B1, then *31* Q—Kt6ch (this move was made possible by removing the Rook Pawn at the 27th move) K—Q1 *32* R—Kt8, and White wins the Queen.

30 ...   Resigns

A curious feature of this game is that Tarrasch won it without making a single move with his King Bishop. What makes this particularly noteworthy is that Tarrasch once said, "As Rousseau could not compose without his cat beside him, so I cannot play chess without my King's Bishop. In its absence the game to me is lifeless and void. The vitalizing factor is missing, and I can devise no plan of attack."

Magnificent Outpost

V. Smyslov · I. Rudakovsky

Moscow 1945, SICILIAN DEFENSE

"The Knight at QB3," says Nimzovich, "is under obligation, the moment the enemy gives him the chance, of undertaking an invasion of the center by Kt—Q5."

Smyslov has a Knight at QB3, but does not intend to sit by idly and wait for such a chance. The key square is heavily guarded, but Smyslov finds a way to get rid of its defenders. Once they are disposed of, Smyslov plants his Knight firmly at Q5, and stabilizes the center. He then turns his attention to the King side, and breaks through quickly with a brilliant attack.

1	P—K4	P—QB4
2	Kt—KB3	P—K3
3	P—Q4	P×P
4	Kt×P	Kt—KB3
5	Kt—QB3	P—Q3

The Scheveningen Variation, a deceptive line of play. It is particularly effective against a premature King-side attack.

6	B—K2	B—K2
7	O—O	O—O
8	B—K3	Kt—B3
9	P—B4	Q—B2
10	Q—K1	

Clears the square Q1 for the Queen Rook, and prepares to develop the Queen at KKt3.

10	...	Kt×Kt

This exchange is not in keeping with the requirements of the Scheveningen. In this line, Black's Queen Knight aims at occupying the square QB5 after suitable preparation, say by ... P—QR3 and ... P—QKt4. From that square the Knight will be in position either to destroy (by exchange) one of White's powerful Bishops, or simply stay there and exert strong pressure on the center.

The ideal set-up for Black is something like this:

The Queen Rook Pawn at R3, to prepare for ... P—QKt4, and to prevent White from attacking the Queen by Kt—Kt5.

The Queen Knight Pawn at Kt4.

The Bishops at Q2 and K2.

The King Knight at KB3.

The Queen Knight at QB5 (by way of B3 and R4).

The Queen at QB2.

The Queen Rook at QB1.

The King Rook at Q1.

Besides seizing the outpost at QB5, Black aims at control of the Queen Bishop file, and a fair share of the center after an eventual ... P—Q4.

The thing to remember is that the Scheveningen is a fighting defense. White's threats on the King-side should be met by counter-attack on the Queen-side.

11 B×Kt   P—K4

A good alternative is *11* ... B—Q2 followed by *12* ... B—B3, with something to say about the center.

12 B—K3

The position is tricky. If *12* P×P, P×P *13* Q—Kt3 (pinning the Pawn) B—B4 is a counter-pin which might induce White to commit hara-kiri by *14* Q×KP, Q×Q.

12 ...   B—K3

This leads to more exchanges, which may have been what Black wanted. Preferable though was quiet development by *12* ... B—Q2 and *13* ... B—B3.

Here is the position:

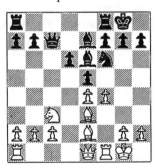

13 P—B5!

Gains a tempo for the pursuit of the King-side attack.

13 ...   B—B5

There was still time for the Bishop to retreat to Q2. In Black's offer to exchange Bishops he loses a guardian of his Q4 square.

14 B×B

White is happy to oblige!

14 ...   Q×B
15 B—Kt5!

And this will get rid of another defender of the vital square. Black cannot avoid the exchange of his Knight.

15 ...   KR—K1
16 B×Kt   B×B
17 Kt—Q5!

The exclamation point is not for the move itself (since it is self-evident) but for the manner in which White attained his objective—control of the center.

"If the defender is forced to give up the center," said Tarrasch (long before this game was played) "then every possible attack follows almost of itself."

The reader will note that the Knight is not only strongly placed, but is almost impossible to dislodge.

17 ...   B—Q1

Black avoids *17* ... Q×BP, as after *18* R—B2, Q—B3 *19* R—QB1, Q—Q2 *20* Kt—B7, he loses the exchange.

18 P—B3   P—QKt4
19 P—QKt3   Q—B4ch
20 K—R1   R—QB1
21 R—B3   K—R1

Black might have played *21* ... P—B3 here, to prevent the break-up of his King-side position. The subsequent play would probably have gone something like this: *22* R—R3, P—QR4 *23* Q—R4, P—R3 *24* Q—Kt4 (threatens *25* R×P) K—R1 *25* R—KB1, B—K2 *26* Q—Kt6, B—B1 *27* P—Kt4, and

Black has no defense.

This is the position, with White to play:

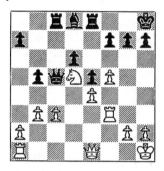

22 P—B6!

A fine sacrifice! It breaks up the enemy Pawn position, and opens up lines leading to his King.

22 ...   P×P

On 22 ... P—Kt3, White has choice between the simple 23 Q—Q2 (threatening 24 Q—R6) and the combinative 23 R—R3 (threatens 24 R×Pch, K×R 25 Q—R4ch, K—Kt1 26 Q—R6 followed by mate) P—KR4 24 Q—Kt3, R—KKt1 25 Q—Kt5, K—R2 26 R× Pch, P×R 27 Q×RP mate.

23 Q—R4   R—KKt1

Otherwise 24 R—R3 is immediately decisive.

24 Kt×P

Threatens 25 Q×P mate.

24 ...   R—Kt2
25 R—Kt3!

Initiates two pretty threats:
(1) 26 Q×Pch, R×Q 27 R—Kt8 mate.
(2) 26 R×R, K×R 27 Q×Pch, K×Kt 28 R—B1ch, K—K2 29 Q×P mate.

25 ...   B×Kt
26 Q×B   R—KKt1
27 R—Q1

White's reserve piece comes out of the corner. The intention is now 28 R×P followed by 29 R×R, R×R 30 R—Q8ch and mate next move.

27 ...   P—Q4

Hoping to prolong the struggle (if there is any merit in prolonging a lost game). If now 28 R×P, Q—KB1 29 R×R, Q×R 30 Q×Qch, K×Q 31 R×KP, P—QR3, and Black can add a few more moves to his score before resigning.

28 R×R!

But White polishes him off neatly by reversing moves!
Now if 28 ... R×R 29 R×P Q—KB1 30 R—Q8, and Black's Queen is pinned.

28 ...   Resigns

The Art of Exchanging Pieces

V. Menchik · J. R. Capablanca

Hastings 1931, QUEEN'S INDIAN DEFENSE

Nothing exciting seems to happen in this game, yet it is a joy to play through. In it we see an interesting aspect of Capablanca's wondrous technique—his inimitable flair for extracting an advantage from the most routine of procedures.

Here for example, Miss Menchik tries to force a draw by exchanging as many pieces as possible. Far from avoiding these attempts to simplify the game, Capablanca welcomes the exchanges, and emerges from each of them with a slightly superior position. By the time most of the pieces have been cleared away, his positional advantage is strong enough to yield a Pawn. One extra Pawn is all Capablanca needs, and since he had an incomparable faculty for making all endings look easy, it is a treat to watch him win this one.

1	P—Q4	Kt—KB3
2	Kt—KB3	P—QKt3

Black indicates that he will try to control the square K5 with his Knight and Queen Bishop. This will make it difficult for White to play P—K4, a desirable objective in Queen Pawn openings.

3	P—K3	B—Kt2
4	B—Q3	P—B4

This attack on the Pawn center is always advisable for Black.

5	O—O	Kt—B3
6	P—B3	P—K3
7	Kt—K5	

This violates the principle that requires each piece be moved only once in the opening. But White is anxious to exchange pieces, even if time is lost thereby.

7	...	P—Q3
8	Kt×Kt	B×Kt

The result of the first exchange is that Black has two pieces in the field against one of White's.

9	Q—K2	B—K2
10	B—Kt5	

Once again White moves a piece twice, neglecting the development of those still on the back rank.

10	...	Q—Q2
11	B×B	Q×B

A couple of Bishops are off the board. The difference though is that White's Bishop has disappeared completely, but Black's has been replaced by another piece—the Queen.

Aside from the fact that White has Castled, she has only one piece in play, while Black has three.

| 12 Kt—Q2 | O—O |
| 13 P×P | |

This makes the Queen file available to Black's Rooks, but if *13 P—K4* at once, then *13 ... P×P 14 P×P, QR—B1*, and White's Knight and Bishop will still have trouble disentangling themselves.

| 13 ... | QP×P |
| 14 P—K4 | QR—Q1 |

What a lovely view the Rook has!

15 P—K5

The Pawn advances so that the Knight is not tied down to its protection. Once the Knight steps out of the way, the Bishop is free to move. After the Bishop is developed, the Queen Rook can get into the game.

| 15 ... | Kt—Q4 |
| 16 Kt—B3 | R—Q2 |

Simple and strong! Black prepares to double Rooks on the open file.

| 17 R—Q1 | KR—Q1 |
| 18 B—Q2 | |

A modest little move, but what else is there? If *18 B—K3, Kt×B 19 R×R, Q×R*, and Black dominates the Queen file, while *18 B—Kt5* succumbs to *18 ... B×B 19 Kt×B, Kt—B5!* (attacks the Queen and

threatens mate) *20 Q—Kt4, R×Rch 21 R×R, R×Rch 22 Q×R, Q×P* mate.

This is the position:

| 18 ... | P—QKt4! |

Vacates the square Kt3 for the convenience of the Knight. From there the Knight can leap to B5 or R5, establishing a strong outpost at one of those squares.

| 19 K—B1 | Kt—Kt3 |
| 20 B—B4 | P—KR3 |

Before continuing matters on the Queen side, Black provides a flight square for his King, meanwhile restricting the activity of White's Knight and Bishop.

21 R×R

White keeps on exchanging pieces, since the position looks quiet and devoid of danger.

21 ...	R×R
22 R—Q1	R×Rch
23 Q×R	Q—K5!

A powerful move! It wins a Pawn by force. The threat (besides *24 ... Q×B*) is *24 ... Q—B5ch* followed by *25 ... Q×RP*.

24 B—Kt3

If instead *24* B—K3 (or *24* B—Q2) Kt—B5 wins either the King Pawn or the Queen Knight Pawn. Or if *24* B—B1 (to protect the Knight Pawn) Q—B5ch *25* Q—K2, Q×RP *26* Q×P, Q—Kt8, and the pinned Bishop is lost.

24 ...	Q—B5ch
25 Q—K2	Q×Qch
26 K×Q	Kt—R5
27 K—Q2	

Certainly not *27* P—Kt3, Kt×Pch, and Black wins two Pawns instead of one.

27 ...	Kt×KtP
28 K—B2	Kt—B5
29 Kt—Q2	

White offers to exchange ...

29 ...	Kt×Kt

... and Black is happy to oblige!

30 K×Kt	P—B5!

In Bishop and Pawn endings, the Pawns should not occupy squares of the color on which the Bishop travels. If they do, the range of activity of the Bishop will be restricted.

Notice how the occupation of K5 by a Pawn hampers the free movement of White's Bishop.

31 B—B4

This is not only an attempt to get the Bishop into active play, but it sets a trap for an over-eager opponent.

This is the position, with Black to play:

31 ...	P—R3

Capablanca does not even go near the trap! If *31* ... B—Kt4 (to exchange Bishops and bring it to a simple Pawn ending) *32* B×B, P×B *33* K—K3, K—B1 *34* K—Q4, K—K2 *35* K—B5, P—R3 *36* P—QR3, and White regains her Pawn.

32 B—K3	K—B1
33 B—Kt6	K—K1
34 K—K3	K—Q2
35 K—Q4	K—B3
36 B—R7	

The only move for the Bishop, since *36* B—R5 allows *36* ... B—B4ch, and Black wins a Pawn.

36 ...	P—B4!

Tightening the coils so that neither the Bishop nor the King may move. If the Bishop moves (*37* B—Kt8) *37* ... B—B4 is mate, or if the King moves (*37* K—K3) *37* ... B—B4ch removes the Bishops and brings it to an ending with Pawns only, and "pure Pawn endings are the easiest endings to win," says Reuben Fine. White also has choice of *37* P×P *e.p.*, but then *37* ... B×Pch *38* K—K4, B×P leaves Black two Pawns ahead.

37 P—QR4

This may look like suicide, but White's moves are running out. Advancing the Pawns on the King-side would delay the inevitable for only a brief while—a move by King or Bishop, either of which is fatal.

37 ...	P—Kt3
38 P—B4	P—KR4
39 P × Pch	K × P
40 P—Kt3	P—R4
41 K—K3	

Or *41* P—R3, P—QR5 *42* K—K3, P—R6, and the Pawn can not be headed off.

41 ...	B—B4ch
42 B × B	K × B
43 Resigns	

The rest, if White is not convinced, could go like this: *43* K—Q2, K—Q4 *44* K—K3, P—QR5 *45* K—Q2, P—R6 *46* K—B2, K—K5 *47* P—R3, P—R7 *48* K—Kt2, K—Q6, and the rest is elementary.

The moral is: Play for a win if you want to get a draw!

The Isolated Pawn

E. Lasker · S. Tarrasch

St. Petersburg 1914, QUEEN'S GAMBIT DECLINED

An isolated Pawn stands all by itself, away from any fellow Pawns. It looks weak, since it can only be protected by pieces. Despite its seeming frailty the isolated Pawn is not easily susceptible to capture. For with every piece that threatens to remove it, there is a friendly piece ready to come to its rescue. It takes ingenuity to find a means of procedure.

Lasker has that ingenuity, and this is how he proceeds: He begins by a direct attack on the Pawn. If that does not succeed he attacks the pieces protecting the Pawn. If that effort is repulsed he attacks the Pawns that protect the pieces that protect the isolated Pawn. This undermining of the defensive structure at the base is bound to cause a fatal weakening and a consequent loss of material. In this case, Lasker wins a Rook for a Knight and two Pawns. It may not seem like a great deal, but in the hands of a fine player it is enough to be decisive. The way Lasker goes about forcing resignation is a lesson in the art of winning a won game.

1 P—Q4	P—Q4
2 Kt—KB3	P—QB4
3 P—B4	P—K3

A favorite defense with Tarrasch, who says of it, "This I hold to be the best, although I must add that I am almost completely alone in holding that opinion. It is based upon the undeniably correct idea that in the Queen's Gambit ... P—QB4 is the freeing move for Black, and must therefore be made as soon as possible. With this defense Black gets a fine free game for his pieces, at the cost of isolating his Queen's Pawn."

4 BP×P	KP×P
5 P—KKt3	Kt—QB3
6 B—Kt2	Kt—B3
7 O—O	B—K2
8 P×P	B×P

Tarrasch is quite pleased with the situation. "White has no positional equivalent," he says, "for the centralized Pawn." So far as its isolation is concerned, his view is that, "He who fears an isolated Queen's Pawn should give up chess."

9 QKt—Q2

The conventional 9 Kt—B3 permits Black to gain a tempo by 9 ... P—Q5. White's idea with the move he does make is to switch the Knight over to QKt3 and then to Q4, where it will blockade the isolated Pawn.

9 ...   **P—Q5**

Wasting a move which should have been devoted to furthering his development, say by *9 ... O—O.*

Nimzovich's wry comment on this move is, "The isolated Pawn has the choice of becoming weak at Q4 or Q5."

10 **Kt—Kt3**   **B—Kt3**
11 **Q—Q3!**

Fixes the Pawn so that it cannot move! Now Lasker threatens to play *12* R—Q1, attacking the Pawn with four pieces.

11 ...   **B—K3**
12 **R—Q1**   **B×Kt**

This exchange removes one of the pieces attacking the Pawn, but it leaves White with the advantage of the two Bishops.

13 **Q×B**

Now Lasker threatens to attack the Queen Pawn by *14* P—K3.

13 ...   **Q—K2**
14 **B—Q2!**

A subtle move, and one that is superior to the obvious development by *14* B—B4.

14 ...   **O—O**
15 **P—QR4!**

"An unusually fine move," says Tarrasch himself. "The Pawn is to be advanced to R5 and then R6, where it will undermine the position of the Queen side pieces, especially that of the Knight."

15 ...   **Kt—K5**

Capturing the King Pawn would

be fatal. After *15 ...* Q×P *16* R—K1, Q—R3 *17* B—KB1, Black's Queen is caught.

16 **B—K1**   **QR—Q1**
17 **P—R5**

Note that the brash Pawn has the support of the Bishop which was shrewdly developed at Q2.

17 ...   **B—B4**
18 **P—R6!**

Attacks the support of the Knight, one of the protectors of the isolated Pawn.

18 ...   **P×P**

The alternative is *18 ...* P—QKt3. Against this Lasker would probably proceed by *19* Q—R4, R—B1 *20* QR—Kt1, and the advance by P—QKt4 will drive off the Bishop and win the Queen Pawn.

19 **QR—B1**

All of Black's minor pieces now hang in the air, and he must guard against loss of one of them by *20* Kt—R4.

19 ...   **R—B1**

This is the position, with White to play:

20 **Kt—R4!**

After this move, something will have to give. The immediate threat is *21* B × Kt, Q × B *22* R × B, winning a piece for White.

20 ...   B—Kt3

Probably as good as there is. If *20* ... Kt—Q1 *21* Kt—B5, Q—K4 *22* B × Kt, Q × B, *23* Kt—Q6, and White wins the exchange by a pretty Pin and Knight Fork. Or if *20* ... B—Q3 *21* Kt—B5 attacks the Queen which protects the Knight, which protects the Bishop. If then *21* ... Q—K4 *22* B × Kt, and Black does not dare recapture by *22* ... Q × B.

21 Kt—B5	Q—K4
22 B × Kt	Q × B
23 Kt—Q6	Q × P
24 Kt × R	R × Kt

Black has lost a Rook for a Knight and two Pawns, but the isolated Pawn has become a passed Pawn and might prove to be dangerous.

25 Q—Q5   Q—K3

The attempt to save the Knight by other means would have provided a little lesson in tactical themes: If *25* ... Kt—K2 (unpinning) *26* R × Rch, Kt × R *27* Q—R8 (pinning) Q—K1 *28* R—B1, Kt—Q3 (unpinning) *29* Q × Qch, Kt × Q *30* R—B8 (pinning) K—B1 *31* B—Kt4ch (driving off the protector) K—Kt1 *32* R × Kt mate (the vulnerable last rank).

26 Q—B3

This is stronger than exchanging Queens; it maintains the pressure.

26 ...   P—R3

27 B—Q2!

Tarrasch does not relish an exchange of Rooks (which he offers next move) but he is faced with this possibility: *28* R—K1, Q—Q2 *29* R—B4 (to double Rooks on the Bishop file) Kt—R4 (or *29* ... Kt—K2 *30* R × Kt winning a piece) *30* R—K7, Q × R *31* R × Rch, K—R2 *32* B × Kt, B × B *33* Q—B5ch, and White picks up the unfortunate Bishop.

27 ...	Kt—K4
28 R × Rch	Q × R
29 Q—K4	Kt—Q2
30 R—QB1	Q—B1

This is the position, with White to play:

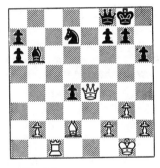

31 B × P!

Lasker is always alert. The exposed position of Black's Knight will cost him a Pawn.

31 ...   Kt—B4

On *31* ... P × B *32* Q—Kt4ch followed by *32* Q × Kt regains the piece and leaves White with a dominating position.

| 32 Q—Kt4 | P—B4 |
| 33 Q—Kt6 | |

This compels Black to offer to exchange Queens, as otherwise he can not beat off the invaders. White has two threats of winning: *34 R—K1* followed by *35 R—K8*, pinning the Queen, and *34 P—QKt4, Kt—Q2 35 R—B8, Q×R 36 Q×P* mate.

33 ...	Q—B2
34 Q×Qch	K×Q
35 B—Kt5	Kt—Q6
36 R—Kt1	

"A miserable move!" says Tarrasch jokingly, "Much prettier is the protection of the Pawn by *36 R—B2*, when Black can reply *36 ... Kt—K8* followed by *37 ... Kt—B6ch*, winning the Bishop."

36 ...	K—K3
37 P—Kt3	K—Q4
38 P—B3	

This move and the previous one keep the King from penetrating further and helping the Queen Pawn.

38 ...	P—R4
39 P—R4	Kt—B4
40 P—R5	P—Q6
41 K—B1	P—R5

Tarrasch's idea is to get rid of White's Knight Pawn, by exchange or otherwise. His King could then move on to B5, B6 and B7. The passed Pawn would then become a real menace.

42 P×P	Kt×P
43 B—B6!	

A little surprise for Tarrasch! It wins a Pawn, and clears a pathway for the Rook Pawn.

43 ...	K—K3

The capture by *43 ... P×B* would lose instantly by *44 P—R6*, as the Pawn could not be headed off. Nor could Black rescue the threatened Pawn by *43 ... B—Q5*, as then *44 B×B, K×B 45 R—Kt4ch* wins the Knight.

44 B×P	K—B2
45 B—K5	Kt—B4
46 R—Q1	Resigns

For *47 B—Q4* followed by *48 B×Kt* will finally win the Queen Pawn (which has had a charmed life, considering the high mortality rate of isolated Pawns).

Both Alekhine and Tarrasch had high praise for the elegance of Lasker's positional and tactical play in this game.

The See-Saw Check, Zugzwang, and Other Tactical Tricks

A. Kupferstich · J. Andreassen

Denmark 1953, VIENNA GAME

Wonderful things go on in this game! There is a series of see-saw checks that is remarkable, an imprisonment of King and Rook that is unique, and a threat of mate requiring at least ten moves to execute, yet so clear-cut a child could carry it out.

Question: Does this game, played so brilliantly come under the heading of "Entertainment" or "Instruction?"

1 P—K4	P—K4
2 Kt—QB3	Kt—KB3
3 B—B4	Kt × P
4 Q—R5!	

This is preferable to *4* Kt × Kt, P—Q4, when Black gets his piece back and retains the initiative.

4 ...	Kt—Q3
5 B—Kt3	Kt—B3
6 Kt—Kt5	

Threatens mate, beginning with *7* Kt × Ktch.

6 ...	P—KKt3
7 Q—B3	Kt—B4

Alekhine favors *7 ...* P—B4, and if *8* Q—Q5, Q—B3 *9* Kt × Pch, K—Q1 *10* Kt × R, P—Kt3, and

Black has "a very strong and probably irresistible attack."

8 Q—Q5

Threatens mate for the third (but not the last) time.

8 ...	Kt—R3
9 P—Q4	

Obviously aiming at *10* B × Kt, B × B *11* Q × BP mate. (What an obsession!)

9 ...	P—Q3
10 B × Kt	B—K3
11 Q—B3	B(K3) × B
12 B × B	B—R5
13 B—Kt7	R—KKt1
14 B—B6	Q—Q2
15 Kt—QR3	Kt × P
16 Q—R3	Q × Q
17 Kt × Q	Kt × Pch

Black tries to collect a few Pawns in return for the piece he has lost.

18 Kt × Kt	B × Kt
19 R—QB1	B—K5
20 Kt—Kt5	

The attack on the Bishop gains a tempo for White.

20 ...	B×P

One would expect White to play *21* R—KKt1, but then Black has time to defend with *21* ... B—B3 *22* Kt×RP, K—Q2. White has a more effective continuation.

This is the position:

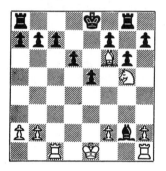

21 R×P!

White sacrifices one Rook for the sake of seizing the seventh rank with the other.

21 ...	B×R
22 Kt×BP	

With three of White's pieces so close to the King there are bound to be mate threats. The one now facing the King is *23* Kt×Pch, K—B1 *24* R—B7 mate.

22 ...	B—Q4
23 Kt×Pch	K—B1
24 B—Kt5	R—R1

The King must have a flight-square!

25 B—R6ch	K—Kt1
26 R—Kt7ch	K—B1
27 R—QB7 dis ch	

Not the quickest way, but it does not matter. Black is helpless.

27 ...	K—Kt1
28 Kt—B8	B—B6
29 R—Kt7ch	K—B1
30 R×QKtP dis ch	

Now he's on the right track!

30 ...	K—Kt1

If *30* ... K—K1 *31* Kt—Q6ch, K—Q1 *32* B—Kt5 mate.

31 R—Kt7ch	K—B1
32 R×QRP dis ch	

"The see-saw can be the cause of frightful devastation," says Nimzovich.

32 ...	K—Kt1
33 R×R!	

An exchange of Rooks when White is behind in material? There is method in his madness though, as we will see.

33 ...	B×R
34 Kt—Q6!!	

Marvellous! The Knight and Bishop stalemate Black's King and Rook. Black can do nothing now but wait for the blow to fall.

This is the position:

White forces mate by marching his King to K7, and then mating at KB6 with the Knight. The Knight reaches that square by way of K8 or K4, Black's Bishop being unable to guard both these squares.

Play would proceed as follows: *34 ...* B—Q4 *35* K—Q2, B×P *36* K—B3, B—K3 *37* K—Kt4, B—R7 *38* K—B5, B—K3 *39* K—Kt6, B—R7 *40* K—B7, B—K3 *41* K—Q8, B—R7 *42* K—K7, B—Q4 *43* Kt—K8, B—R7 *44* Kt—B6 mate.

Black could delay this a bit by sacrificing his Pawns, but since he could not give away his Bishop, there is no hope of drawing by stalemate. Therefore:

34 ...   **Resigns**

The Two Bishops

S. Rosenthal · W. Steinitz

Vienna 1873, THREE KNIGHTS' GAME

This is one of the earliest, and still one of the most impressive examples of the superiority of two Bishops to two Knights, or to Knight and Bishop.

Steinitz's Bishops lurk in the background, but their presence is felt. They exert a baleful influence the length of the board, just by being there. His opponent's lone Bishop on the other hand, confined to squares of one color, is sadly circumscribed, while his Knight, struggling to get a foothold in the center, is harried by the adverse Pawns, and driven from the field of battle.

1 P—K4	P—K4
2 Kt—QB3	Kt—QB3
3 Kt—B3	P—KKt3

The book move is 3 ... B—Kt5, but Steinitz preferred to throw his opponents on their own resources.

4 P—Q4	P×P
5 Kt×P	

A more aggressive line is *5* Kt—Q5, with this likely sequence: *5* ... B—Kt2 *6* B—KKt5, QKt—K2 *7* P—K5, P—KR3 *8* B×Kt, Kt×B *9* Q×P, Kt×Kt *10* Q×Kt, P—QB3 *11* Q—Q6, B—B1 *12* Q—Q4, and White retains the initiative.

5 ...	B—Kt2
6 B—K3	KKt—K2

This is better than *6* Kt—B3, shutting off the Bishop's view.

7 B—QB4

This can not be completely bad, since a piece is developed, but the move is not in consonance with the requirements of the position. Steinitz himself suggested *7* P—KR4, an attack on the fianchettoed formation, and a revolutionary concept in strategy. Nobody in those days relinquished voluntarily the privilege of Castling on the King-side, when King-side Castling was almost automatic.

Another good line is *7* Q—Q2, P—KR3 *8* O—O—O, P—Q3 *9* B—K2, and White has a fine game.

7 ...	P—Q3
8 O—O	O—O
9 P—B4	

White's Pawn center looks impressive, but the Pawns interfere with the free movement of the pieces. The Queen Bishop for example, has had its mobility lessened and is an exposed (unprotected) piece.

9 ...	Kt—R4!

A fine move, whose object is to get in ... P—Q4, the freeing move in King Pawn openings.

10 B—Q3

The Bishop should retreat to K2, but White seems to have no idea of what is coming.

10 ...   P—Q4!

Not only does this break up White's Pawn center, but it initiates an attack on the Queen file.

11 P×P

Pushing on by *11 P—K5* would be fatal, as *11 ... P—QB4 12 Kt—B3*, P—Q5 wins a piece for Black.

11 ...	Kt×P
12 Kt×Kt	Q×Kt
13 P—B3	R—Q1

The heavy pieces bear down on the Queen file. Black threatens *14 ... P—QB4 15 P—B4, Q—Q2*, winning a piece.

14 Q—B2

Ready to meet *14 ... P—QB4* with *15 B—K4* followed by *16 Kt—B3*. This would rescue the pieces on the Queen file.

This is the position, with Black to move:

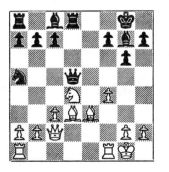

14 ...   Kt—B5!
15 B×Kt

Blithely allowing his opponent the two-Bishop racket (as Pollock called it). Rosenthal was apparently unfamiliar with the game won by Paulsen trom Hannah in the 1862 London tournament, in which the advantage of retaining both Bishops was convincingly demonstrated. Did Steinitz know this game, I wonder, or did Steinitz think that he discovered this concept in chess strategy?

15 ...   Q×B

Now Black threatens to win a piece by *16 ... B×Kt 17 B×B*, R×B.

16 Q—B2   P—QB4

The beginning of a campaign to make life miserable for the Knight. The Knight is to be driven away from any outpost (such as Q4 or K5, where it has the support of a Pawn) and forced into retreat.

This move evicts the Knight from the square Q4.

17 Kt—B3   P—Kt3

Steinitz's Pawn chain on the Queen-side greatly limits the scope of White's Bishop. Note that the Bishop is blocked on the other diagonal by White's own Bishop Pawn.

18 Kt—K5	Q—K3
19 Q—B3	B—QR3
20 KR—K1	

This is the position, with Black to play:

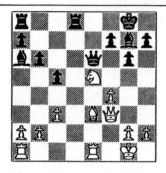

20 ...   P—B3

This will dislodge the Knight from another fine outpost.

21 Kt—Kt4

The Knight must retreat: If 21 Kt—B6, KR—QB1 ends its gay career, or if 21 Q—B6, Q×Q 22 Kt×Q, R—Q3 23 Kt—K7ch, K—B2 24 B—B2, R—K1, and the stranded Knight will be captured.

21 ...   P—R4

Another thrust by a Pawn, and the Knight must go still further back.

22 Kt—B2   Q—B2

Steinitz prepares to force the Queen off the long diagonal by ... B—Kt2, and seize it for himself.

23 P—B5

Plausible, since White needs elbow-room desperately, but the Pawn becomes weak and is soon captured.

23 ...   P—KKt4
24 QR—Q1   B—Kt2
25 Q—Kt3   R—Q4!

Much better than 25 ... Q×RP 26 Q—B7, R×R 28 R×R, B—Q4 29 Q—Q7, and White might become obstreperous.

26 R×R   Q×R
27 R—Q1

On 27 Q—R3, P—Kt5 wins the Bishop Pawn, as White must guard aginst the threat of mate.

27 ...   Q×BP
28 Q—B7

With the Knight and Bishop sadly out of play, this attempt to counter-attack can have little meaning.

28 ...   B—Q4
29 P—QKt3   R—K1
30 P—B4   B—B2
31 B—B1

Deplorable, but protecting the Bishop by 31 R—K1 yields to 31 ... R×B 32 R×R, Q—Kt8ch, and Black gets two pieces for a Rook.

31 ...   R—K7!

A powerful blow! Black seizes the seventh rank and also threatens mate in two moves.

32 R—B1   Q—B7

Now the threat is 33 ... R×Kt 34 R×R, Q×Bch, and Black wins two pieces for the Rook.

33 Q—Kt3   Q×RP
34 Resigns

Variety of Themes

S. Tartakover · R. Domenech

Sitges 1934, COLLE SYSTEM

This game flows along with such grace, charm and wit, it is hard to realize that it offers more than mere entertainment. In the short space of 37 moves it offers an insight into such useful ideas in chess strategy as:

(1) The Advantage of the Two Bishops,

(2) Pressure on the Black Squares,

(3) Majority of Pawns on the Queen-side,

(4) Sacrifice of a Piece to Create Passed Pawns, and (to crown it all),

(5) The Triumphal March of the Passed Pawns.

1	P—Q4		Kt—KB3
2	Kt—KB3		P—K3
3	P—K3		P—B4
4	B—Q3		Kt—B3
5	P—B3		P—Q4
6	QKt—Q2		

The Colle system of opening begins quietly enough, but it can easily turn into a whirlwind attack. Its tactical objective is an attack on Black's Castled position on the King-side. Its strategical objective is to create a majority of Pawns on the Queen-side, which can be decisive in the endgame.

The characteristic formation is as follows:

The Queen Pawn in the center, supported by the Bishop Pawn as an understudy.

The King Pawn at K3, enabling the development of the King Bishop. Later on, the Pawn advances to K4 to let the Queen Bishop come into the game.

The King Knight develops at KB3, ready to seize the outpost K5, or perhaps to attack by Kt—Kt5.

The Queen Knight develops at Q2 to support the thrust P—K4.

The Queen is best posted at K2, to back up the King Pawn and to permit the Rooks to get in touch with each other.

The Rooks are generally most useful at K1 and Q1, on files which are likely to be opened.

6	...		B—Q3
7	O—O		O—O
8	Q—K2		

Preparing to advance the King Pawn, which will open up the game and release White's pieces.

8	...		P—K4

This sort of move, according to the annotators, is "a premature attempt to seize the initiative" if Black loses, but "a well-timed counter-attack" if Black wins.

9	P×BP		B×P
10	P—K4		B—KKt5
11	P×P		B×Kt

There is no reason for this exchange, which lets White have the two Bishops, unless Black thought that fewer pieces on the board would give him more drawing chances.

12 Q×B   Q×P

If *12* ... Kt×P *13* Kt—Kt3, B—K2 *14* R—Q1, and Black has no defense against the threats of winning the Knight by *15* B—K4, *15* B—QB4 or *15* P—B4.

13 Kt—K4

This is the position, with Black to play:

Even at this early stage Black can easily go wrong. The immediate threat is *14* Kt×Ktch, discovering an attack on his Queen. If he defends against this by *13* ... QR—Q1 (hoping to lure White into *14* Kt×Ktch, P×Kt *15* Q×P, Q×B *16* B—R6, when he averts the threat of mate by *16* ... Q—Kt3) he gets a painful lesson when the continuation *14* Kt×Ktch, P×Kt *15* Q—Kt4ch, K—R1 *16* B—K4, Q—Q2 *17* B—B5, Q—Q4 *18* Q—R5 leaves him helpless.

13 ...   Kt×Kt
14 B×Kt   Q—Q2

15 R—Q1   Q—B2
16 P—QKt4   B—Kt3

Safer than *16* ... B—K2, when this might occur: *17* Q—R3, P—KR3 (if *17* ... P—KKt3 *18* R—Q7, Q—B1 *19* B×Kt, Q×B *20* R×B, and White wins a piece) *18* B×P, P×B *19* Q—B5, K—Kt2 (or *19* ... KR—Q1 *20* Q—R7ch, K—B1 *21* Q—R8 mate) *20* Q—R7ch, K—B3 *21* Q×RP mate.

17 P—QR4   P—QR3
18 P—R5   B—R2
19 Q—R3   P—KKt3

But not *19* ... P—R3 *20* B×P, P×B *21* R—Q7!, Q—B1 *22* Q—B5, and White mates quickly.

20 B—R6   KR—Q1
21 Q—B3

With an eye to *22* Q—B6 (control of the black squares) and mate at Kt7.

21 ...   R×Rch
22 R×R   R—Q1
23 B—Q5   Q—K2
24 P—R4!

An advance which provides the King with a flight square in case of need. It also incorporates two threats—*25* B—Kt5 winning the exchange, and *25* P—R5 breaking up Black's Pawns on the King-side.

24 ...   P—K5
25 Q—B4   B—Kt1

The last two moves have enabled Black to get his Bishop back into active play.

This is how things stand:

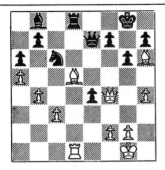

The position is tricky. White must not be lured into playing *26* B × Pch, hoping for *26* ... Q × B *27* R × Rch, Kt × R *28* Q × B, and he wins the pinned Knight. The reply to *26* B × Pch would be *26* ... K—R1, after which *27* R × Rch, Q × R *28* Q—Q2, Q × KRP leaves Black with a slight advantage.

26 Q—Kt5!

This forces an exchange of Queens, after which the rash King Pawn will fall.

| 26 ... | Q × Q |
| 27 B × Q | R—Q2 |

On *27* ... R—K1 *28* R—K1 wins the King Pawn.

28 R—Q2	B—K4
29 B × KP	R × R
30 B × R	

White has the two Bishops, three Pawns to two on the Queen side, and is a Pawn ahead. What more could mortal crave!

| 30 ... | Kt—Q1 |
| 31 P—QB4 | |

The customary procedure. Pawns are to be exchanged by *32* P—Kt5,

P × P *33* P × P, later on by P—R6, P × P P × P, leaving White's passed Pawn only two steps away from the coronation.

| 31 ... | K—B1 |
| 32 P—Kt5 | K—K1 |

The King rushes over to head off the Pawns, but Tartakover's next move cuts the journey short.

This is the position, with White to play:

33 B × QKtP!

"A bolt from the blue!" as the fellows used to say.

| 33 ... | P × P |

If *33* ... Kt × B *34* P × P, B—Kt1 *35* P × Kt, K—Q2 *36* P—R6, K—B3 *37* B—K3 (threatens *38* P—R7) B—K4 *38* B—R7, and White wins.

34 P—R6

Threatens to win at once by *35* P—R7.

| 34 ... | B—Kt1 |

Or *34* ... B—Q5 *35* B—K3,

Kt×B *36* B×B, K—Q2 *37* P—R7, and White wins.

35 P×P	Kt×B
36 P—Kt6!	

Very pretty! The passed Pawns are now all-powerful.

36 ...	K—Q2
37 P—R7	Resigns

Systematic Strangulation

S. Tarrasch · J. Showalter

Vienna 1898, HUNGARIAN DEFENSE

"This is a game in which there are no combinations. Yet, after a modest beginning, White cramps his opponent's game more and more until it is completely crippled—and all this without any noticeable blunder on Black's part. That is the highest triumph of chess strategy."

Tarrasch said this, believed it and lived by it. In this positional masterpiece, Tarrasch does not let Showalter develop his pieces properly, stifles attempts at counterattack, cramps his opponent's game move by move, and finally crushes him to the wall.

There are combinations in the game, despite Tarrasch's assertion, but they are hidden away in the notes. They show what might have happened to Showalter, had he not played as well as he did.

1 P—K4	P—K4
2 Kt—KB3	Kt—QB3
3 B—B4	B—K2

The usual move is *3* ... B—B4, leading into the Giuoco Piano, but Black wants to avoid openings familiar to Tarrasch.

4 P—Q4	P—Q3

Blocks the King Bishop, but the alternative *4* ... P×P surrenders the center.

5 P—Q5	

"White plays to stalemate his opponent," says Tarrasch, "who has himself made a start toward that object by playing *3* ... B—K2 and *4* ... P—Q3."

5 ...	Kt—Kt1

One would now expect Tarrasch to proceed by *6* Kt—B3, developing another piece. This is what a lesser master would do automatically and unthinkingly. Tarrasch is interested though in maintaining his Pawn chain (Pawns at K4 and Q5) which has a restraining effect on Black's game. So he moves a piece twice in the opening!

6 B—Q3!	

"The first principle of attack—" says Reuben Fine, "Don't let the opponent develop!"

White's move prevents *6* ... P—KB4, an attack on the base of the Pawn chain. It also prepares to meet *6* ... P—QB3 (an attempt to break up the center Pawns) with *7* P—B4. Then if Black plays *7* ... P×P, the recapture by *8* BP×P keeps the Pawn chain intact.

6 ...	Kt—KB3
7 P—B4	O—O
8 P—KR3!	

Another prophylactic move! This one prevents Black from developing his Queen Bishop by 8 ... B—Kt5, and limits it to the square Q2. It also prepares for the advance P—KKt4, against an attempt by Black to free himself with 8 ... Kt—K1 and 9 ... P—KB4.

8 ...	P—B3
9 Kt—B3	Kt—R3

Black hopes for counter-play by 10 ... Kt—B4 11 B—B2, P—QR4. His Queen Knight would then be strongly posted, and not easily driven away.

10 B—K3

Puts an end to that idea, since 10 ... Kt—B4 would allow 11 B×Kt, P×B 12 Kt×P, and White wins a Pawn.

10 ...	Kt—B2
11 O—O	Kt(B3)—K1

Black's intention is to free his cramped position by getting in ... P—KB4 after suitable preparation, say by ... P—KKt3 followed by ... Kt—Kt2.

Tarrasch will of course direct all his energies to make this breakthrough impossible.

12 Q—B2!

The Queen backs up the Bishop and King Pawn in bearing down on the key square.

12 ...	P×P
13 BP×P	

Obviously the proper way to recapture, as 13 KP×P allows Black to play 13 ... P—B4 at once.

13 ...	P—KKt3

Black prepares to play ... P—B4 either next move, or after the Knight reaches Kt2 and adds its support to the advance.

How does White play to restrain the Bishop Pawn?

14 B—KR6!

This attack on the Rook will force the Knight to interpose at Kt2. The Knight's support of the Bishop Pawn will then be meaningless, as it will be pinned and helpless to move or capture.

14 ...	Kt—Kt2

This is the position, with White to play:

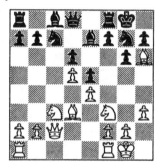

15 P—KKt4!

Definitely puts an end to Black's hopes of playing 15 ... P—B4.

The next step for Tarrasch is to reap the benefit of his positional advantage, which now consists of his greater command of space.

15 ...	Kt(B2)—K1

The desperate 15 ... P—B4 leads to 16 B×Kt, K×B (on 16 ... P× KP 17 B×R wins a whole Rook for White) 17 KtP×P, P×P 18

P×P, and White has won a Pawn.

16	K—R2	K—R1
17	R—KKt1	

Tarrasch (always a careful man) places his Rook on the King Knight file, so that he can benefit from the opening of the file, if Black does manage to get ... P—B4 in.

17	...	B—Q2
18	R—Kt2	R—B1
19	QR—KKt1	P—Kt3

Good moves are getting scarce, and this one does not help, as it weakens Black's QR3, QKt4, and QB3 squares. Tarrasch of course takes this into account, and will exploit the weaknesses of these white squares later on.

In the meantime, Tarrasch would like to cramp his opponent still more on the King-side by playing Kt—K1 followed by P—B4 and P—B5. But if he were to play 20 Kt—K1 at once, the reply 20 ... B—KKt4 would force an exchange of Bishops and free Black's game somewhat.

The plan needs a preparatory move, so Tarrasch plays ...

20	Q—Q2!

Now that the square Kt5 is controlled by Queen and Bishop, White's King Knight is free to move away, releasing the Bishop Pawn.

20	...	Kt—B3
21	Kt—K1	Kt—Kt1
22	B—K3	P—KKt4

This prevents the advance 23 P—B4, but the cost is high. For one thing, the square KB4 (counting from the Black side) has been weakened, and will surely be seized as an outpost by one of White's Knights. For another, the Pawn placed at Kt4 stands in the way of Black's King Bishop, greatly limiting its activity.

23	Kt—B3

Now that 23 P—B4 is not feasible, the Knight returns to the attack.

23	...	P—B3
24	P—KR4!	P—KR3

This and the previous move weaken Black's white squares more and more, and allow his pieces less and less mobility, but the prospect after 24 ... P×P 25 Kt×RP followed soon by Kt—B5 was not appetizing.

25	R—KR1	K—R2

The King prepares to flee, rather than face the possibility of the Rook file being opened against him.

26	K—Kt1	K—Kt3
27	Kt—R2	

The Knight is headed for KB5, which he will reach by way of B1 and Kt3.

27	...	R—QB2
28	Kt—B1	Q—B1

Double attack on White's Knight Pawn—Black's first threat in the game!

29	Q—K2

This way of protecting the Knight Pawn is superior to the natural move 29 P—B3. The square KB3 must not be blocked by a Pawn, but left open for use by pieces.

29 ...	K—B2
30 B—R6	Q—Kt1

This is the position, with White to play:

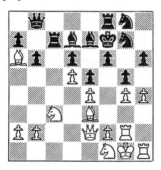

31 Kt—Kt5!

This attack on the Rook (which has no safe square to run to) forces an exchange of Bishop for Knight.

31 ...	B × Kt
32 B × B	

The foregoing exchange of pieces highlights certain features in the position:

(1) The disappearance of Black's Queen Bishop (which travelled on white squares) accentuates the weakness of Black's white squares. Tarrasch can now settle pieces on those squares without fear of their being dislodged.

(2) Black's remaining Bishop is completely imprisoned by Pawns standing on black squares.

(3) Black's King cannot flee to safety by way of K1.

(4) White has two active Bishops against Black's two ineffectual Knights.

32 ...	KR—B1
33 P × P	RP × P
34 B—B6!	

Blockade! The Rooks are doubled on the open file, but can make no use of it.

34 ...	B—B1
35 Q—B3!	

Threatens to capture the King Knight Pawn.

35 ...	R × B

A desperate move, but he has no good reply: If *35 ... K—Kt3* (to protect the Knight Pawn) *36 R(Kt2)—R2, Kt—K2 37 R—R6ch, K—B2 32 Q × Pch, K—Kt1 33 R—R8 mate.*

Another possibility is *35 ... K—Kt3 36 R(Kt2)—R2, R—Q1 37 R—R8, B—K2 38 R(R1)—R7* (threatens *39 Q—B5ch, Kt × Q 40 KtP × Kt* mate) *Q—B1 39 R × Ktch, K × R 40 Q—R3, K—B1 41 Q—R6ch, K—B2 42 R—R7 mate.*

36 P × R	Kt—K3
37 R—R7ch	B—Kt2

On *37 ... K—K1 38 Q—B5, Kt—B4 39 B × Kt, KtP × B 40 Q—Q7* is mate.

38 Kt—Kt3	R × P
39 Kt—B5!	

Finally the Knight arrives at the ideal square!

39 ...	Q—QB1
40 R(Kt2)—R2	Kt—K2

Here too *40 ... K—Kt3* loses by a combination: *41 B × KKtP, P × B* (if *41 ... Kt × B 42 R × B mate*) *42 Kt—R4ch, K × R 43 Q—B5ch, K—R1 44 Kt—Kt6 dble check and mate* (Reinfeld).

Another line (after *40* . . . K—Kt3) is *41* B × KKtP, P × B *42* Kt—K7ch, Kt × Kt *43* R(R2)—R6ch, B × R *44* Q—B7 mate (Chernev).

> *41* Kt × B   Kt × Kt
> *42* B × KKtP

Threatens *43* Q × Pch and mate next move, as well as *43* B—R6 winning the Knight.

> *42* . . .   Q—K3

Showalter made this move and then resigned without waiting for a reply. Tarrasch might have played the simple *43* B—R6, winning a piece, or the more interesting *43* B × P, Q × B *44* R × Ktch, K—K3 (if *44* . . . K × R *45* R—R7ch, K—Kt3 *46* R—R6ch wins the Queen) *45* R × Ktch!, K × R (if *45* . . . Q × R *46* Q—B5 is mate) *46* R—R7ch, K—K3 *47* Q—Kt3ch, P—Q4 *48* Q × P mate.

Good Bishop and Bad Bishop

L. Barden · N. Rossolimo

Hastings 1950, SICILIAN DEFENSE

Some of our modern concepts in chess strategy might have shocked the old-timers. Take this game for instance, where Rossolimo exchanges pieces to rid the board of an enemy Bishop standing quietly at its home square! It turns out though that Barden is left with the bad Bishop (one hemmed in by Pawns) against a powerful Knight of Rossolimo's.

In the hands of a fine player, this is practically the equivalent of being a piece ahead, so Rossolimo quickly works up an attack. In the ensuing complications he wins a Pawn, and then proceeds to cut down all the pieces in sight. The ending, with Pawns only, is no problem at all. This is pro chess of a high order!

1 P—K4	P—QB4
2 Kt—KB3	P—Q3
3 P—Q4	P×P
4 Kt×P	Kt—KB3
5 Kt—QB3	

Another way to protect the King Pawn is by 5 P—KB3. Then if 5 ... P—KKt3 6 P—QB4, B—Kt2 7 Kt—B3, and White has the Maroczy Bind—a favorable formation.

5 ...	P—QR3

A refinement, introduced by Najdorf, in the Boleslavsky line, the characteristic move of which is ... P—K4.

If at once 5 ... P—K4, then 6 B—Kt5ch, QKt—Q2 7 Kt—B5 is in White's favor.

6 P—B4	

Now if Black plays 6 ... P—K4, the Knight can return to B3 without obstructing the Bishop Pawn.

6 ...	P—K3
7 B—K2	

A good alternative is 7 B—Q3, with this likely continuation: 7 ... Q—B2 8 Q—B3!, Kt—B3 9 B—K3, B—Q2 10 O—O, and White has fine attacking possibilities.

7 ...	Q—B2
8 O—O	Kt—B3
9 B—K3	B—Q2

Black's aim (if let alone!) is to control the Queen Bishop file with Queen and Rook, post his Queen Knight at QB5 (supported by a Pawn at QKt4) and bear down on the Queen side of the board. His pressure on that wing can give him the superior ending, provided he can survive the King-side attack that is sure to come in the midgame.

10 P—KKt4	

Threatens to push on to Kt5, and drive the Knight back to the first rank.

Nevertheless the move seems a bit impulsive since it initiates a King-side attack against a King that has not yet Castled on that wing.

| 10 ... | Kt × Kt |

The exchange makes the square QB3 available to the Bishop. The Bishop in turn will vacate Q2, leaving that as a flight square for the King Knight, if attacked.

| 11 B × Kt | B—B3 |
| 12 B—B3 | P—K4! |

The key move in the Boleslavsky System. Black establishes a Pawn in the center. True, he is left with a backward Queen Pawn, but the Pawn is much healthier than it looks.

| 13 B—K3 | B—K2 |

Pieces must be developed, even if they take only one step.

| 14 P—B5 |

White hopes to follow this move with *15 P—Kt5*, and the Pawn-roller looks threatening, but he never gets a chance to carry out his plan.

He might have fared better with *15 P—Kt5, Kt—Q2 16 Kt—Q5*, and Black must part with one of his Bishops.

| 14 ... | P—R3! |

Nips that little scheme in the bud! If White persists in playing *15 P—Kt5*, the continuation *15 ... P × P 16 B × P, Q—Kt3ch 17 K—R1, Q × P*

wins a Pawn for Black.

| 15 Q—Q2 |

This is the position, with Black to play:

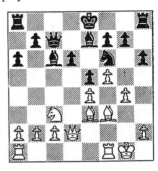

| 15 ... | P—QKt4! |

A subtle move! The Pawn will make a fine support for the Knight when it arrives at QB5. Meanwhile, the square Kt2 is made available to the Queen, who will strengthen the attack on White's center.

| 16 QR—Q1 | R—QB1 |

Increases the pressure on the Queen Bishop file.

| 17 P—QR3 | Q—Kt2 |

Threatens the life of the King Pawn.

| 18 Q—Q3 | Kt—Q2! |

Two possibilities are now open to the Knight:

(1) To attack the King Pawn once more by *19 ... Kt—B4*, forcing White to give up his good Bishop for the Knight, and,

(2) To swing the Knight over to the outpost QB5, by way of Kt3.

| 19 P—Kt4 |

Eliminates the first possibility.

19 ...   Kt—Kt3

But not the second!

20 B—B1

White avoids the attractive-looking *19 Kt—Q5*, as after *19 ... B×Kt 20 P×B*, *Kt—R5!*, the threats of winning the exchange by *21 ... Kt—Kt7*, or of dominating the Bishop file by *21 ... R—B6*, would be difficult to parry.

20 ...   Kt—B5

The Knight attacks nothing, since the Rook Pawn is protected. Its occupation of QB5 is enough by itself though to exercise a paralyzing influence on White's entire Queen side.

21 Kt—Q5   B×Kt
22 P×B

This is the position, with Black to play:

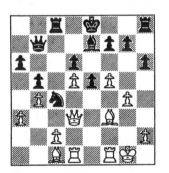

At this point Rossolimo decides to do away with White's good Bishop. Despite the fact that it stands on its original square, and its function is purely defensive, it is a potential danger. Once it is removed, Barden will be left with the impotent King Bishop, hemmed in by Pawns of its own color.

22 ...   B—Kt4!
23 KR—K1   Q—K2
24 B—K4   B×B
25 R×B   P—KR4!

Clever play! The Rook file will be opened whether White captures or not.

26 Q—KKt3   P×P
27 Q×KtP

Care is needed at all times in the wonderful but sometimes exasperating game of chess! Black's hasty protection of the Knight Pawn by *27 ... K—B1* would evoke *28 P—B6* in immediate reply—and Black could resign!

27 ...   Q—B3

This puts an end to the Pawn's ambitions.

28 B—Q3   R—R5
29 Q—Kt3   Kt—Kt3

The Knight prepares to take part in the attack on the King-side.

30 R—K4

If *30 B—K4* (to protect the Queen Pawn) *R—QB5 31 Q—Kt2* (on *31 B—B3, Kt×P 32 B×Kt, R(B5)— Kt5* wins the Queen) *R(B5)×B 32 R×R, R×R 33 Q×R, Q—Kt4ch*, and Black picks up the other Rook and wins.

30 ...   R—R4
31 R—Kt4

There is no way to save the Queen Pawn, so White tries to get behind the lines.

31 ...	Kt × P
32 R × P	Kt—B5
33 R—Kt8ch	K—Q2
34 R × R	K × R
35 Q—Kt8ch	K—Kt2!

But not *35 ...* K—B2, when *36* Q—QR8 not only threatens to harass the King, but also guards White's critical KKt2 square.

36 K—R1

Avoids loss of the Queen by *36 ...* R—Kt4ch.

36 ...	Q—R3
37 Q—Kt1	

Forced, as after *37* Q × Pch, K—Kt3, the Queen could not return to the defense of the Rook Pawn.

37 ... Kt × B!

The finish a player dreams about! All the pieces are cleared away, leaving an ending with a Pawn ahead and an easy win!

38 P × Kt	R × Pch
39 Resigns	

The finish, if White played on, would be: *39* Q × R, Q × Rch *40* Q—Kt1 (if *40* K—Kt2, Q—Q7ch forces the exchange of Queens) Q × Qch *41* K × Q, K—B3 *42* K—B2, K—Q4 *43* K—K3, P—B3 *44* K—K2, K—Q5 *45* K—Q2, P—K5 *46* P × P, K × P, and Black wins.

Coup de Grâce

A. Alekhine · F. D. Yates

London 1922, Queen's Gambit Declined

Alexander Alekhine

Even the mighty Alekhine, who played more brilliant games than any other man who ever lived, did not pluck combinations out of thin air. Even he had to abide by Lasker's dictum: "In the beginning of the game ignore the search for combinations, abstain from violent moves, aim for small advantages, accumulate them, and only after having attained these ends search for the combination—and then with all the power of will and intellect, *because then the combination must exist, however deeply hidden.*"

Note how Alekhine, ever alert for opportunity, anchors pieces on strong squares, seizes open files, doubles Rooks on the seventh rank, and centralizes his King.

Centralizes his King? Good Heavens! Alekhine's King walks up the board practically in the midgame and steals a Rook in broad daylight!

If there are combinations to be found (and Lasker assures us there are) Alekhine is the man who can find them.

1 P—Q4	Kt—KB3
2 P—QB4	P—K3
3 Kt—KB3	P—Q4
4 Kt—B3	B—K2
5 B—Kt5	O—O
6 P—K3	QKt—Q2

White has a happy time of it in this line of the Queen's Gambit. All he has to do to get a good game is make natural moves.

Black, on the other hand, usually has trouble developing the pieces on the Queen-side. The Queen Knight stands awkwardly at Q2, and shuts in the Bishop. Bringing the Knight out at QB3 though would be far worse. It would block the Bishop Pawn whose job it is to attack the center by ... P—B4, while the plight of the Queen Bishop would not be mitigated—it would still be shut in.

7 R—B1	P—B3
8 Q—B2	R—K1
9 B—Q3	P×P

With this move and the next (Capablanca's freeing maneuver) Black has a fair chance of achieving equality. Other lines are less promising, e.g.

(1) *9* ... P—QR3 (in order to get counter-play on the Queen-side by *10* ... P×P *11* B×P, P—QKt4 *12* B—Q3, P—B4) *10* P×P!, KP×P (not *10* ... Kt×P *11* B×Pch winning a Pawn) and the position is in White's favor.

(2) *9* ... P—KR3 *10* B—B4!, P—R3 *11* P×P!, Kt×P *12* Kt×Kt, KP×Kt *13* O—O, Kt—B3 *14* P—KR3, and White can play for the minority attack by R—Kt1, P—QKt4, P—QR4 and P—Kt5,

with good winning chances.

10 B×P	Kt—Q4
11 Kt—K4	

The theorists, including Alekhine, consider *11* B×B to be White's best move, but Alekhine often plays inferior or little-analyzed moves to throw his opponents on their own resources, or to bring about complications in which they are not quite at home.

11 ...	P—KB4

This move is not good, since it weakens his black squares, and saddles Black with a backward King Pawn. An enemy Knight can establish itself on his K4 square, without fear of being driven away by Pawns.

"From this point," says Alekhine, "Black's game may be considered strategically lost, which is not to say that the realization of victory will be an easy matter."

A preferable defense was *11* ... B×B *12* Kt(K4)×B, Kt—B1, though Black still faced the prospect of a long, hard winter.

12 B×B	Q×B
13 QKt—Q2	P—QKt4

Another strategical error, and again an important black square (QB4) is weakened. White, as we shall see, utilizes this square as a pivot for his pieces—the Knight, the Queen and then one of the Rooks.

White also obtains control of the only open file. It makes a fine avenue of entry into the adverse position.

14 B×Kt!

Very good! Alekhine gets rid of a Knight that is posted strongly in the center, and prepares to operate on the open file.

14 ...	BP × B
15 O—O	P—QR4
16 Kt—Kt3	

This must be played at once, as otherwise *16* ... P—R5 keeps the Knight out. The Knight is of course headed for QB5, the magic square.

16 ...	P—R5
17 Kt—B5	

This forces an exchange of Knights, after which White's other Knight can settle on B5 (or on K5) without fear of being disturbed.

17 ...	Kt × Kt
18 Q × Kt!	

The right way to capture! "Weak points or holes in the opponent's position," says Tarrasch, "must be occupied by pieces, not by Pawns."

18 ...	Q × Q
19 R × Q	

White has the advantage in force, space and time.

In force: the Knight, which will be posted unassailably at K5, supported by a Pawn, is stronger than a Bishop—especially this one, which is limited purely to defense.

In space: his Rooks will dominate the only open file.

In time: two of his pieces are in active play, while Black has none.

19 ...	P—Kt5
20 KR—B1	B—R3

Black hopes to oppose Rooks on the Queen Bishop file.

This is the position, with White to play:

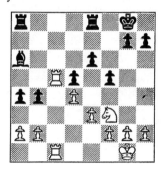

21 Kt—K5!

The Knight arrives just in time to put a stop to any such fancies! If Black tries to dispute possession of the Bishop file by *21* ... KR—B1, the continuation would be *22* R × Rch, R × R *23* R × Rch, B × R *24* Kt—B6, and the attack on the Knight Pawn as well as the threat of winning the Bishop by *25* Kt—K7ch would gain a Pawn for White.

21 ...	KR—Kt1
22 P—B3!	

Another advantage for White: he can bring his King into active play, while Black's King may not emerge.

22 ...	P—Kt6
23 P—QR3	P—R3

Here if *23* ... R—QB1 *24* R × Rch, R × R *25* R × Rch, B × R *26* K—B2, K—B1 *27* K—K1, K—K2 *28* K—Q2, K—Q3 *29* K—B3, and Black cannot save his Queen Rook Pawn.

24 K—B2!

The starting point of mate threats, in which the King himself takes part!

| 24 ... | K—R2 |
| 25 P—R4 | R—KB1 |

Black still cannot oppose Rooks. After *25 ... R—QB1 26* R × R, R × R *27* R × R, B × R *28* Kt—Q3, B—Q2 *29* Kt—B5, and Black loses either his King Pawn or his Queen Rook Pawn.

| 26 K—Kt3 | R(B1)—QKt1 |

Black can do nothing but wait and hope.

27 R—B7

"The chief advantage of the possession of an open file," says the good book, "is that the Rook may be able to penetrate to the seventh rank."

| 27 ... | B—Kt4 |
| 28 R(B1)—B5! | |

Intends the following maneuver: *29* R—K7, R—K1 *30* R—KB7, R(R1)—Kt1 (to protect the Bishop) *31* R(B5)—B7, and the Rooks are doubled on the seventh rank.

| 28 ... | B—R3 |
| 29 R(B5)—B6 | |

Step by step White approaches his goal. Black must protect his King Pawn, as an attempt to exchange Rooks by *29 ... R—QB1* loses instantly by *30* R × B!, and White wins a piece.

| 29 ... | R—K1 |
| 30 K—B4! | |

Now that the doubling of his Rooks cannot be prevented, Alekhine takes time to bring his King closer to the center.

| 30 ... | K—Kt1 |
| 31 P—R5! | |

Tightens the net around the King (Black's, of course!).

| 31 ... | B—B8 |
| 32 P—Kt3 | B—R3 |

If *32 ... B—K7* instead, White protects the Bishop Pawn by bringing his Knight to KKt6 and then KR4, after which he moves his King to K5, winning the King Pawn as a start.

| 33 R—B7 | K—R2 |
| 34 R(B6)—B7 | |

At last the Rooks are doubled! What remains now is to break through the last barrier—the Knight Pawn that shields the King.

| 34 ... | R—KKt1 |
| 35 Kt—Q7! | |

Threatens to win the exchange by *36* Kt—B6ch.

| 35 ... | K—R1 |

Now comes a brilliant combination, with the characteristic Alekhine sting at the tail-end of it.

This is the position, with White to play:

36 Kt—B6!   R(Kt1)—KB1

Of course not *36* ... P×Kt as *37* R—R7 is mate on the spot, but Black's actual move seems to force an exchange of Rooks.

37 R×P!!

This calls for two exclamation marks.

37 ...   R×Kt
38 K—K5!

The point of the combination. White wins a whole Rook! If Black moves *38* ... R—KB1 (either Rook!) he is mated in two moves by *39* R—R7ch, K—Kt1 *40* R(B7)—Kt7 mate.

38 ...   Resigns

The Powerful Passed Pawns

Aganalian · T. Petrosian

Tiflis 1945, OLD INDIAN DEFENSE

The modern master tries to accumulate slight advantages, though they may not promise an immediate reward.

In this game, Petrosian's positional superiority consists in having two Bishops against Knight and Bishop, and in the pressure that his Rooks exert on an open file. It is little enough, but a sudden sacrifice of the exchange transforms these somewhat intangible advantages into one that can be turned quickly into account. Petrosian is left with two connected passed Pawns in the center, facing an enemy Rook. This Rook, strangely enough, is helpless to stop at least one of the Pawns from reaching the Queening square.

1 P—Q4	Kt—KB3
2 P—QB4	P—Q3
3 Kt—QB3	P—K4
4 P×P	P×P
5 Q×Qch	K×Q

Loss of the Castling privilege is no disadvantage once Queens are off the board. The King is in no danger of being mated, and is well-placed for the endgame.

6 B—Kt5	P—B3
7 Kt—B3	QKt—Q2
8 O—O—O	

White develops with gain of time:

he threatens 9 Kt × P.

8 ...	K—B2
9 P—QR3	

White's troubles begin with this move, which is intended to prevent pressure being put on his Knight by 9 ... B—Kt5. His game begins to disintegrate from this point, though his moves have been plausible enough.

Can it be that this last move (which might better have been replaced by 9 P—K3) is enough to lose the game? Or did he envision this possibility: 9 P—K3, B—Kt5 10 B × Kt, Kt × B! 11 Kt × P, B × Kt 12 P × B, Kt—K5 13 Kt—Q3, B—K3, with the better game for Black?

9 ...	Kt—Kt5!
10 B—R4	P—B3

Protects the King Pawn, freeing the Knights of that job, and also cuts down the range of White's Queen Bishop.

11 P—KR3	Kt—R3
12 P—KKt4	

Otherwise, 12 ... Kt—KB4 follows, and Black is assured of the two Bishops.

12 ...	Kt—B2
13 B—Kt3	P—QR4

Preparation for *13 ... Kt—B4*, which if played at once would be met by *14 P—Kt4*, dislodging the Knight immediately.

14 Kt—Q4	Kt—B4
15 P—K3	Kt—Q3!

This involves a threat! It is not the capture of the Knight, for *16 ... P×Kt* is met by *17 P×P* followed by *18 P—B5*, and White regains his piece. It is a positional threat.

16 Kt—B2

This is the position, with Black to play:

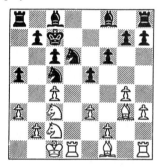

16 ...	Kt(Q3)—K5!

The Knight invades enemy territory with two threats:

(1) *17 ... Kt×Kt*, ruining White's Pawn position on the Queen side after the recapture.

(2) *17 ... Kt×B*, saddling White with an isolated King Pawn after the reply *18 P×Kt*.

17 Kt×Kt	Kt×Kt
18 B—R4	

White fights hard to prevent the exchange of his Bishop. He might better have submitted to fate though, and played *18 R—Kt1*, in order to recapture the Knight with his Rook.

18 ...	P—KKt4
19 B—Kt3	P—R4!

A valuable *zwischenzug* (interposition). The threat of winning a Pawn by *20 ... P×P* forces White to capture first, and opens a file for Black's King Rook. The Bishop will not run away, as Nimzovich used to say.

20 P×P	Kt×B

At one stroke (or so it seems) Black leaves his opponent with an isolated Pawn, and obtains for himself the two Bishops, and an open file for his King Rook!

21 P×Kt	R×P
22 B—Kt2	

The Bishop emerges—but only for a moment!

22 ...	B—K3
23 B—B1	P—R5

Fixes White's Pawns on the Queenside.

24 R—Q2	B—QB4
25 R—B2	P—B4
26 R—Kt1	QR—R1
27 K—Q2	P—B5
28 P—KKt4	

This is the position, with Black to play:

28 ...   R × P!

A fine sacrifice of the exchange to effect a breakthrough.

29 B × R   R × B

White is ahead in material, but only for a little while.

Black threatens *30* ... B × BP, as well as *30* ... P × Pch *31* Kt × P, B × Ktch *32* K—K1, B × Rch *33* K × B, B × BP, leaving him two Pawns ahead and with an easy win.

30 K—Q3   B × KP
31 Kt × B   R × Ktch!

This drives the King back to the second rank, and nets the Bishop Pawn.

32 K—Q2   B × BP
33 R—K1   R × R
34 K × R   P—K5
35 Resigns

If White were skeptical and play continued, it would go somewhat like this: *32* R—R2, P—K6 (in Bishop and Pawn endings, the Pawns should occupy squares different in color from those on which the Bishop travels) *33* R—R5, P—B6 *34* R—R2, P—B7ch *35* R × P, P × Rch *39* K × P, K—Q3, and the rest plays itself.

Another interesting possibility is *32* R—R2, P—K6 *33* R—R3 (to stop *33* ... P—B6) B—K3 *34* R—R5, P—B6 (better than *34* ... B × P) *35* R—R2, P—B7ch *36* K—B1, B—B5ch, and it's all over.

Bishop and a Half

I. Bondarevsky · V. Smyslov

Moscow 1946, RUY LOPEZ

Strictly speaking, this is not a two-Bishop game, although it has most of the attractive features connected with games where two Bishops oppose two Knights, or a Knight and Bishop.

Smyslov takes it out of that category by exchanging one of his Bishops for a Knight. Of course he punishes the Pawn that removed his Bishop by capturing it ten moves later.

In the midgame, Smyslov's Pawns swarm over the board like little black ants, and make things uncomfortable for the opponent, whose pieces can find no resting place on any decent central square.

In the ending, Smyslov's lone Bishop (one is all he needs, apparently) travelling along the white squares, spreads terror among the enemy's Pawns on the Queen side, fixed as they are on white squares.

The whole game is in Smyslov's best style, which is to say that it is a delight to play over.

1 P—K4	P—K4
2 Kt—KB3	Kt—QB3
3 B—Kt5	P—QR3
4 B—R4	Kt—B3
5 O—O	B—K2
6 B×Kt	

More usual is either *6* R—K1 or *6* Q—K2. In this delayed-exchange variation, Black has the two Bishops in compensation for his doubled Pawns.

6 ...	QP×B
7 R—K1	

Besides this, White has other good moves in *7* P—Q3, *7* Kt—B3 and the curious-looking but effective *7* Q—K1.

7 ...	Kt—Q2
8 P—Q4	P×P
9 Q×P	O—O
10 B—B4	Kt—B4
11 Q×Q	B×Q
12 Kt—B3	P—B4!

A good move. It will either increase the range of Black's pieces after *13* P×P, B×P, or reduce White's after *13* P—K5, Kt—K3.

13 P—K5

Instead of this, White should have played to simplify the position, according to Smyslov, who suggests this possibility: *13* B—Kt5, B×B *14* Kt×B, P—R3 *15* P—QKt4, Kt×P *16* KKt×Kt, P×Kt *17* Kt×P, B—B4, with an approximately even position.

13 ...   Kt—K3!

Blockades the passed Pawn. "The passed Pawn," says Nimzovich, "is a criminal, who should be kept under lock and key."

The Knight makes an ideal blockader here, as it complies with the requirements specified by Nimzovich:

(1) It prevents the approach of enemy pieces, say at Black's Q5 and KKt4 squares.

(2) It exercises threats from the post where it is stationed.

(3) It is elastic in its movements.

14 B—Q2   P—KKt4

The Pawns begin to move! The plan is to dislodge White's pieces from any good squares they now occupy, and deprive them of the possibility of reaching others where they might be effective.

Black's immediate threat is *15 ...* P—Kt5, winning the Knight.

15 Kt—K2

Obviously in order to meet *15 ...* P—Kt5 with *16 Kt(B3)—Q4*, rescuing the beast.

15 ...   P—B4

Black takes away that square, and renews the threat against the Knight.

16 B—B3

This prepares Q2 as a flight-square for the Knight.

Here is the position, with Black to play:

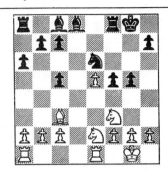

16 ...   P—Kt4

The advance of the Pawns on both sides of the board is embarrassing to White, whose pieces keep getting in each other's way.

Black's new threat is *17 ...* P—QKt5 *18 B—Q2*, P—Kt5, and again the Knight has no escape.

17 P—QKt3	B—Kt2
18 Kt—Kt3	P—KKt5
19 Kt—Q2	B—K2

Black is now ready to centralize his King, and bring his Rooks into play.

20 Kt—R5

There being no squares in the center available to White's minor pieces, this Knight hopes to accomplish some good by occupying KB6.

20 ...	K—B2!
21 Kt—B1	K—Kt3

Practically compelling the Knight's next move, as the retreat to Kt3 would allow *22 ...* P—KR4 followed by *23 ...* P—R5, driving the Knight still further back.

22 Kt—B6   QR—Q1

White's Knight occupies an advanced post, but the drawback is that its retreat has been cut off!

23 QR—Q1	R×R
24 R×R	R—Q1
25 R×R	B×R

The exchange of Rooks has simplified the position, but left White with problems. He must guard against 26 ... Kt—B5, which attacks the Knight Pawn with two pieces, and also threatens 27 ... Kt—K7ch, winning the Bishop.

26 Kt—K3

This meets with a clever refutation. This is the position on the board, with Black to play:

26 ...   P—KB5!

This must have come as a shock to White, who hoped to get the Knight into active play.

27 Kt—Q1

Abject retreat, but what else is there? If 27 Kt(K3)×P, P—KR4 wins the Knight, whose escape is cut off by enemies (and a few friends). Or if 27 Kt(K3)—Q5, P—B3 follows, and again the poor Knight finds himself surrounded.

27 ...   B×Kt!

Smyslov gives up one of his fine Bishops, for the sake of later winning a Pawn.

| 28 P×B | B—K5 |
| 29 B—Kt2 | |

Clears the square B3 for the Knight.

29 ...   P—Kt5

But Smyslov deprives the Knight of that square! And, as if that were not enough, he threatens to play 30 ... B×BP, and then capture the Knight, which may not move away and cannot be protected.

30 P—KB3	B×QBP
31 Kt—B2	P×P
32 P×P	B—Kt8
33 Kt—K4	B×P
34 Kt—Q2	

This protects the Knight Pawn, and imprisons the Bishop. But all this has taken time, and Black has meanwhile won two Pawns.

34 ...   P—QR4!

Preparation to return one of the Pawns, if necessary, and free his Bishop.

| 35 K—B2 | Kt—Q5 |
| 36 B×Kt | |

If 36 Kt—K4, Kt×KtP 37 Kt—Kt5 (threatens to win by 38 P—B7!) Kt—Q5 38 Kt—K4, Kt—K3, and White can resign.

| 36 ... | P×B |
| 37 K—K2 | K×P |

The Pawn falls at last.

38 K—Q3	K—K4
39 K—B2	

On *39* K—B4, P—R5 *40* K×P, B×P wins easily for Black.

39 ...	P—R5
40 P×P	P—B4
41 P—R5	P—B5
42 P—R6	P—Q6ch
43 Resigns	

No man can hold out against three connected passed Pawns—although, come to think of it, Edward Lasker drew against Janowsky's three connected passed Pawns on the seventh rank, at New York in 1924!

If Bondarevsky played on though, this would be the finish: *43* K—Kt2, P—B6ch *44* K×B, P×Kt *45* P—R7, P—Q8(Q) *46* P—R8(Q), P—Kt6ch *47* K—Kt2, Q—B7ch *48* K—R1 (if *48* K—R3, Q—R7ch wins the Queen) Q—B8 mate.

Prophetic Strategy

S. Tarrasch · J. Mieses
A. Schottlander · W. Paulsen
C. von Bardeleben · F. Riemann
T. von Scheve · H. von Gottschall

Leipzig 1888, SLAV DEFENSE

It is always exciting to come across an unknown masterpiece, especially when the strategy it features is so far ahead of its time.

I like the way pieces are manipulated, and an open file utilized, to establish a strong outpost at QKt7. I particularly relish the way combination play at one end of the board culminates in the gain of a Pawn at the other. I find the climax amusing, with Black's Knight imprisoned by a Bishop, while his King struggles desperately to be in two places at once.

Amusing—if you are not yourself caught in a like dilemma.

1 P—Q4	P—Q4
2 P—QB4	P—QB3
3 Kt—QB3	Kt—B3
4 B—Kt5	

Instead of this, *4* P—K3 is simple and strong. If then *4* ... B—B4, to get the Bishop into play, (the development of this piece always presents a problem in the Queen's Gambit) the continuation *5* P×P, P×P *6* Q—Kt3 forces the return of the Bishop to B1, as occurred in the

game Alekhine–Capablanca at New York in 1924, and as far back as the fifth match game between Zukertort and Steinitz in 1886.

White would then be ahead in development.

4 ...	P—K3
5 Kt—B3	B—Q3

Somewhat better was *5* ... B—K2, to relieve the pin on his Knight.

6 P—K3	O—O
7 B—Q3	QKt—Q2
8 O—O	R—K1
9 Q—B2	

Threatens *10* B×Pch, winning a Pawn.

9 ...	Q—B2

A natural enough attempt to unpin the Knight, but he gets a cramped game after this. Nor is *9* ... B—K2 a good alternative. The sequel would be *10* B×Kt, Kt×B *11* Kt—K5, followed by *12* P—B4, and White gets a Pillsbury-bind on the position. The safest move to meet the threat was simply *9* ... Kt—B1.

10 P—B5!

This is very much in order, now that the Bishop cannot retreat to B2.

10 ...   B—K2
11 B—KB4   Q—Q1
12 P—QKt4   Kt—B1
13 P—KR3!

Provides a flight-square for the Bishop, against a threat of its exchange by *13 ... Kt—R4.*

13 ...   B—Q2

Black is quite limited in choice of moves. This is one of only six moves which his pieces can make without incurring loss. White's superiority in mobility is such that he can choose any of thirty-three possible moves for his pieces!

14 P—Kt5   Q—B1
15 P—QR4   Kt—R4

Futile, since the Bishop can run away, but good moves are hard to find.

16 B—R2   B—Q1
17 P—R5   B—B2

A good idea: Black rids the board of a long-range Bishop, in return for his that was miserably placed. This accords with the principle that the player with a cramped game should try to free his position by exchanging pieces.

On *17 ... P×P* instead, there follows *18 Kt×KtP, B×Kt 19 B×B, Kt—Q2 20 P—R6*, and White will obtain a passed Pawn on the Bishop file.

18 B×B   Q×B

This is the position, with White to play:

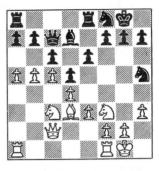

19 P—R6!   P—QKt3

If *19 ... P×RP 20 P×BP, B×P 21 R×P*, and White has a strong passed Pawn.

20 P×BP   B×P

On *20 ... Q×P 21 Kt—K5, Q—B1 22 Kt×B, Kt×Kt* (better than *22 ... Q×Kt 23 B—Kt5*, and White wins the exchange) *23 B×Pch*, and White wins a Pawn.

21 P×P   Q×P

Capturing by *21 ... P×P* not only provides White with a passed Rook Pawn, but permits him quick material gain by *22 Kt—Kt5, Q—B1* (on *22 ... Q—Q2 23 Kt—K5* wins the Bishop, which is doubly-attacked) *23 Kt—Q6*, and White wins the exchange.

22 KR—Kt1   Q—Q1

But not *22 ... Q—B2*, as the reply *23 Kt—Kt5* (as in the previous note) wins the exchange or the Bishop. "Admittedly, after the text-move," says Tarrasch, "the Queen-side attack has not resulted in the establishment of a passed Pawn, but it has opened lines of attack. Furthermore, the Queen Rook Pawn is very strong and provides support for White's pieces. White's superiority is very, very great."

23 Kt—K5   B—Q2

Forced, as protecting the Bishop by 23 ... R—B1 leads to 24 Kt × B, R × Kt 25 B—Kt5, and Black loses the exchange.

Notice how combinations appear of themselves once a player has a strategically superior position.

24 Kt × B   Kt × Kt

Capturing with the Queen is penalized by 25 B—Kt5 (repetition of a theme) and again the Rook is a victim.

25 B × Pch!

Remarkable! Combinations at one end of the board win a Pawn at the other!

25 ...   K—R1
26 B—Q3

Evades the trapping of the Bishop by 26 ... P—Kt3.

26 ...   Kt—Kt3
27 Kt—R4

To exchange Knights, and clear away the obstruction on the Knight file.

27 ...   Kt × Kt
28 Q × Kt   R—K2

This is the position, with White to play:

29 R—Kt7!

A fine outpost! The Rook exerts great pressure from this square—pressure which cannot be relieved by an exchange of Rooks. For if 29 ... R × R, there follows 30 P × R, R—Kt1 31 Q × P, and White's threat of 32 Q × R followed by 33 R—R8 is decisive.

29 ...   R—B1
30 R(R1)—Kt1   R(K2)—B2

White's game is so strong that he has choice of more than one forcing line of play. For instance, 31 R × R, and then if:

(1) 31 ... Q × R 32 R—Kt7, Q—B8ch 33 K—R2, Q—Q7 34 Q—Q7, R—B1 35 Q × BP!, and White wins (mate is threatened, the Knight and Rook are attacked, and Black dares not take the Queen).

(2) 31 ... R × R 32 Q—Kt4 (threatens 33 Q—Kt8) R—B1 33 Q—Kt7, R—B2 34 Q—Kt8, Q—QB1 35 Q × Qch, R × Q 36 R—Kt7, and White has a winning advantage.

31 Q—R5

The Queen is quite safe here. An

attempt to win the Queen by *31 ...*
R—B8ch *32* R × R, R × Rch *33*
K—R2, Q × Q succumbs to *34*
R—Kt8ch and mate in two.

31 ...	P—Kt3
32 B—B1	Kt—B3
33 R × R	Q × R

But not *33* ... R × R *34* R—Kt7,
R—Q2 *35* Q × Qch, R × Q *36* R × BP,
Kt—Q2 *37* B—Kt5, and White
wins easily.

| *34* Q × Q | R × Q |
| *35* R—Kt7 | |

The key square in White's combination and position play.

Black is now forced to exchange
Rooks, as *35* ... Kt—K1 is met by
36 B—Kt5, and something has to
give way.

| *35* ... | R × R |
| *36* P × R | |

Transformation! The Pawn which
was blocked a moment ago has
become a passed Pawn, only a step
away from turning into a Queen!

| *36* ... | Kt—Q2 |
| *37* B—Kt5 | Kt—Kt1 |

This is the situation, with White
to play:

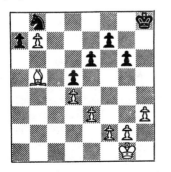

38 P—R4!

With his Knight cornered by the
Bishop and unable to emerge, action
for Black on the Queen-side is
temporarily suspended.

White therefore prepares to create
a passed Pawn on the King-side
(by means of P—Kt4, followed
sooner or later by P—R5) to keep
Black's King occupied in that area,
and unable to come to the rescue
of his Knight. In the meanwhile,
White would have all in the time in
the world to march his King up
the board and capture the Knight.

| *38* ... | K—Kt2 |
| *39* P—Kt4 | K—B3 |

Driving the Bishop away accomplishes nothing, viz: *39* ... P—R3
40 B—R4, P—R4 *41* B—Kt5, P—R5
42 B × P, Kt—R3 *43* B—Kt5, and
the Knight must return to Kt1.

40 P—B4	K—K2
41 K—B2	K—Q1
42 K—K2	K—K2

The King dares not attack the
Pawn by *42* ... K—B2, as after
43 P—R5, K × P *44* P—R6, the
new passed Pawn could not be headed
off.

43 K—Q3	K—Q3
44 K—B3	P—B3
45 K—Kt4	P—K4
46 QP × Pch	P × P
47 P × Pch	K × P
48 K—B5	K—K3
49 P—R5	Resigns

After *49* ... P × P *50* P × P, K—B3
51 K—Q6, P—R3 *52* K—B7 (the
quickest) it's all over.

Problem-like Finale

J. Foltys · H. Golombek

London 1947, SICILIAN DEFENSE

The student of chess strategy will be fascinated by the way certain elements of position play—centralization, weaknesses on the black squares, Knight outpost at K5, Bishop hemmed in by Pawns—are treated here.

The connoisseur of grace and ease of style will find sufficient incentive to play this game over (more than once, I am sure) in Leonard Barden's comment on it in his excellent book *A Guide to Chess Openings*, "The whole game runs with a smooth logic characteristic of the greatest masterpieces."

1 P—K4	P—QB4
2 Kt—KB3	P—Q3
3 P—Q4	P×P
4 Kt×P	Kt—KB3
5 Kt—QB3	P—KKt3
6 B—K2	B—Kt2
7 B—K3	Kt—B3
8 O—O	O—O

The attempt to simplify by *8* ... Kt—KKt5 lands Black in a trap: *9* B×Kt!, B×B (if *9* ... B×Kt *10* B×QB wins a piece for White) *10* Kt×Kt, B×Q (or *10* ... P×Kt *11* Q×B, and White is a piece ahead) *11* Kt×Q, and White wins a piece.

9 Q—Q2	Kt—KKt5

Black would not have an easy time of it after *9* ... P—Q4 when the play might run: *10* Kt×Kt, P×Kt *11* P—K5, Kt—Q2 *12* P—B4, followed by Kt—R4 and Q—B3 with lasting pressure on the squares Q4 and QB5.

10 B×Kt	B×B
11 P—B4	

Threatens to shut the door on the Bishop by *12* P—B5.

11 ...	B—Q2
12 QR—Q1	K—R1
13 P—KR3	P—B4
14 P×P	P×P

This capture, which limits the range of Black's Queen Bishop, is inferior to the natural *14* ... B×P, keeping the lines open. Black may have been prompted though by a desire to keep the two Bishops.

15 KR—K1	Q—K1
16 Kt—Q5!	

This move gets an exclamation mark (to which it is entitled) from Foltys himself. The Knight clears the way, with gain of tempo, for an advance of the Queen Bishop Pawn which proves to have decisive effect.

16 ...   Q—B2
17 P—B4

White's moves are simple and strong. They are hard to meet, because they involve no immediate threats. Later on, when his pieces seize the best squares, there are threats.

17 ...   QR—B1
18 Kt—KB3   P—KR3

This is the position, with White to play:

19 P—B5!

Very good! White threatens to exchange Pawns, leaving Black with a frail Queen Pawn which could not long survive.

More than that, it leaves no palatable alternative to the opponent.

19 ...   P—K3

This limits still further the scope of Black's Queen Bishop, but if instead *19* ... P×P there follows *20* B×P, KR—K1 *21* Kt×P, Kt×Kt *22* B×Kt, R×B *23* R×R, Q×R *24* Q×B, and White, a Pawn up, wins the ending.

20 Kt—B3   P—Q4

Of course *20* ... P×P *21* Q×B is unthinkable, but now the Queen Bishop is badly hemmed in by the Pawns on white squares.

21 Kt—QKt5   R—QKt1

Guards against *22* Kt—Q6, an attack on Queen and Rook—to say nothing of the Knight Pawn.

22 P—QKt4   B—B3
23 Kt—Q6   Q—Kt2
24 P—Kt5!

Not content with strengthening his position move by move, White seeks to dislodge any adverse pieces which might be well-placed.

24 ...   Kt—Q1

The Knight must retreat, since the tempting counter-attack by *24* ... B—B6 meets this harsh fate: *25* Q×B!, Q×Q *26* P×Kt (threatens to regain the Queen by *27* B—Q4ch) Q—R4 *27* P×B, and White, who has three pieces for his Queen and threatens to get an overwhelming position with *28* Kt—K5, should win easily.

25 B—Q4   Kt—B2
26 B×B   Q×B

White now gets a strong grip on the black squares, now that Black's King Bishop that dominated those squares is off the board.

27 Kt×Ktch   Q×Kt
28 Kt—K5!

The first reward: a fine outpost for the Knight, on a black square.

| 28 ... | Q—Kt2 |
| 29 Q—Q4 | |

Threatens *30 Kt—Kt6ch*, winning the exchange, as well as the brusque *30 Kt × B*, removing a piece and then taking one of the Rooks.

| 29 ... | K—R2 |
| 30 P—B6 | R—Kt1 |

Threatens nothing less than mate.

| 31 R—Q2 | P × P |
| 32 Q × RP! | |

Very effective! It pins the Bishop, which is doubly attacked, and restricts its defense to one move.

| 32 ... | QR—Q1 |

The only way to save the Bishop. A move by the Bishop loses the Queen Rook immediately, while defending the Bishop by *32 ... KR—Q1* allows this pretty win: *33 P × P, B—K1 34 Q × Qch, K × Q 35 P—B7!*, and the Pawn fork wins a whole Rook.

33 P × P	B—B1
34 Q × Qch	K × Q
35 R—Kt1	B—R3

The Bishop is finally ready to take part in the game, but it's much too late.

| 36 R—Kt6 | R—QR1 |

Forced, since *36 ... B—B5* loses a Pawn after *37 Kt × B, P × Kt 38 R × R, R × R 39 P—B7, R—QB1 40 R—B6*.

| 37 R(Q2)—Kt2 | K—B3 |

This is the position, with White to play:

38 R × B!

Ends the Bishop's inglorious career, and starts a pretty combination.

| 38 ... | R × R |
| 39 R—Kt7 | |

Threatens *40 R—KB7*—mate on the move.

39 ...	R—Kt2
40 P—B7	R—R1
41 R—Kt8	R—Kt1
42 R × R(R8)	Resigns

For if *42 ... R × R 43 Kt—Q7ch, K—K2 44 Kt—Kt8*, and the Pawn becomes a Queen next move.

A Pawn Is a Pawn Is a Pawn

I. Kashdan · H. Steiner

Pasadena 1932, COLLE SYSTEM

The mental attitude of a modern master can be summed up in one crisp sentence: Win a Pawn early in the game, and nurse it along to victory!

In the game that follows, Kashdan does this, and does it beautifully. There are intervening difficulties of course, and how he resolves them we shall see as the game unfolds.

1 P—Q4	Kt—KB3
2 Kt—KB3	P—Q4
3 P—K3	P—K3

A line that takes the sting out of the Colle is *3* ... B—B4 *4* B—Q3, P—K3 *5* B×B, P×B *6* Q—Q3 (attacks the Bishop Pawn, and also threatens *7* Q—Kt5ch) Q—B1 *7* P—QKt3, Kt—R3 *8* O—O, B—K2 *9* P—B4, O—O *10* Kt—B3, P—B3 *11* B—Kt2, Kt—K5 *12* KR—B1 (but not *12* P×P, Kt—Kt5 *13* Q—K2, Kt×Kt *14* B×Kt, Kt×QP, with the better game for Black) as Euwe played against Alekhine in the 17th game of their 1935 match.

4 B—Q3	QKt—Q2
5 QKt—Q2	B—K2
6 Q—K2	

Prepares for P—K4, the key move of the Colle, which opens the position and liberates White's Queenside pieces.

6 ...	P—B4
7 P—B3	O—O
8 O—O	P—QKt3
9 P—K4	P×KP

This is more or less forced. If *9* ... P×QP *10* P—K5 (this advance is nearly always favorable for White, as it dislodges the strongest defender of the Castled position) Kt—K1 *11* P×P, followed by R—Q1, Kt—B1 and Kt—Kt3 leaves White with the superior position.

10 Kt×P	B—Kt2
11 R—Q1	

With pressure that can be felt the entire length of the file. One threat for example: *12* Kt×Ktch, B×Kt (if *12* ... Kt×Kt *13* P×P wins a Pawn as Black must guard against loss of his Queen by *14* B×Pch) *13* P×P, P×P *14* B—QKt5, B—B1 *15* B—K3 (Black is to be denied even the pleasure of keeping his isolated Pawn) B—K2 (if *15* ... Q—B2 *16* B×Kt, B×B *16* B×P wins a Pawn) *16* B×Kt, B×B *17* Kt—K5, and the pinned Bishop is lost.

11 ...	Q—B2

The Queen steps aside nervously.

12 B—KKt5	KR—K1

Not at once *12 ... Kt×Kt*, as after *13 B×B, R—K1 14 B—R4*, White keeps his long-range Bishops.

13 P×P

First Step: White gets the advantage of three Pawns to two on the Queen-side.

13 ...   B×Kt
14 B×B

But not *14 P×P, B×Kt*, and Black wins a piece.

14 ...   Kt×B
15 Q×Kt

Here too, the attempt to steal a Pawn by *15 P×P* would lose a piece, this time by *15 ... Q—B3.*

15 ...   Kt×P
16 Q—QB4   B×B
17 Kt×B

Even in this simplified position, there are tactical threats. Black must guard against *18 P—QKt4, Q—K4 19 Kt—B3, Q—K5 20 R—Q4*, and his Knight is lost.

17 ...   Q—K2
18 Kt—B3

"The smoke has cleared," says Kashdan, "and the battle is to be resumed with diminished forces. What White has played for is an advantage of Pawns on the Queen-side. These he will advance, eventually obtaining a passed Pawn, or else isolating one of the remaining Black Pawns, and attempting to win it. Black can similarly advance his King-side Pawns, but there are two difficulties. In the middle game, he would endanger his King. In the endgame, the distance of his King from the other side might well prove the deciding factor in White's favor. A Pawn majority on the Queen-side is therefore worth obtaining when the opportunity offers."

18 ...   KR—Q1
19 Kt—Q4   Q—R5

On *19 ... QR—B1* instead, Kashdan had prepared these pretty combinations:

(1) *20 P—QKt4, Kt—R5 21 Kt—B6, Q—B2 22 R×Rch, R×R (or 22 ... Q×R 23 Kt—K7ch, and the Rook falls) 23 P—Kt5, Kt—Kt7 24 Q—Kt3*, and White wins the exchange.

(2) *20 P—QKt4, Kt—R5 21 Kt—B6, R×Rch 22 R×R, Q—B2 23 Kt—K7ch, K—B1 24 Kt×R!, Q×Q 25 R—Q8 mate.*

After Black's actual move he threatens *20 ... P—K4*, winning the pinned Knight.

20 Q—K2   QR—B1
21 P—QR4

Second Step: White advances the Queen-side Pawns at every opportunity.

21 ...   Q—B3
22 P—QKt4   Kt—Q2
23 Kt—Kt5   Kt—B1

If Black tries to win the Bishop Pawn by *23 ... P—QR3*, then *24 Kt—Q6, R×P 25 Kt—K4* wins the exchange and teaches him a lesson.

24 Q—K3

Protects the Bishop Pawn and threatens to win a Pawn by *25 R×R, R×R 26 Kt×P.*

| 24 ... | P—QR3 |

This is the position, with White to play:

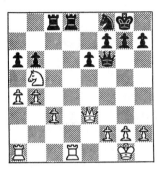

| 25 Kt—Q6 | R—Kt1 |

Much as he would like to, Black still must not touch the Bishop Pawn. If 25 ... R×P 26 Kt—K4, R×Q 27 Kt×Qch, P×Kt 28 P×R, and Black has a lost game.

26 R—Q2	Q—K2
27 QR—Q1	Q—B2
28 P—QB4	

Third Step: Pressing on to create a passed Pawn.

28 ...	R—Q2
29 Q—QB3	P—R3
30 Kt—K4	

In order to advance 31 P—B5, and recapture with the Knight in the event that Black plays 31 ... P×P. This would avoid the splitting up of the remaining Pawns.

30 ...	R×R
31 R×R	R—B1
32 Kt—Q6	R—Q1

This is the position, with White to play:

33 P—B5!

"This had to be carefully analyzed," says Kashdan. "Such an advance, if it does not bear immediate fruit may result in the Pawn becoming a weakness.

If 33 ... P×P 34 Q×P, Q×Q 35 P×Q, R—Q2 (otherwise at once 36 P—B6 and 37 P—B7) 36 P—B6, R—B2 37 R—B2, Kt—Kt3 38 Kt—K8 (to drive off the blockader) R—B1 39 P—B7, Kt—K2 40 Kt—Q6, and White wins."

| 33 ... | Q—B3 |
| 34 Q—B3 | |

This is strong, but Kashdan misses the immediately decisive 34 Kt—B5! The threat of 35 Q×P mate as well as the discovered attack on the Rook would result in White's winning the exchange.

We may be grateful though that Kashdan played as he did, for otherwise we would be deprived of a finely played ending.

Strangely enough, the idea of a discovered attack on the unprotected Rook comes up *twice* in the next few moves, as shown in the notes.

| 34 ... | Q×RP |

Black does not exchange Queens, as that would lose by the play shown in an earlier note.

35 Q×Pch   K—R2
36 P—R3

Provides a flight-square for the King, and sets a little trap.

36 ...   P×P

Black avoids the poisoned Pawn, as after 36 ... Q×P, the reply 37 Kt—K4! discovers an attack on the Rook and also threatens mate in two by 38 Kt—B6ch, K—R1 39 Q—Kt8 mate.

37 P×P   R—Kt1

And now he sidesteps 37 ... Q—R8ch 38 K—R2, Q—K4ch 39 P—B4, Q×QBP, when 40 Kt—K4! endangers the lives of Black's King, Queen and Rook!

38 K—R2   Kt—Kt3
39 R—K2

Of course not 39 Q×KP, as then 39 ... Q—B5ch wins the unprotected Rook—this time of White's!

39 ...   R—KB1
40 Q×KP

Fourth Step: White gains a Pawn.

40 ...   Q—B5ch
41 P—Kt3   Q—Q5
42 Q—K3!   Q×Q
43 P×Q   Kt—K4
44 K—Kt2   P—QR4
45 R—QB2

This follows the rule laid down by Tarrasch: The Rook's place is *behind* the passed Pawn; behind the enemy Pawn in order to keep it under attack, behind one's own in order to support its advance.

45 ...   Kt—B3

The ending is not too easy. White's passed Pawn is blockaded, and his King shut out. It will take endgame wizardry (which luckily Kashdan has) to win it.

46 Kt—Kt5

Fifth Step: Preparing to remove the blockader.

46 ...   R—Q1

To prevent White from trying to drive off the blockader by 47 Kt—Q4, as that would cost him a Pawn.

This is the position, with White to play:

47 Kt—Q4!

Sixth Step: White returns the extra Pawn in order to further the career of the passed Pawn.

47 ...   Kt×Kt

There is not much fight in 47 ... R—QB1 48 Kt×Kt, R×Kt 49 K—B3, K—Kt3 50 K—K4, K—B3 51 K—Q5, and the blockading Rook is easily driven off.

48 P×Kt	R×P
49 P—B6	R—Q1
50 K—B3!	

Pushing on would be premature, as Kashdan shows: *50* P—B7, R—QB1 *51* K—B3, P—R5 *52* K—K4, P—R6 *53* K—Q5, P—R7, and White must play *54* R × P, allowing a draw.

50 ...	P—R5

Black's King cannot help out, for if *50* ... K—Kt3 *51* K—K4, K—B3 *52* P—B7, R—QB1 *53* K—Q5, K—K2 *54* K—B6, P—R5 *55* R—K2ch, K—B2 *56* K—Q7, and White wins.

51 K—K4	P—R6
52 K—K5	

Threatens to win quickly by *53* P—B7, R—QB1 *54* K—Q6 followed by *55* K—Q7.

52 ...	R—Q6
53 P—B7	P—R7
54 R × P	R—QB6
55 K—Q6	R—Q6ch
56 K—B6	R—B6ch
57 K—Kt7	R—Kt6ch
58 K—R8	R—QB6
59 R—R7	

Builds a bridge for the King, as Nimzovich calls this maneuver. If now *59* ... K—Kt3 *60* K—Kt8, R—Kt6ch *61* R—Kt7, and the King is sheltered from any further checks. The passed Pawn would then cost Black his Rook.

59 ...	Resigns

Board with Excitement

P. Keres · A. Tarnowski

Helsinki 1952, Ruy Lopez

Paul Keres

From the very start of this magnificent game, Keres does not allow his opponent a moment's breathing spell. He threatens the King-side, he threatens the Queen-side, he threatens the center, and the whole board vibrates with the fury of his attack.

When the decisive combination does materialize (as inevitably it must when a Rook on the seventh rank controls the Queen side, a Knight at KB5 terrorizes the King-side, and the Queen dominates the center) it is a pleasing one, and a fitting climax to the impeccable strategy that made it possible.

1 P—K4	P—K4
2 Kt—KB3	Kt—QB3
3 B—Kt5	P—QR3
4 B—R4	Kt—B3
5 O—O	B—K2

The Strong Point variation, the central idea of which is to maintain the Pawn at K4 as a strong point, and as a pivot for future action.

The line is popular now, but not so long ago it was censured by Tarrasch (who considered 5 ... Kt × P the only tenable defense) in these ringing words, "All lines of play which lead to the imprisonment of a Bishop are on principle to be condemned!"

6 Q—K2

A strong alternative to the usual 6 R—K1. The King Rook is to move to Q1, there to exert lasting pressure on the Queen file.

6 ...   P—QKt4

Castling instead lands Black in a trap: *6* ... O—O *7* B × Kt, QP × B *8* Kt × P, Q—Q5 *9* Kt—KB3, Q × KP *10* Q × Q, Kt × Q *11* R—K1, and White wins a piece.

7 B—Kt3	P—Q3
8 P—B3	Kt—QR4
9 B—B2	P—B4
10 P—QR4	

Keres leaves the books (including his own book on the Ruy Lopez) with this diversion on the flank, the customary move being *10* P—Q4.

10 ...	P—Kt5
11 P—Q3	Kt—B3
12 QKt—Q2	O—O
13 R—Q1	P—R3
14 Kt—B4	

The Knight is on its way to KB5, an ideal square for the Knight in this form of the Ruy Lopez.

Watch the peregrinations of this Knight, who is destined to play an important role in the concluding combination.

14 ...   Q—B2

An attempt to free his game by *14* ... P—Q4 would cost Black a Pawn after the reply *15* Kt(B4) × P.

| 15 Kt—K3 | R—K1 |
| 16 Kt—R4 | |

Not at once *16* Kt—B5, as after *16* ... B × Kt *17* P × B, White would have a Pawn instead of a piece occupying the square KB5. Tarrasch says (and I have faith in Tarrasch) "Weak points or holes in the opponent's position must be occupied by pieces, and not by Pawns."

16 ...   B—B1

Black avoids another little pitfall: If *16* ... Kt × P (expecting to win a Pawn after *17* P × Kt, B × Kt) White interpolates *17* Kt—Q5, and after *17* ... Q—Q1 *18* Kt × Bch, Q × Kt, wins a piece by *19* Q × Kt, his Knight now being protected.

17 Q—B3

This is stronger than the immediate *17* Kt(R4)—B5, when Black might free his game by *17* ... B × Kt *18* Kt × B, P—Q4.

The move by the Queen puts further restraint on Black's Queen Pawn.

17 ...	Kt—K2
18 Kt(R4)—B5	Kt × Kt
19 Kt × Kt	

The threats begin! The one now in

sight is *20 Kt×RPch, P×Kt 21 Q×Kt*, and White wins a Pawn.

This is how the board looks:

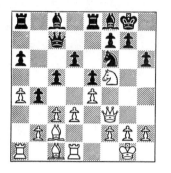

The position of the Knight is classic in the Ruy Lopez. The control of this outpost has led to such famous victories as Capablanca–Marshall 1909 (sixth game of the match), Capablanca–Bernstein, San Sebastian 1911, Capablanca–DusChotimirsky, St. Petersburg 1913, Capablanca–Fonaroff, New York 1918, and Teichmann–Schlechter, Carlsbad 1911, among others.

19 ...   Kt—R2
20 B—Kt3

The Bishop switches to another diagonal, where it can be more effective. Its attack on the Bishop Pawn ties Black's Queen down to the protection of the second rank. If for example, *20 ... Q—Q1 21 Kt×Pch, P×Kt* (or *21 ... K—R1 22 Kt×Pch* and White wins the Queen) *22 Q×Pch*, and White mates next move.

20 ...   B—K3
21 B—QB4

This is better than *21 B×B*, as after the recapture by *21 ... P×B,*

the attacked Knight would be forced to leave.

21 ...   P×P
22 P×P   B×B
23 P×B

White is saddled with a doubled Pawn, but in return his Rook exerts pressure on the Queen file, with particular emphasis on the backward Pawn on that file.

Black's compensation lies in the open Queen Knight file, which he hopes to occupy with Queen and Rook.

23 ...   R—K3
24 P—R4

Keres starts the Pawns rolling on the King-side. His attack on the wing is justified by the fact that it cannot be met by play in the center (the usual recipe in such situations).

24 ...   R—Kt1
25 P—Kt4   R—Kt6
26 B—Q2   Q—Kt2

Black seems to be getting counter-play on the Queen-side. Keres not only shrugs this off, but manages to drive the heavy pieces from the Queen Knight file and seize it for himself.

27 Q—Q3

"The key to White's deep plan," says Barden. "Black now finds not only that he has no points of attack on the Queen Knight file, but that he can do nothing to prevent White using it to break through himself. With the aid of this extra attacking avenue, the advance of White's King-side Pawns, by itself not conclusive, becomes decisive."

27 ...	R—KKt3
28 P—B3	P—KR4
29 P—Kt5	P—B3
30 K—B1	P×P
31 P×P	

Black had expected to win a Pawn, but now sees that on *31 ... Kt×P*, the reply *32 Kt—R4*, driving the Rook away from the Knight's protection, would be painful.

| 31 ... | R—K3 |
| 32 KR—Kt1 | |

Forces Black to exchange Rooks, in view of White's threat: *33 R×R, Q×R 34 Q—Q5, K—B2 35 P—Kt6ch, K—B3 36 P×Kt*, and White gets another Queen next move.

32 ...	R×R
33 R×R	Q—KB2
34 Q—Q5	

Now that the Queen Knight file is in his possession, White brings his Queen to a vital square in the center.

The Queen is not only centralized, but ready to support an invasion of the seventh rank by the Rook.

| 34 ... | P—Kt3 |

This is the position, with White to play:

35 R—Kt7!

The Rook crashes into the game, breaking down all resistance in its path.

| 35 ... | Q—K1 |

Forced, since *35 ... B—K2 36 Kt×Bch, R×Kt 37 R×R* costs Black his Rook, the pinned Queen being helpless to recapture.

| 36 Kt—K7ch! | K—B2 |

The King must run into a discovered check, or leave the Rook unprotected.

| 37 Kt—B6 dis ch | K—Kt1 |

Interposing the Bishop would be ruinous, as after *37 ... B—K2 38 R×Bch, Q×R 39 Kt×Q, K×Kt 40 Q—Kt7ch* follows, and White picks up the Knight hiding behind the King.

| 38 Kt—Q8! | |

Fancy stepping by the Knight!

38 ...	Q×Kt
39 Q×Rch	K—R1
40 Q—B7	Resigns

Elegant Simplification

M. Botvinnik · I. Boleslavsky

Moscow 1941, FRENCH DEFENSE

Mikhail Botvinnik

This is one of the great Botvinnik games, notable for the originality of its opening strategy and the brilliance of its midgame combinative play. It is the superb clarity of the endgame phase though that will appeal particularly to the student. It is a Rook and Pawn ending, the study of which is bound to increase anyone's playing strength.

"The crystalline simplicity of the winning process," says Reinfeld, "has an enchanting logic which is easy to appreciate but hard to explain!"

1 P—K4	P—K3
2 P—Q4	P—Q4
3 Kt—Q2	

The fashionable move nowadays. It avoids the pin by *3* ... B—Kt5, and leaves the Bishop Pawn free to support the Queen Pawn.

3 ...	P—QB4
4 P×QP	KP×P

This is probably preferable to *4* ... Q×P, after which White develops quickly by *5* KKt—B3, P×P *6* B—B4, Q—Q1 *7* Kt—Kt3, Kt—KB3 *8* O—O.

5 B—Kt5ch	Kt—B3
6 KKt—B3	B—Q3
7 O—O	KKt—K2
8 P×P	B×P
9 Kt—Kt3	B—Kt3
10 B—K3!	

A remarkable move! White practically forces an exchange which leaves him with a sickly-looking King Pawn.

10 ...	B×B
11 B×Ktch!	P×B

On *11* ... Kt×B, the continuation *12* R—K1, P—Q5 *13* Kt(B3)×P wins a Pawn for White.

12 P×B

In return for his isolated Pawn, White exerts pressure on the squares Q4 and QB5, the strategical importance of which will be evident later.

12 ...	O—O
13 Q—Q2!	Q—Kt3
14 Q—B3	

The point of Botvinnik's subtle position play. Black must not be permitted to get in the freeing move ... P—QB4.

Botvinnik also contemplates anchoring his Knights on Q4 and QB5, squares from which they cannot be dislodged by Pawns.

14 ...	R—Kt1

Temporarily prevents *15* Kt—B5, the reply to which would be *15* ... Q×P.

15 QR—Kt1

Protects the Knight Pawn, and renews the threat of planting the Knight at B5.

15 ...	R—K1
16 KR—K1	Kt—Kt3

Black's aim is to establish *his* Knight strongly in the center, where it will have some neutralizing effect on the position.

17 Kt—B5	B—Kt5
18 Kt—Q4	Kt—K4

This is the position, with White to play:

19 P—Kt4

White is now firmly entrenched on the black squares, but that is not enough in itself to assure victory. He must now find a way to open lines for his Rooks without allowing his opponent too much freedom.

19 ...	QR—Q1
20 P—K4!	P×P
21 R×P	P—QR4
22 P—QR3!	P×P
23 P×P	P—B3

This re-enforces the Knight and guards against *24* Q—KKt3—threats against the loose pieces.

24 R(Kt1)—K1   K—R1

Black misses his chance. The way to consolidate his position was to play *24* ... B—R4 (adding protection to the King Rook) followed by *25* ... B—B2, making his K3 square unavailable to an enemy Knight.

25 K—R1

After this, there are all sorts of ways for Black to go wrong. For instance:

(1) *25* ... R—Q4 *26* R×B wins a piece.

(2) *25* ... B—B1   *26*   Kt—R4, Q—R3 *27* Q×P, Q×Q *28* Kt×Q, and White wins a Pawn.

(3) *25* ... B—R4 (recommended by Muller, Czerniak, Coles, Oskam, Belavienetz, Yudovich, Reinfeld and other noted annotators), *26* Kt(Q4)—K6, R—QKt1 *27* R×Kt!, P×R *28* Q×P, (threatens mate) R×Kt *29* Kt×R, and Black must give up his Bishop to prevent mate.

25 ...   B—Q2
26 Kt×B   R×Kt
27 Q×P!

This wins a Pawn, thanks to the vulnerable last rank, and begins a delightful combination.

27 ...   Q—Q1

Certainly not *27* ... Kt×Q, when *28* R×R is checkmate.

28 Kt—B3   R—QB2

After this plausible move, Botvinnik unfolds a startling combination which clears away most of the pieces like magic, and leaves a Rook and Pawn ending, with Botvinnik a Pawn ahead.

This is the position, with White to play:

29 Kt×Kt!   P×Kt

If *29* ... R×Q *30* Kt—B7ch, K—Kt1 *31* Kt×Q, R×Kt *32* P—B4, P—B4 *33* R—B4, and White wins. Or if *29* ... R×Kt *30* R×R, P×R (on *30* ... R×Q *31* R—K8ch forces mate) *31* Q—K4, and White should win.

30 Q×Rch!   Q×Q
31 R×P   Q—KKt1

Strangely enough, there was no way for Black to avoid returning his Queen for a Rook.

32 R—K8   R×P
33 R×Qch   K×R
34 R—QKt1

The Rook belongs behind the passed Pawn. Not only does the Rook support the Pawn, but its range of power increases with every step forward of the Pawn.

34 ...	K—B2
35 P—Kt5	K—K3
36 P—Kt6	

The passed Pawn will keep Black's King and Rook occupied. In the meantime, White can bring his King into active play, eventually to threaten the abandoned Pawns on the King-side.

36 ...	R—B1
37 P—R3	

Botvinnik shows that *37 P—Kt7* would be premature, the play after that running as follows: *37 ... R—QKt1 38 K—Kt1, K—Q3 39 K—B2, K—B2 40 K—Kt3, R×P 41 R×Rch, K×R 42 K—B4, K—B3 43 K—K5, K—Q2*, and White's advantage has been dissipated.

37 ...	R—QKt1
38 K—R2	K—Q4
39 K—Kt3	K—B3
40 K—Kt4	K—Kt2

Blockades the Pawn with his King, and releases the Rook for some sort of counter-play.

Capturing the Pawn would be ruinous, as after *40 ... R×P 41 R×Rch, K×R 42 K—B5*, the King gets to the Pawns and removes them.

41 R—K1!

The Rook shifts over to the King file, where it will assume a more active role, while still watching over the Pawn.

White's immediate threat incidentally is *42 R—K7ch, K×P 43 R×P*, followed by capture of the helpless Rook Pawn.

41 ...	R—Kt1

Here too, *41 ... K×P* loses by *42 R—Kt1ch*, followed by exchanging Rooks.

42 R—K6!

The Rook not only defends the passed Pawn from this horizontal position, but is prepared to help out in the attack on Black's King-side Pawns. Black's King and Rook, on the other hand, are separated and reduced to defensive functions.

42 ...	K—R3

Black defends as well as he can. Moving either of the Pawns lets White's King in, i.e. *42 ... P—R3 43 K—R5* followed by *44 K—Kt6*, or *42 ... P—Kt3 43 K—Kt5* followed by *44 K—R6*.

43 K—Kt5	K—Kt2
44 P—R4	K—R3
45 P—R5	K—Kt2
46 P—Kt4	K—R3
47 K—R4	K—Kt2
48 P—R6!	

This will break up the Pawns!

48 ...	P×P

Or *48 ... P—Kt3 49 R—K7ch, K×P 50 R×P, K—B4 51 R—KKt7, R—KR1 52 R×P*, and Black may resign.

49 R×P	R—Kt2
50 K—R5	K—R3

If *50 ... R—KB2 51 R—K6, R—Kt2 52 P—Kt5, K—R3 53 K—R6, R—Q2 54 R—K8, K×P 55 R—KR8*, and White wins.

51 R—QB6!	R—K2

If 51 ... K—Kt2 52 R—B7ch, R×R 53 P×R, K×P 54 K—R6, and White wins easily, Black's King being too far away to cause trouble.

52 R—B7	R—K4ch
53 P—Kt5	K×P
54 R×P	K—B3
55 K—R6	K—Q3
56 P—Kt6	R—K8
57 R—KB7	K—K3
58 R—B2	

Thus far and no further! The King is prevented from approaching the Pawn.

58 ...	R—QR8
59 P—Kt7	R—R8ch
60 K—Kt6	R—Kt8ch

61 K—R7	R—R8ch
62 K—Kt8	K—K2
63 R—K2ch	K—Q2

On 63 ... K—B3 64 K—B8 does the trick.

64 R—K4!	

Discovered by Lucena in 1497, this magic move is still potent today!

64 ...	R—R7
65 K—B7	Resigns

Boleslavsky does not wait to be shown, but this is how the win is completed: 65 ... R—B7ch 66 K—Kt6, R—Kt7ch 67 K—B6, R—B7ch 68 K—Kt5, R—Kt7ch 69 R—Kt4, and the Pawn is assured of becoming a Queen.

Four Endings in One

J. H. Blackburne · M. Weiss

New York 1889, RUY LOPEZ

This game and the next were played between Blackburne and Weiss in the first two rounds of a double-round tournament.

This game, the first between them, was won by Weiss, who played the Bishop ending beautifully. Blackburne, on the other hand, conducted the ending indifferently, hemming in his own Bishop with Pawns.

In the second round, the game once again came down to a Bishop ending. What happened in the interval I don't know, but this time it was Blackburne who demonstrated the win in classic style. He played it like the man who wrote the book, or at least that chapter in it called, "How to win a Bishop ending with a Pawn ahead."

Incidentally, this Bishop ending was preceded by an ending of two Bishops against Knight and Bishop, followed by a Queen ending, and finally by a Pawn ending. Four endings in one game!

1 P—K4	P—K4
2 Kt—KB3	Kt—QB3
3 B—Kt5	Kt—B3
4 P—Q4	P×P
5 O—O	B—K2
6 R—K1	O—O
7 Kt×P	

Nothing is to be gained from *7* P—K5, Kt—K1 *8* Kt×P, Kt×Kt *9* Q×Kt, P—Q4, and Black has equalized.

7 ...	Kt×Kt
8 Q×Kt	P—Q4
9 P×P	Kt×P
10 B—QB4	

There is no reason to move this piece twice in the opening. White should simply go about the business of continuing his development, say by *10* Kt—B3.

10 ...	B—K3
11 B×Kt	

And for this—letting the opponent have the two Bishops—there is simply no excuse!

11 ...	B×B
12 Kt—B3	

Obviously, *12* R×B, Q×R *13* Q×B, Q—K8 mate won't do!

12 ...	B—K3
13 Q—K4	P—QB3
14 B—B4	R—K1
15 QR—Q1	Q—Kt3
16 Kt—R4	Q—Kt5
17 Q×Q	

This exchange is bound to help Black, whose Bishops gain in power as the board becomes cleared. Instead of this, Steinitz suggests *17* R—Q4, Q—Kt4 *18* B—K5, and if then *18* ... B—Q4, *19* Kt—B3, B×Q *20* Kt×Q, and Black must part with one of his Bishops, to prevent loss of the exchange by *21* Kt—B7.

17 ...	B×Q
18 R—K4	B—KKt5!

"Herr Weiss is one of the greatest masters of simplifying positions," says Steinitz, "and he can well rely on his judgment in the ending, which he conducts with exemplary skill."

19 R×Rch	R×R
20 P—KB3	B—KB4
21 P—B3	B—K2

There are poisonous threats in the air, one of them being *22* ... P—QKt4, winning the Knight.

22 P—QKt3	P—QKt4
23 Kt—Kt2	B—B3
24 B—Q2	

Not very attractive, but the alternatives are worse:

(1) *24* R—QB1 (to save the Bishop Pawn) R—K7 *25* Kt—Q1, R×RP, and White has lost a Pawn.

(2) *24* R—Q6, B×P *25* Kt—Q1, B—QKt5 *26* R—Q4 (or *26* R×P, R—K8ch winning the Knight) B—B4, and Black wins a whole Rook.

24 ...	R—Q1
25 P—QKt4	

This is the position, with Black to play:

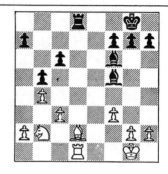

25 ...	P—KR4

Provides the King with a flight-square, a necessary prelude to the threat of winning a piece by *26* ... B—B7.

26 B—K1	R×Rch
27 Kt×R	B—B7
28 Kt—K3	B—Kt8
29 P—QR3	K—B1
30 K—B2	B—Q6

Further reducing White's mobility! Now his King is kept from coming closer to the center, his Knight can move but only to retreat, while his Bishop is confined to a zig-zag excursion from K1 to QR1 and back again, in problem-like style.

31 P—Kt3	K—K2
32 P—KB4	

White should have avoided making this move. It places *all his Pawns* on black squares, greatly limiting the scope of his Bishop, which travels on black squares. The advance of the Pawn also relinquishes control of the square K4, making it now possible for the adverse King to enter strongly into the position by way of that square.

32 ...	K—K3
33 K—B3	B—Q1
34 B—B2	P—R4
35 Kt—Q1	B—B7
36 Kt—K3	B—Kt6
37 K—K4	P—B4ch
38 K—Q3	

Clearly *38* Kt × P would not do, as *38* ... B—B7ch wins the rash creature.

38 ...	P—QR5
39 Kt—Kt2	B—B5ch
40 K—Q2	

The King is forced to retreat, as *40* K—K3 loses by *40* ... B—Kt3ch *41* K—B3, B—Q4ch *42* K—K2, B × B *43* K × B, B × Kt *44* K × B, K—Q4, followed by the removal of White's Queen-side Pawns, while the alternative *40* K—Q4 allowing *40* ... B—Kt3 mate is even worse.

40 ...	K—Q4

White's King meanwhile advances steadily into enemy territory.

41 B—Q4	P—Kt3
42 Kt—K3ch	

White intends to get rid of one of the Bishops, but the exchange leaves him with the bad Bishop!

42 ...	K—K5
43 Kt × B	P × Kt

Black has lost one of his fine Bishops, but the dominating position of his King more than makes up for it. Note too that his Bishop is not hampered by Pawns, since all of them occupy white squares, while the Bishop travels on black squares.

All six of White's Pawns, on the other hand, stand on squares of the color used by the Bishop. Not only does this limit the scope of the Bishop, but it allows White no control of the white squares. *His Bishop and all six Pawns attack black squares only.*

44 K—K2

The only move, as otherwise *44* ... K—B6 followed by *45* ... K—Kt7 wins easily for Black.

44 ...	P—Kt4!
45 B—K3	

If *45* P × P, B × P (threatens *46* ... B—B8) *46* K—Q1, B—K6, and it's all over.

45 ...	P × P
46 B × P	

Obviously *46* P × P loses a Pawn at once after the reply *46* ... B—B2.

46 ...	B—B3
47 B—Q2	

This is the position, with Black to play:

47 ...	P—R5!

This forces an exchange of Pawns,

after which Black will have a passed Pawn on the King Bishop file.

48 P×P

On *48 B—K1*, Black wins nicely by *48 . . . P×P 49 P×P, B—K4*, and White is out of moves—in zugzwang! His Bishop must stay where it is to protect the Pawns on either side of it, while any move by the King allows Black further entrance, either by *50 . . . K—B6* or *50 . . . K—Q6*, in each case winning a Pawn.

48 . . .	B×RP
49 B—K3	B—B3
50 B—Q2	P—B5
51 B—K1	P—B6ch
52 K—B2	

If *52 K—Q1, K—K6 53 B—Q2ch, K—B7 54 B—K1ch, K—Kt7 55 P—R4, P—B7*, and Black wins. Or if *52 K—Q2, B—Kt4ch 53 K—Q1, B—K6*, followed by *54 . . . P—B7* is decisive.

52 . . .	B—R5ch

This begins a fifteen-move combination. Despite its length, it is easy enough to visualize and understand it, if we break it down. This is the series of ideas:

(1) Bishops are exchanged to bring about a Pawn ending.

(2) A count-up of moves shows that each side will Queen a Pawn, but that Black's Pawn becomes a Queen with check.

(3) A series of checks will force an exchange of Queens.

(4) The new Pawn ending will be in Black's favor, his King being near the adverse Pawns.

(5) White's Rook Pawn will fall,

leaving Black with a passed Pawn.

(6) The passed Pawn (after a bit of jockeying) will reach the Queening square.

53 K—B1	B×B
54 K×B	K—Q6
55 P—R4	K×P
56 P—R5	K—Kt6!

But not *56 . . . K—Kt7*, as that allows White to win in fine style by *57 P—R6, P—B6 58 P—R7, P—QB7 59 P—R8(Q)ch, K—Kt8 60 Q—R7* (the beginning of a pretty zig-zagging maneuver) *K—Kt7 61 Q—Kt7ch, K—Kt8 62 Q—Kt6, K—Kt7 63 Q—B6ch, K—Kt8 64 Q—B5, K—Kt7 65 Q—K5ch, K—Kt8 66 Q—K4, K—Kt7 67 Q—Q4ch, K—Kt8 68 Q—Q3, K—Kt7 69 Q—Q2, K—Kt8 70 P—Kt5!, P×P* (if *70 . . . P—B8(Q)ch 71 Q×Qch, K×Q 72 P×P*, and White wins) *71 Q—Kt4ch* (the Queen reaches this square, thanks to the Pawn sacrifice on the previous move) *K—R7 72 K—Q2, P—B7 73 K×P, P—B8(Q) 74 Q—Kt2 mate*.

Now back to this position, with White to play:

57 P—R6	P—B6
58 P—R7	P—QB7
59 K—Q2	

If *59* P—R8(Q), P—B8(Q)ch *60* K—B2, and *61* ... Q—Kt7ch forces the exchange of Queens.

59 ...	P—B7
60 P—R8(Q)	P—QB8(Q)ch
61 K×Q	P—B8(Q)ch
62 K—Q2	Q—B7ch
63 K—Q3	

The only other move is *63* K—Q1, when *63* ... Q—B7ch *64* K—K1, Q—B6ch follows, and the Queens come off the board.

63 ...	Q—QB7ch
64 K—K3	Q—B6ch

This does the trick.

65 Q×Qch	K×Q
66 K—K4	K—Kt6
67 K—Q4	K×P
68 K—B3	

If *68* K—B4, K—Kt7 *69* K—B5, K—Kt6, and Black wins.

68 ...	K—R7
69 K—B2	P—R6
70 K—B1	

On *70* K—B3, K—Kt8 followed by *71* ... P—R7 wins for Black.

70 ...	K—Kt6
71 Resigns	

Bishop and Pawn Ending Deluxe

M. Weiss · J. H. Blackburne

New York 1889, CENTER COUNTER GAME

Blackburne lost his first-round game against Weiss in the great New York Tournament of 1889, but got his revenge when the players met again in the second round. What made the victory particularly sweet was the fact that Blackburne achieved it by using the very weapons with which he was beaten—Bishop and Pawns against Bishop and Pawns.

It is doubtful that even Rubinstein in his palmiest days could have played the ending in more convincing style.

1 P—K4	P—Q4
2 P×P	Kt—KB3
3 P—Q4	Q×P
4 Kt—QB3	Q—QR4
5 Kt—B3	P—B3

A safety measure, to provide a retreat for the Queen.

6 Kt—K5	QKt—Q2
7 Kt—B4	Q—Q1

Sorrowful homecoming, but 7 ... Q—Kt5 loses the Queen by 8 P—QR3, while 7 ... Q—R3 does likewise by 8 Kt—Q6ch and 9 B×Q.

8 B—K2	P—KKt3
9 P—Q5	

Simple development by 9 B—K3 was preferable. The exchanges that now follow will increase the scope of Black's King Bishop.

9 ...	P×P
10 Kt×P	Kt×Kt
11 Q×Kt	B—Kt2
12 P—KR4	

This may have been meant to discourage King side Castling, but it doesn't disturb Blackburne, who goes about his business.

12 ...	O—O
13 P—R5	Kt—B3
14 Q×Q	R×Q
15 P×P	RP×P
16 B—Q3	B—K3
17 B—Q2	QR—B1

The Rook develops with gain of tempo—the threat of winning a piece by 18 ... B×Kt.

18 Kt—K5	Kt—Q2

Forces an exchange which favors Black, all of whose pieces are in active play.

19 Kt×Kt	R×Kt
20 B—QB1	

A wretched move, but how else can White save his Queen Knight Pawn? If 20 B—B3, R×B 21 P×R, B×Pch 22 K—K2, B×R 23 R×B wins a Pawn for Black, while 20 O—O—O loses at once by 20 ... R×B.

This is the position, with Black to play:

20 ... B—B5!

A fine move which wins a Pawn.

21 R—R3

If *21* B×B, R×B *22* P—QB3, R×P *23* P×R, B×Pch, and Black wins two Pawns.

21 ...	B×B
22 R×B	R×R
23 P×R	R—B7!

Rook on the seventh—a paralyzing move!

24 R—Kt1 B—Q5

Black's Rook and Bishop work beautifully together, attacking Pawns on both sides of the board.

25 B—Q2 R×P

Of course not *25 ...* B×KtP, as *26* K—Q1 in reply wins the exchange for White.

26 R×R

White has no choice. If he avoids the exchange of Rooks by playing *26* R—R1 (to protect the Rook

Pawn) the reply *26 ...* R×B costs him a piece immediately.

26 ... B×R

"The rest is a matter of technique." Hundreds of annotators have said this about thousands of games where one side was a Pawn ahead in an ending. Now we can see how the process of winning works out in real life.

27 B—K3	P—R3
28 K—Q2	K—B1
29 K—B2	B—K4
30 K—Kt3	K—K1
31 K—B4	K—Q2
32 K—B5	B—B2

Stops further penetration by the King. That in itself is not enough. The King must be driven back, and the Pawns (Black's, of course) carefully advanced.

33 P—B3 P—K3

Notice how careful Blackburne is (in contrast to his play in the previous game) to place his Pawns on squares *opposite in color* to those on which his Bishop operates.

34 P—R4

Not the best move, since Black would have more difficulty getting a passed Pawn if this Pawn remained on its original square.

34 ...	P—Kt3ch
35 K—B4	K—B3
36 B—B2	P—B3
37 B—K3	B—Q3

This is the position, and it is a curious one:

Is the formula for winning placing all the pieces in one row?

38 B—Q4	P—K4
39 B—K3	P—Kt4ch
40 P × Pch	P × Pch

And so, a passed Pawn is brought into being.

41 K—Kt3	K—Q4
42 B—Q2	P—B4
43 B—B3	P—Kt4

If let alone, Black might very well play 44 ... B—B4 next move, once again placing all his pieces in a row.

| 44 P—Kt4 | P × P |
| 45 P × P | B—B4 |

(I refrain from stressing the obvious.)

46 B—K1	P—K5!
47 P × Pch	K × P
48 B—Q2	

Black can easily go wrong at this point. If he protects the threatened Pawn instinctively by 48 ... B—K2, then 49 B × P (this would come in a flash!) B × B 50 K—Kt4 forces a draw.

| 48 ... | B—K6 |

Offers an exchange which White doesn't dare accept.

49 B—K1	K—B6
50 K—Kt4	K × P
51 K × P	K—B6

The last phase: getting the Pawn through without allowing White to sacrifice his Bishop for it.

52 K—B4	P—Kt5
53 K—Q3	B—B7
54 B—R5	P—Kt6
55 B—B7	P—Kt7
56 B—R2	B—Kt3

"The ending is a fine study and is played with masterly skill by Mr. Blackburne," says Steinitz at this point.

| 57 K—Q2 | K—Kt5 |
| 58 Resigns | |

There is no way to prevent 58 ... K—R6, followed by Queening the Pawn.

Brilliant Career of a Pawn

V. Panov · M. Taimanov

Moscow 1952, SICILIAN DEFENSE

The major theme of this game, with suitable sub-heads, could very well be:

THE PASSED PAWN

(1) Creation of the Pawn.

(2) Blockade of the Pawn.

(3) Removal of the Blockade.

(4) Triumph of the Pawn.

Another phase of this game (a minor theme?) I find even more interesting. Early in the play, instead of the usual struggle for positional advantage as the necessary preliminary to a decisive combination later on, we have here a series of little combinations whose purpose is to acquire ultimately an advantage in position! A good deal of sharp fighting revolves about the efforts of one side to limit, and the other side to increase the attacking range of Black's King Bishop.

This seeming reversal of theory is typical of the play of today's masters, who refuse to let their thinking be bound by convention.

I like this sort of chess, I think it's great, I think it's exciting!

1 P—K4	P—QB4
2 Kt—QB3	Kt—QB3
3 P—KKt3	P—KKt3
4 B—Kt2	B—Kt2

5 P—Q3	P—Q3

Both sides are content to develop quietly, making no effort to tangle with each other.

6 KKt—K2

The Knight develops here (instead of at B3) in order not to block the Bishop Pawn. The Pawn must be free to advance to B4 and B5, in the event that White starts a King-side attack.

6 ...   R—Kt1

The Rook leaves! Not only to get out of the range of White's King Bishop, but to support a counter-attack by 7 ... P—QKt4 and 8 ... P—QKt5.

7 O—O	P—QKt4
8 P—B4	P—Kt5
9 Kt—Q5	

White intends to continue with *10* P—B3 and *11* P—Q4. These last two moves would build up a strong Pawn center, and shorten the range of Black's King Bishop.

9 ...   Kt—Q5!

A clever reply which practically forces White to exchange Knights, and renders it difficult for him to play P—B3 for quite a while.

10 Kt × Kt

If White persists, and does try
10 P—B3, then *10* ... Kt × Ktch *11*
Q × Kt, P—K3 *12* Kt—K3, P × P
wins a Pawn for Black.

10 ...	B × Ktch
11 K—R1	P—K3
12 Kt—K3	Kt—K2

White's position is a bit uncomfortable, for the moment. He cannot
develop his Queen Bishop, as *13*
B—Q2, B × P loses a Pawn, nor can
he drive off the troublesome Bishop,
whose pressure on the long diagonal
is annoying.

But he finds a pretty little move,
which enables him either to dislodge
the Bishop by P—B3, or open a
file for his Queen Rook, affording
him counter-play.

This is the position, with White to
play:

13 P—QR3!

A subtle trap! If *13* ... P × P *14*
R × P (threatens *15* P—B3) B × P
15 B × B, R × B *16* Q—R1! (a strange
attack on both Rooks!) Q—Kt3 *17*
Kt—B4, and White wins a whole
Rook.

13 ...	O—O
14 P × P	P × P
15 Q—K1	

Again with the idea of playing *16*
P—B3 followed by *17* P—Q4.

15 ...	Q—B2

Which Black of course prevents!

16 Kt—B4

Screens off the opposing Queen,
and once more prepares to play *17*
P—B3.

16 ...	P—Q4

Apparently forcing the Knight to
return. Has White wasted time with
his last move?

17 B—K3!

Not after this move! Suddenly
the skies are clear, and the birds
begin to sing!

17 ...	B × B

What else is there? If *17* ...
P × Kt *18* B × B (threatens *19* B—K5
winning the exchange, as well as
19 R × P) Kt—B3 *19* B—B6, and
now it's White's Bishop that dominates the long diagonal.

Or if *17* ... B—KKt2 *18* R × P snips
off a Pawn, without compensation
for Black. Finally, if *17* ... Kt—
B3 (protects the Bishop as well as
the Rook Pawn) *18* P × P, P × P *19*
B × P, and White wins a Pawn.

18 Kt × B	P × P
19 P × P	R—Q1

Black's once-powerful King Bishop
is off the board, and its absence

leaves a weakness on the black squares, particularly Black's KB3 and KR3 squares. White's next move is an attempt to exploit that weakness.

20 P—Kt4

Intending to follow with *21* P—Kt5, *22* Kt—Kt4 and *23* Kt—B6ch, anchoring his Knight on a strong outpost.

20 ...   P—B4

Disposes of that threat, but opens the way for White to secure another sort of advantage—one which could hardly have been foreseen earlier.

21 KtP×P   KP×P

Preferable to *21* ... KtP×P, which opens a file against Black's King—not a palatable prospect!

22 Kt—Q5!   Kt×Kt
23 P×Kt

The climax of the combination play. White has a passed Pawn, a positional advantage. Black's counter-play in such situations is always tempered by the fact that he must always keep a watchful eye on the Pawn. Its menace grows greater with every step it takes.

23 ...   R—Kt3
24 Q—K5   R(Kt3)—Q3

This is better than *24* ... R(Q1)—Q3, after which *25* KR—K1 (threatens to win the Queen by *26* Q—K8ch, K—Kt2 *27* R—K7ch) is

strong for White, while the alternative *24* ... Q×Q *25* P×Q, allowing White to have two connected passed Pawns, is unthinkable.

Note how one little Pawn (true enough, it's a passed Pawn) can tie up nearly all of the opposing forces.

This is the position, with White to play:

25 P—B4!

The next step: White plays to establish two connected passed Pawns.

25 ...   P×P *e.p.*

Capturing with the Queen instead leads to this: *25* ... Q×P *26* R×P, R(Q1)—Q2 *27* R×R, R×R *28* P—Q6, and the check by the Bishop will be fatal.

26 P×P   Q—B4

Hoping to develop the Bishop next move. If at once *26* ... B—Kt2 *27* R×P wins a Pawn, or if *26* ... B—Q2 *27* R×P, Q×R *28* Q×R does likewise, while *26* ...

B—R3 loses immediately by *27* R × B, since Black dares not recapture the Rook.

| 27 P—B4 | B—R3 |

The passed Pawns are now heavily blockaded—but White finds a way to lift the blockade!

| 28 R × B! | R × R |
| 29 P—Q6! | |

Both of White's Pawns are perfectly safe! If *29* ... Q × BP *30* B—Q5ch wins the Queen, while *29* ... Q × QP is drastically punished by *30* B—Q5ch, K—B1 *31* Q—R8ch, K—K2 *32* Q—Kt7ch, K—K1 *33* Q—B7 mate.

| 29 ... | Q × Q |
| 30 P × Q | |

White now has three connected passed Pawns—a more than adequate return for his sacrifice of the exchange.

| 30 ... | R—R4 |

Temporarily restraining all three dangerous Pawns.

| 31 B—Q5ch | K—B1 |
| 32 R—QKt1! | |

White brings up the reserves!

| 32 ... | K—Kt2 |

The King goes into hiding, to avoid the effects of *33* R—Kt7, P—R4 *34* R—R7, K—K1 *35* B—B6ch, and Black loses a Rook.

33 R—Kt7ch	K—R3
34 K—Kt2	R—R7ch
35 K—B3	R—R6ch
36 K—K2	P—B5

Threatens *37* ... R—K6ch followed by *38* ... R × KP, removing one of his tormentors.

| 37 K—Q2 | R—K6 |
| 38 R—K7 | R—QKt1 |

Black tries to get the other Rook into active play, with threats of drawing by perpetual check, or even of mating, if White is not careful.

| 39 B—Kt7! | |

Destroys that hope!

| 39 ... | P—R4 |
| 40 P—Q7 | |

Clearly indicating his intentions— *41* R—K8, followed by Queening the Pawn.

The Bishop is indirectly protected: if *40* ... R × B *41* P—Q8(Q) wins easily.

| 40 ... | R—QKt6 |
| 41 B—B6 | |

This is better than *41* R—K8, the sequel to which could be *41* ... R(Kt6) × B *42* R × R, R × Pch! (but not the tempting *42* ... R × R, after which *43* P—K6, R—Q1 *44* K—K2, K—Kt2 *45* P—K7 wins for White) and Black should have no trouble drawing the game.

41 ...	R—Kt7ch
42 K—B3	R(Kt1)—Kt6ch
43 K—Q4	R—Q7ch
44 K—B5	P—B6
45 R—B7	P—B7
46 R × BP	R × R
47 P—Q8(Q)	

Black could resign here, but "Hope springs eternal in the human breast," as Alexander Pope remarked.

47 ...	R—B4	
48 K—Q6	R—Q6ch	
49 B—Q5	P—R5	
50 P—K6	R—K6	
51 Q—R4ch	K—Kt2	
52 Q—Q4ch	R(B4)—K4	
53 Q×Rch	R×Q	
54 K×R	P—R6	
55 P—B5	Resigns	

Dispatching the King's Musketeers

T. Petrosian · V. Smyslov

Moscow 1961, QUEEN'S INDIAN DEFENSE

There is nothing prosaic in the way Petrosian handles a King-side attack. He can discover witty ideas in the most well-worn positions.

In this game, he finds an original means of breaking into the opponent's territory. He begins by making three aggressive moves in a row with his Queen. These three moves uproot the three Pawns protecting the King in the Castled position. There still remains one strong defender of the King to be disposed of—the enemy Queen! Petrosian lures the Queen away by an offer of his Bishop, and then storms the bastions.

1 P—QB4	Kt—KB3
2 Kt—QB3	P—K3
3 Kt—B3	P—QKt3
4 P—Q4	B—Kt2
5 P—QR3	P—Q4
6 P×P	Kt×P

This is probably preferable to *6* ... P×P, blocking the Bishop's view of the long diagonal.

7 P—K3	B—K2
8 B—Kt5ch	P—B3

Interposing the Knight could be fatal: *8* ... Kt—B3 *9* Kt—K5, Q—Q3 *10* Kt—K4, and the pinned Knight will fall, or *8* ... Kt—Q2 *9* Kt×Kt, P×Kt *10* Kt—K5, B—QB1 *11* Kt—B6, and the Queen is smothered.

9 B—Q3	P—QB4
10 Kt×Kt	Q×Kt
11 P×P	Q×P

Black avoids *11* ... B×P, after which *12* B—Kt5ch, B—B3 *13* Q×Q, P×Q *14* B—Q3, leaves him with an isolated Pawn.

12 B—Q2	Kt—B3
13 R—QB1	Q—Q3
14 Q—B2	R—QB1
15 O—O	

This is the position, with Black to play:

At this point, Black seems to have a tremendous move in *15* ... Kt—K4. He does not play it though, as it might lead to disaster, thus:

(1) *15* ... Kt—K4 *16* B—Kt5ch, K—B1 *17* Q×Rch, B×Q *18* R×Bch, B—Q1 *19* B—Kt4, and Black's

Queen is pinned.

(2) *15 ... Kt—K4 16 B—Kt5ch,
Kt—Q2 17 Q×Rch, B×Q 18 R×
Bch, B—Q1 19 B—Kt4, Q—Q4*
(the only move for the poor Queen)
20 B—B6, Q—Q6 (if *20 ... Q—KB4
21 R—Q1* wins) *21 Kt—K5,* and
Black's game is in ruins.

(3) *15 ... Kt—K4 16 B—Kt5ch,
K—Q1 17 Kt×Kt, R×Q* (*17 ...
Q×Kt 18 Q—Q3ch, Q—Q3* might
save Black) *18 Kt×Pch, K—B2 19
Kt×Q, R×R 20 R×Rch, K×Kt
21 B—Kt4ch, K—K4 22 B×B,* and
White wins.

Smyslov might have seen these
beautiful combinations, or on principle, might have spent little time
analyzing the possibilities. The
principle is one that Capablanca
expressed when he said this about a
powerful-looking move that Winter
made against him, "My opponent
should have considered that a
player of my experience and strength
could never allow such a move if it
were good."

15 ...	P—KR3
16 KR—Q1	O—O
17 B—B3	Q—Kt1
18 Q—R4!	

The first in a series of ingenious
moves which leads to a devastating
King-side attack.

18 ...   KR—Q1

Black prepares to meet *19 Q—
KKt4* with *19 ... B—B1,* but White
has other ideas.

19 Q—K4

First threat: *20 Q—R7ch,* and
mate next move.

19 ...   P—Kt3

The best reply, but now one of the
Pawns has been uprooted, and the
position weakened.

20 Q—KKt4

Second threat: *21 B×P, P×B 22
Q×KtPch, K—B1 23 B—Kt7ch,
K—Kt1 24 B×P dis ch, K—R1 25
Q—Kt7* mate.

This is the position, with Black to
play:

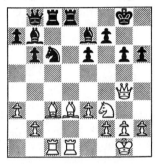

20 ...   P—KR4

Another Pawn is dislodged. De-
fending the Knight Pawn by *20 ...
K—R2* instead leads to some pretty
combinations, the logical result of
Petrosian's fine position play: *20 ...
K—R2 21 B×Pch, P×B 22 Q×KP*
(threatens *23 Q—B7* mate) *R—B1
23 R—Q7* (threatens *24 R×Bch* and
quick mate) *R—QB2 24 Kt—K5!
Kt×Kt 25 Q×Kt* (the goal is *26
Q—Kt7* mate) *R—B2 26 R×R,* and
Black is helpless.

Even prettier is this line: *20 ...
K—R2 21 B×Pch, P×B 22 Q×KP,
R—B1 23 R—Q7, QR—K1 24
Kt—Kt5ch!, P×Kt 25 Q—R3ch,
K—Kt1 26 Q—R8ch, K—B2 27
Q—B6ch, K—Kt1 28 Q—Kt7* mate.

21 Q—R3

Third threat: *22* B×P, P×B *23* Q×KPch, K—B1 *24* Q×P, and White wins.

21 ...   P—B4

A third Pawn is displaced. Here too, a different defense meets with retribution by combinative means: If *21* ... R—Q3 (to protect the King Pawn) *22* P—KKt4, QR—Q1 *23* P×P, R×B *24* R×R, R×R *25* P×P, P×P *26* Q—R8ch, K—B2 *27* Kt—K5ch!, and Black must give up his Queen, either by *27* ... Q×Kt directly, or by *27* ... Kt×Kt, unguarding the Queen.

22 B—B4   R×Rch
23 R×R   K—B2
24 P—K4!

Everybody wants to get into the act! The attack is directed against Black's vulnerable Pawn at K3. The immediate threat is *25* P×P, KtP×P *26* Q×BPch, K—K1 (if *26* ... K—Kt1 *27* B×P is mate) *27* Q—Kt6ch, K—B1 *28* B—Kt7ch, K—Kt1 *29* B×P mate.

24 ...   Q—B5
25 R—K1   Q—Kt5

Can Black force an exchange of Queens, and stifle the attack?

26 P×P   Q×B

What else was there? If *26* KtP×P *27* B×Pch followed by *28* B×R

wins, or if *26* ... Q×BP *27* B×Pch wins the Queen. Finally, if *26* ... Q×Q *27* B×Pch, K—B1 *28* P×Q, R—Q1 *29* P×P, and White is three Pawns ahead, with an easy win.

27 P×KtPch   K—K1

Black avoids the elegant loss by *27* ... K×P *28* R×Pch, K—B2 *29* R×Kt!, and Black may capture the Rook in any of three ways, only to lose his Queen by the Knight fork *30* Kt—K5ch.

28 P—Kt7   P—K4

If *28* ... K—Q2 *29* R—Q1ch, K—B2 *30* Q—Kt3ch, P—K4 *31* B×Pch, Kt×B *32* Q×Ktch, K—B3 *33* Kt—Q4ch, and Black must give up his Queen, or be mated.

29 Q×Pch   K—Q2
30 R—Q1ch   B—Q3

There is no hope in *30* ... K—B2 *31* B×Pch, Kt×B *32* Q×Ktch, K—B3 *33* Kt—Q4ch (reproducing the position in the previous note) K—Q2 *34* Kt—B5 dis ch, K—B3 *34* Kt×B mate.

31 B×P   Kt—Q5

Loses a piece, but so does everything else.

32 Kt×Kt   Resigns

Masterly attacking play by Petrosian.

The Sheltering Pawn

Schlage · R. Réti

Berlin 1928, SICILIAN DEFENSE

Réti's endings are always wonderfully instructive. He is two Pawns down in this one, but the aggressive position of his King, Rook and passed Pawn give him the advantage. For practical purposes Réti is a King ahead!

There are clever touches in this exquisite ending. An appreciation of their fine points will do more to improve your game than learning by heart the quickest way to mate with a Knight and Bishop, especially since an opportunity to do so may never occur in your lifetime!

1 P—K4	P—QB4
2 Kt—KB3	Kt—KB3
3 Kt—B3	P—Q4
4 P×P	Kt×P
5 B—Kt5ch	B—Q2
6 B×Bch	Q×B
7 Kt×Kt	Q×Kt
8 P—Q4	P—K3
9 O—O	Kt—B3
10 P×P	Q×Q
11 R×Q	B×P

The players skip the midgame and go right into the ending, with the chances about even.

12 B—B4	K—K2
13 Kt—K5	Kt×Kt

14 B×Kt	P—B3
15 B—B3	KR—Q1
16 B—R5	

To tempt *16 ... P—QKt3* in reply, but Réti wants the third rank free for his Rook.

16 ...	R×Rch
17 R×R	R—QB1
18 P—QR4	B—Q3
19 R—Q2	

White must also be careful about moving his Pawns. If he plays *19 P—QB3* to save his Pawn, then *19 ... P—QKt3 20 B—Kt4, B×B 21 P×B, R—B5 22 P—R5, R×P* wins a Pawn for Black.

19 ...	R—B3

With an eye to *20 ... R—R3 21 B—B3* (of course not *21 P—QKt4, P—QKt3*, trapping the Bishop) *R×P*, and Black wins a Pawn.

20 B—B3

White is careful! The natural move *20 P—QKt3* protects the Rook Pawn, but makes a victim of the Bishop after the reply *20 ... P—QKt3*.

This is the position, with Black to play:

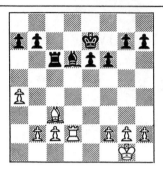

20 ...   P—K4

Prepares for this attack: 21 ... R—B5 22 P—R5, B—Kt5 23 B×B, R×B 24 P—QKt3, R—Kt4, and Black wins a Pawn.

Réti does not play 20 ... R—B5 at once, as 21 R—Q4 in reply rescues the Pawn.

21 R—Q3

This defense of the Bishop frees the Knight Pawn from that duty. Now if 21 ... R—B5, 22 P—QKt3 holds everything.

21 ...	K—K3
22 R—R3	P—KR3
23 R—Kt3	P—KKt4
24 R—R3	B—B1
25 R—Q3	R—B5!

Induces White to play ...

26 P—QKt3

Bolsters the Rook Pawn, but now the Bishop's position has been weakened as it lacks the support of the Knight Pawn.

26 ...	R—B3
27 P—B3	P—B4

The Pawns take on a menacing look. Black's immediate threat is 28 ... P—K5 29 P×P, P×P 30 R—R3, P—Kt5 31 R—Kt3 (the Rook must stay on the third rank to keep in touch with the Bishop) B—Q3 32 R—K3, B—B4, and the pin by the Bishop wins the exchange for Black.

28 P—KKt4	P—B5
29 K—B1	B—Kt2

Clearly intending 30 ... P—K5, a discovered attack which wins a piece or the exchange.

30 B—Kt4

White offers a Pawn in the hope of getting counter-play after its capture (30 ... R×P) by 31 R—Q6ch, K—B2 32 R—Q7ch.

30 ...   P—K5!

A fine sacrifice (of the Rook Pawn and Knight Pawn, as it turns out), which clears the way for the King to come strongly into the game.

31 P×P	R×P
32 R—Q6ch	K—K4
33 R—KKt6	B—B3
34 R×RP	B—Q1
35 R—R8	B—B2
36 P—R4	

And we have this position, with Black to play:

White is willing to give up a couple of Pawns, if he can thereby obtain a passed Pawn. Naturally, he expects Black to take whatever Pawns he can get, and that the game might take this course: *36* ... P × P *37* P—Kt5, K × P *38* P—Kt6, K—B6 *39* P—Kt7, R—B8ch *40* B—K1, B—R4 *41* R—K8, P—R6 *42* P—Kt8(Q), P—R7 *43* Q—Kt2 mate.

Or, if this is too much to expect, that Black will play the straightforward *36* ... K × P, Pawns being so valuable in the endgame.

36 ...	**K—Q5!**

But Réti crosses him up! Instead of capturing the Pawn, *the King goes around it*! In this way the King advances to a dominating position, *sheltered by the opponent's Pawn*, which acts as a buffer against annoying Rook checks.

37 P × P	**K—K6**
38 R—R3ch	**P—B6**

Despite the fact that he is two Pawns behind, Black's position is powerful. His King and passed Pawn are strongly placed in the opponent's territory, and his Rook dominates the seventh rank. In addition to this, he threatens to finish matters off by *39* ... R—B8ch

40 B—K1, B—R4.

Black has everything in his favor.

39 B—R3

Prepared to meet *39* ... R—R7 (an attack on the Bishop and a threat to mate by *40* ... R—R8ch) with *40* B—B1ch.

But Black can trump this trick, too!

39 ...	**B—Q3!**
40 P—Kt4	**P—R4**
41 R—R6	**B × P**
42 B × B	**P × B**

Black now has a passed Pawn on each side of the board. Meanwhile he threatens instant mate!

43 K—Kt1	**P—Kt6**
44 R—QKt6	**P—Kt7**
45 P—Kt6	**K—K7!**

This is more accurate than *45* ... R—B8ch *46* K—R2, P—Kt8(Q) *47* R × Q, R × R *48* P—Kt7, P—B7 *49* P—Kt8(Q), and White still needs subduing.

46 P—Kt7	**P—B7ch**
47 K—R2	**P—B8(Q)**
48 Resigns	

If White Queens the Pawn, the finishing touch is *48* ... K—B6, discovered check and mate.

The Power of Position Play

J. R. Capablanca
(*Simultaneous*)

· T. Germann
· D. Miller
· W. Skillicorn

London 1920, QUEEN'S GAMBIT DECLINED

This is a typical Capablanca game. Which is to say, that its outward appearance of classic simplicity may conceal inner workings of fiendish ingenuity.

Capablanca squeezes out a win from a position where his advantage, acquired in the opening, and carried through the midgame into the ending, is so slight as to be almost imperceptible. It consists in having a King that is situated closer to the center, and a Rook that is more active than his opponent's. This is little enough, but it enables Capablanca to set his sights on a Pawn, surround it and remove it. Once he is a Pawn ahead, and a road cleared for the advance of a passed Pawn, the win is easy for Capablanca.

All this is done smoothly and effortlessly, as though Capablanca were demonstrating a composed ending whose terms were, "White to move and win."

We may not hope ever to play like Capablanca, but we can learn a great deal about the technique of winning by watching him in action.

| 1 | P—Q4 | P—Q4 |
| 2 | P—QB4 | P—K3 |

3	Kt—KB3	Kt—KB3
4	B—Kt5	QKt—Q2
5	P—K3	B—K2
6	Kt—B3	P—QR3

Ready to start the Pawns rolling on the Queen-side by 7 ... P×P 8 B×P, P—Kt4 9 B—Q3, P—B4, with vigorous (but perhaps premature) counter-play. A safer line is 6 ... O—O 7 R—B1, P—B3, which does not reveal his hand so soon.

| 7 | Q—B2 | O—O |
| 8 | R—B1 | |

The Rook moves to a file where it can be useful. Sooner or later an exchange of Pawns will open the Bishop file, and the Rook's presence will be felt.

8	...	P×P
9	B×P	P—Kt4
10	B—Q3	B—Kt2
11	P—QR4!	

This attack weakens Black's Pawn structure on the Queen-side, and will make it difficult for him to get in the freeing move ... P—B4.

11	...	P—Kt5
12	B×Kt	Kt×B
13	Kt—K4	

This brings about more exchanges, as White threatens either to win a Pawn by *14* Kt × Ktch, B × Kt *15* B × Pch, or to play *14* Kt—B5, getting a powerful grip on the position.

13 ...	B × Kt
14 B × B	Kt × B

Once again compulsory, as the alternatives are:

(1) *14* ... R—B1 *15* B—Kt7, and White wins a Pawn.

(2) *14* ... R—R2 *15* Kt—K5, Kt × B *16* Kt—B6, Q—R1 (what else is there, with everything *en prise*?) *17* Kt × Bch, K—R1 *18* Kt—B6, and White wins the exchange.

15 Q × Kt	P—QB4

Win or lose, Black must advance the Bishop Pawn, or be left with a strategically lost position. Any delay will allow White to play *16* Q—B6 with intolerable pressure.

16 P × P	Q—R4

This is the position, with White to play:

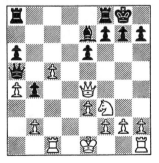

17 P—QKt3!

Simple and strong! Black will have to lose time capturing the Bishop Pawn, and in consequence his pieces will be somewhat awkwardly placed.

An attempt to hold on to the passed Pawn though, leads to complications which are not clear: If *17* P—B6, Q × P *18* O—O, KR—B1 *19* R—B4, R—B2 *20* KR—B1, QR—B1 *21* Kt—Q4, and White has no definite advantage.

17 ...	B × P
18 Kt—Kt5	

This is not the beginning of a King-side attack, even though White does threaten *19* Q × P mate. The object of this, and the next move, is to force a loosening of Black's Pawn structure on the King-side.

18 ...	P—Kt3
19 Q—R4	P—R4
20 Kt—K4	

This is better than the plausible attempt to break up Black's King-side by *20* P—Kt4 followed by *21* P × P. Black meets *20* P—Kt4 with *20* ... B—K2 (pinning the Knight) and after *21* P—B4, B × Kt deprives White of a valuable piece.

20 ...	KR—B1
21 Q—Kt5!	

Guards against loss of a Pawn by *21* ... B × P *22* R × Rch, R × R, and White may not capture the Bishop.

The triple attack on the Bishop will force an exchange of Queens, simplifying the position to White's advantage.

21 ...	B—Kt3
22 Q × Q	B × Q
23 K—K2	

There are always threats against exposed pieces in the most innocent-looking positions. The unprotected Bishop in this case is a likely candidate for abduction. One possibility is: *24 Kt—Q6, R—Q1* (to control one of the open files) *25 Kt—Kt7* (attacks Rook and Bishop) *R—Q4 26 P—K4* (attacks the defender of the Bishop) *R—K4 27 P—B4, R×Pch 28 K—B3,* and White wins a piece.

23 ...	B—Q1
24 Kt—Q6	R—B2
25 R—B4	R—Q2

Abandons the Bishop file, but exchanging Rooks instead is not very attractive: *25* ... R×R *26 Kt×R, K—B1 27 R—Q1, K—K2 28 P—B4* (if *28 Kt—K5, K—K1* defends against the threats of winning a Pawn by *29 Kt—B6ch* or by *29 R—Q7ch*) and White has the edge.

26 Kt—K4	B—K2
27 R—Q1!	

Naturally, Capablanca does not try to win a Pawn by *27 R×P,* when *27* ... P—B4 (but not *27* ... B×R *28 Kt—B6ch,* regaining the Rook) winning a piece for Black is the penalty.

27 ...	R×R

Here though, if *27* ... QR—Q1 *28 R×R, R×R 29 R×P,* and White wins a Pawn, as *29* ... P—B4 is met by *30 R—Kt8ch.*

28 K×R	R—Q1ch
29 K—K2	R—Q4
30 R—B6	P—R4

If Black defends the Pawn by *30* ... R—R4, the reply *31 Kt—Q2* followed by *32 Kt—B4,* drives the Rook away and wins the Pawn.

This is the position, with White to play:

White has a target in the Queen Rook Pawn. He can attack it by moving his Rook behind the Pawn, and posting his Knight at QB4. Black can defend the Pawn with Rook and Bishop, but the Rook can be driven off, and the Pawn then captured.

31 Kt—Q2	K—Kt2
32 Kt—B4	B—Q1
33 P—K4	R—Q5

The Rook must leave the fourth rank, and the defense of the Pawn. If it tries to remain, and moves to KKt4, then *34 P—Kt3* threatens Black with loss of a whole Rook by *35 P—B4, R—Kt5 36 K—B3,* followed by *37 P—R3.*

34 P—B3	R—Q2
35 R—R6	K—B3
36 Kt×P	B×Kt

Black exchanges to bring about a Rook ending, which may be difficult to win even with an extra Pawn.

37 R×B	R—Q5

Protecting the Knight Pawn by *37* ... R—Kt2 succumbs to *38 R—QKt5, R×R 39 P×R, K—K4*

40 K—Q3, followed by *41* K—B4, and another Pawn bites the dust.

| *38* R—QKt5 | P—K4 |

On *38* ... K—K2 instead, *39* K—K3 evicts the Rook again—this time from the fifth rank.

| *39* P—R5 | K—K3 |
| *40* P—R6 | R—Q3 |

Or *40* ... R—Q2 *41* R—Kt6ch, K—K2 *42* R—Kt7, K—Q1 *43* R × Rch, and the Pawn cannot be stopped.

| *41* P—R7 | R—R3 |

There is no hope in *41* ... R—Q1, since *42* R—Kt8 in reply forces the Pawn through. So Black moves his Rook behind the Pawn to stop its mad rush.

Capablanca has a pretty answer to that move!

| *42* R—Kt6ch! | Resigns |

This unknown game of Capablanca's is as beautifully precise as his familiar masterpieces.

That Old Black Magic

O. S. Bernstein · J. Mieses

Coburg 1904, SICILIAN DEFENSE

This is the finest game I know of to reveal the mysteries of the black squares.

In this game, White gets a stranglehold on the position through his control of the black squares. His opponent's Pawns are held in a grip of steel, and are unable to move without loss. The consequence is that the pieces behind the Pawns are helpless to come into the game. White's pieces, on the other hand, are unrestrained, and free to roam all over the board.

The exploitation of White's superiority is quite entertaining, the King himself giving a remarkable display of his powers in the ending.

1 P—K4	P—QB4
2 Kt—QB3	P—K3
3 Kt—B3	Kt—QB3

This cannot be bad, since a piece is developed. More to the point though, is the vigorous *3 . . . P—Q4*, to establish a Pawn firmly in the center.

4 P—Q4!	P×P
5 Kt×P	Kt—B3
6 Kt×Kt	KtP×Kt
7 P—K5!	

Excellent! This evicts the Knight from its fine post, and strengthens White's grip on the square Q6.

This is the first step in White's campaign for control of the black squares.

7 . . .	Kt—Q4
8 Kt—K4	

Intensifies the pressure on Q6—reason enough for moving a piece twice in the opening.

8 . . .	P—KB4

If *8 . . . Q—B2 9 P—B4* (but not *9 Kt—Q6ch, B×Kt 10 P×B, Q×P 11 P—QB4*, when Black escapes from the pin by *11 . . . Q—K4ch*).

9 P×P *e.p.*	Kt×P
10 Kt—Q6ch	B×Kt
11 Q×B	

The exchange of pieces has left Black with the bad Bishop, one which is ineffective because its pathway is cluttered up by Pawns. A Bishop can have little mobility if the squares to which it is limited are occupied by Pawns.

Black must also cope with the fact that his King may not Castle, and his Queen Pawn is blockaded.

11 . . .	Kt—K5

The Queen must be driven off, or Black will choke for lack of air.

There is no relief in *11 . . . Q—K2 12 B—KB4, Q×Q 13 B×Q, Kt—K5*

14 B—R3!, and White still bears down with a heavy hand.

12 Q—Q4	Kt—B3
13 Q—Q6	Kt—K5
14 Q—Kt4!	

Very strong! If the Queen cannot establish permanent residence at Q6, this square is the next best thing. At QKt4 (odd place though it is) the Queen attacks the Knight, controls a diagonal which makes Castling impossible for Black, and in a third direction prevents Black's Queen Rook from seizing the open file.

14 ...   P—Q4

Quite plausible, since it seems to bring about equality. The Knight is protected, and Black intends to continue with *15* ... Q—Q3, enabling him to Castle.

15 B—Q3

An ideal move, as a piece is developed with a threat—*16* B × Kt, P × B *17* Q × P, and White wins a Pawn.

15 ...	Q—Q3
16 Q × Q	

White is happy to simplify. He will still enjoy the advantages accruing from two powerful Bishops, and an enduring grip on the black squares.

16 ...   Kt × Q

Black is content with his part of the bargain: his Rooks have open files on which to operate, and the cluster of Pawns in the center should limit the scope of the opposing Bishops.

17 P—KB4!

This prevents *17* ... P—K4, and the release of Black's Bishop.

It was about moves of this sort that the great annotator Marco said, "An eye for the microscopic betokens the master."

17 ...   P—QR4

Obviously preparing to bring the Bishop into play on the starboard side.

18 B—K3!

An excellent move! It prevents the advance of Black's Queen Bishop Pawn, while two more black squares (Q4 and QB5) come under White's domination.

18 ...   B—R3

This is the position, with White to play:

19 K—Q2!

The King is a strong piece and should be used aggressively in the ending. As the number of pieces on the board diminishes, so is the danger lessened of the King being exposed to a mating attack, and its own power as a fighting piece magnified. In the ending, the King is unexcelled as a means of causing damage by getting in among the enemy Pawns.

19 ...   Kt—B5ch

Black's plan becomes manifest: he wants to force an exchange of Knight for Bishop. This would leave Bishops of opposite colors on the board, a circumstance generally leading to a draw.

Black is also playing for a swindle: if *20* K—K2 (hoping for *20 ...* Kt×P, when *21* B×B, R×B *22* QR—QKt1, Kt—B5 *23* R—Kt8ch followed by *24* R×R wins for White), Black crosses him up by the simple *20 ...* Kt×B, getting rid of the Bishop that is holding back his Pawns.

20 B×Kt   B×B
21 P—QR4!

Blockade! The Rook Pawn is stopped dead in its tracks. It is now a fixed target, always in danger of being attacked by B—Kt6. Black must watch over the Pawn constantly with his Queen Rook, as loss of the Pawn allows White a passed Pawn on the Rook file. Black is thereby deprived of the active services of his Queen Rook.

21 ...   K—Q2

The King comes to the center for the endgame.

The Rooks are now united, while the King heads for Q3 to support the Bishop Pawn, whose advance would help free his game.

22 P—QKt3   B—R3

The only flight square open to the unhappy Bishop!

23 B—Kt6!

And now an attack on the Pawn!

23 ...   B—B1

Which can only be met by further retreat of the Bishop!

24 K—K3

Continues the trek to Q4, K5, and as we shall see, points north!

White is ready to meet *24 ...* K—Q3 with *25* K—Q4, after which Black's center Pawns are held tight.

24 ...   R—R3
25 B—B5!

Dominates every important square on the board!

Black's King cannot reach Q3, his Rooks cannot seize any open files, his Bishop has little scope (one square as against eight by White's) and his Pawn center is paralyzed.

White has a won game, strategically. What remains is the matter of winning it, a technique the masters take for granted, but one not always easily demonstrated. It is done here in magnificent style.

25 ...   K—B2
26 K—Q4!

Tightens the noose! The strengthening of White's grip on the black squares prevents the opponent's center Pawns from moving, and this in turn keeps the pieces behind the Pawns from taking an active part in the game.

The King's last move also clears the way for the entrance of the King Rook, who will make good use of the King-file.

26 ...   B—Q2

Black will try to maneuver the Bishop over to the King-side, say to KKt3.

His King Rook seems to have a great deal of scope, but what does it avail him? If it moves to QKt1 (as good a file as there is) at what point can it penetrate? There is no useful square on that file for the Rook.

27 KR—K1

Much stronger than the immediate occupation of K5 by the King. White intends to use this key square as a transfer point for his Rook on its way to the King Knight-file. After the Rook gets there, White will settle his King at K5, and tighten his grip on the black squares.

27 ...   P—R4
28 R—K5

Second stop on the way to Kt5.

28 ...   P—Kt3
29 R—Kt5

Attacks the Knight Pawn, and simultaneously makes room for further entry by the King.

29 ...   R—KKt1

The Pawn must be protected, and this is of course preferable to *29 ... R—R3*, and the Rook has no mobility to speak of.

30 K—K5

Further penetration along the convenient black squares. The threat is now *31 K—B6* (double attack on the Knight Pawn) B—K1 *32 R—K1* (stronger than *32 K × P*) followed by

33 R × KP.

30 ...   B—K1

Black abandons the King Pawn, as he cannot hope to save all his Pawns. There is a slight chance, if White takes the Pawn at once, of putting up some resistance by *31 ... B—Q2ch 32 K—B6, B—B4.*

Black's poor Bishop is sadly shut in by the five Pawns standing on the same color as the Bishop.

31 R—K1

Before committing himself to decisive action, White applies more pressure. Notice how a master player puts every piece to work before he strikes a blow.

31 ...   R—QR1

To get back into the game, this Rook has to return home!

There was no satisfactory defense in *31 ... K—Q2*, as the reply *32 K—B6* uncovers the Rook's attack on the King Pawn.

This is the position, with White to play:

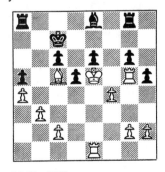

32 K—B6!

This completes the concept of encirclement. Notice the effects of the arrangement of Black's Pawns at K3, Q4 and QB3. Black's own pieces are kept under restraint, while White's can utilize the weakened black squares QB5, Q4, K5 and KB6 to effect an entrance into the vitals of the enemy position. Notice also that these black squares are "holes" (as Steinitz called them), squares from which pieces can not be dislodged by the opponent's Pawns.

White does not resort to brutal attack or to intricate combination to accomplish his purpose, but puts his trust in the dynamic power inherent in a crushing positional superiority.

32 ...   **B—Q2**

Hoping to lure White into playing *33 R × KtP*, when *33 ... R × Rch 34 K × R, R—Kt1ch 35 K × P, R × P*, turns Black suddenly into the aggressor.

33 P—Kt3   **R(R1)—K1**
34 R(K1)—K5

Further blockade of the King Pawn, making it almost impossible for Black to free himself. This is stronger than capturing the Knight Pawn, since that Pawn is doomed anyway.

Four of Black's Pawns are now stopped dead in their tracks, while the remaining two can advance but only to be captured.

34 ...   **R—KR1**

"While there's life ..."

35 R × KtP   **R—R2**
36 R—Kt7

White keeps on gaining ground.

Now he invades the seventh rank.

36 ...   **R(K1)—KR1**
37 R × R

Simplest, hence the scientific way to force the win. In endings where one side has a material advantage, the prescribed strategy is to exchange pieces, not Pawns, and bring it to a position with Pawns only.

Endings with Pawns only on the board are the easiest endings to win.

37 ...   **R × R**
38 K—Kt6!

With every reduction of pieces from the board, the power of the King increases. Now the King threatens the Rook and helps attack the Rook Pawn.

38 ...   **R—R1**

Does White settle the issue now by taking the Rook Pawn?

No, no, a thousand times no! If *39 R × RP*, B—K1ch, and Black wins a whole Rook and the game. How easy it is to go wrong in a simple ending!

White's actual move banishes the Rook from the premises.

39 K—Kt7!

Look at that King!

39 ...   **R—Q1**
40 R × RP   **B—K1**
41 R—R7

A well-trained Rook settles down on the seventh rank instinctively.

41 ...   **R—Q2ch**

This leads to an exchange of Rooks,

but otherwise the continuation *42 K—B6 dis ch*, B—Q2 *43 P—KKt4*, wins easily for White, as the Pawn has a clear road ahead.

42 K—R6	R × Rch
43 K × R	B—R4

A flicker of hope! The Bishop rushes to get at White's Queen-side Pawns.

44 P—R4

The Pawns on the Queen's wing cannot be rescued, so White starts the Pawns on the King-side rolling.

44 ...	B—Q8
45 P—B3	B × P
46 P—Kt4	K—Q2

The King hastens to stop the Pawns. If instead *46 ... B × P 47 P—B5*, B—B7 *48 K—Kt6*, K—Q2 *49 P—R5*, and the Rook Pawn reaches the last square. Or if *46 ... B × P 47 P—B5*, K—Q2 *48 P—B6*, K—K1 *49 K—Kt7*, and the Bishop Pawn will Queen.

47 P—Kt5	P—K4

Desperation, but there is no promising defense. If *47 ... K—K1 48 P—Kt6*, B—B7 *49 P—R5*, B—B4 *50 K—Kt7*, and White wins.

48 P—B5	B × P

Or *48 ... B—B7 49 K—Kt6* followed by *50 P—R5*.

49 P—B6

There is no answer to this, as after *49 ... K—K1 50 K—K7* sees the Pawn through.

49 ...	Resigns

The whole game is played with beautiful consistency by Bernstein.

The Singular Strategy of Steinitz

W. Steinitz · A. G. Sellman

Baltimore 1885, FRENCH DEFENSE

"Place the contents of the chessbox in your hat," said Bird, "shake them up vigorously, pour them on the board at a height of two feet, and you get the style of Steinitz."

Bird may have been joking, but to players brought up on the straightforward attacking and combination play of Anderssen and Morphy, the weird-looking, time-wasting maneuvers of Steinitz to obtain a trivial advantage in position seemed far removed from the gallant "when Knights were bold" spirit of chess.

And yet it is from Steinitz and his queer moves that we learn so much about game-winning strategy. It is from Steinitz, whose play might have horrified La Bourdonnais and Morphy, that we discover the fundamentals of position play.

In the early part of the following game, we may be amused by the unconventionality of Steinitz's play—the delayed Castling, the absurd-looking moves, the quixotic journey of a Knight over five squares to reach a remote outpost at the side of the board. But by the time we get to the end of the game, we will have learned a great deal about modern chess strategy.

1 P—K4	P—K3
2 P—Q4	P—Q4
3 Kt—QB3	Kt—KB3
4 P—K5	KKt—Q2
5 P—B4	

Steinitz improves on the play of the time, which was to keep the Pawn chain intact by *5 QKt—K2, P—QB4 6 P—QB3*. Later researches showed that Black could break the chain and get the better game by continuing *6 ... P×P 7 P×P, P—B3 8 P—B4, P×P 9 BP×P, Q—R5ch 10 Kt—Kt3, B—Kt5ch 11 K—B2, O—Och.*

Steinitz's idea (with *5 P—B4*) is to support the King Pawn (which cramps Black) without compromising his own position.

5 ...	P—QB4
6 P×P	

Steinitz gives up the center voluntarily, with the hope of later centralizing a Knight at Q4.

6 ...	B×P
7 Kt—B3	P—QR3

This provides a flight square for the King Bishop. In the event of *8 Kt—QR4*, the reply is *8 ... B—R2*, and the Bishop remains on the fine long diagonal.

8 B—Q3	Kt—QB3
9 Q—K2	Kt—Kt5

Obviously to exchange Knight for Bishop, and assure himself of the two Bishops.

10 B—Q2	P—QKt4
11 Kt—Q1	Kt × Bch
12 P × Kt	Q—Kt3

A better line was *12* ... P—Kt5, followed by *13* ... P—QR4, to prepare for the development of the Queen Bishop at QR3.

Black's actual move is plausible enough, since it increases the pressure on the diagonal, but it meets with a sharp reply.

This is the position, with White to play:

13 P—QKt4!

Bayonet attack, à la Alekhine!

13 ... B—K2

The Bishop must retreat! If instead *13* ... B—Q5 *14* R—QKt1, Q—R2 (creates a flight-square for the Bishop, but it's too late!) *15* Kt × B, and White wins a piece in a curious way. For if Black recaptures by *15* ... Q × Kt, the reply *16* R—K3 traps the Queen in the center of the board!

14 P—QR3	P—B4

This move is a strategic error. It renders the King Pawn backward, so that a piece is always tied down to its defense.

In addition, the fixing of so many Pawns on white squares greatly circumscribes the activity of the Queen Bishop.

15 QR—B1	B—Kt2
16 B—K3!	

This move, seizing control of the black squares, marks the beginning of White's positional attack.

White plans to win the game by taking possession of the most important squares in sight, eventually leaving his opponent without a single playable move.

16 ...	Q—Q1
17 Kt—Q4	

The Knight leaps to the center, gaining a move by the attack on the King Pawn.

17 ...	Kt—B1
18 O—O	P—KR4

This move, intended to prevent the opening of an attack by *19* P—Kt4, is a weakening of Black's Pawn structure.

It also accentuates the weakness of his black squares, on which White's pieces can settle with impunity, since no Pawns can drive them away. The sole guardian of the black squares in fact is the King Bishop—and Steinitz intends to do away with that piece!

This is the position, with White to play:

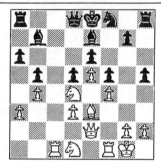

19 Kt—QB3!

The beginning of a remarkable Knight's Tour. The Knight is headed for QR5, an important black square located at the edge of the board! From there the Knight will be in position to dispatch the King Bishop—the one that guards the black squares.

19 ...   K—B2

Defends the King Pawn with the King, so that the Knight can get back into the game.

20 Kt—Kt1!   P—Kt3

A necessary precaution before the Knight can emerge. If at once *20 ... Kt—Q2*, White sacrifices the Knight (temporarily) by *21 Kt×BP*, and after *21 ... P×Kt*, plays *22 P—K6ch* recovering the piece with advantage (if *22 ... K×P*, the reply *23 B—Kt6 dis ch* is terribly painful).

After Black's actual move, all seven of his Pawns stand on white squares. They not only are helpless to prevent an intrusion on the black squares, but they confine the Queen Bishop, who is lost in a forest of Pawns!

21 Kt—Q2   Kt—Q2

Black might have tried *21 ... P—R4*, to free his Queen Bishop, and to prevent White's Knight from settling down at QR5. Steinitz was ready to refute this though, with this interesting line of play: *22 Kt×KtP, P×P 23 P×P, B×P 24 Kt—Q6ch, B×Kt 25 P×B, Q×P 26 B—Q4, KR—Kt1 27 Kt—B3* followed by *28 Kt—Kt5ch* and *B—B5,* and White regains the Pawn with a winning attack.

22 Kt(Q2)—Kt3   QR—B1
23 Kt—R5!

The Knight has taken five moves to get to R5, a square at the edge of the board, but there is method to Steinitz's madness. The Knight is bound for QB6, to kill off the King Bishop.

(I have explained the purpose of the remarkable Knight maneuver earlier, but it is worth repeating.)

23 ...   B—R1
24 R×R   Q×R
25 R—B1

The exchange of Rooks enables White to attack the Queen with his remaining Rook, drive her off (there is no room for gallantry in chess), and seize control of the file.

25 ...   Q—QKt1
26 Q—QB2!

This move gives White undisputed possession of the only open file.

26 ...   B—Q1

To prevent further invasion by *27 Q—B7,* but Steinitz (like love) will find a way.

27 Kt(R5)—B6!

If Black should now play 27 ...
B×Kt (to rid himself of the bad
Bishop), this would follow: *28
Q×B, Kt—B1 29 Kt×KP!, Kt×Kt
30 Q—Q7ch, B—K2 31 R—B6,
Kt—B1 32 R—B6ch, K—Kt2 (if
32 ... K—Kt1 33 Q×QPch, K—R2
34 Q—B7ch wins easily) 33 Q×Bch,
K—R3 34 R—B7, Kt—R2 35
Q—Kt5ch, Kt×Q 36 P×Kt mate.*

27 ...	Q—Kt2
28 Kt×Bch	

White removes the Bishop—guardian of the black squares, and in
particular the square QB7 (from
White's side of the board).

Now it will be possible to establish
one of White's heavy pieces (Queen
or Rook) on that square, with a view
to dominating the seventh rank.

28 ...	R×Kt
29 Q—B7!	Q—Kt1

Black tries to avoid an exchange of
Queens, as "a Rook on the seventh
rank is even more unpleasant than a
Queen."

30 B—B2!

This Bishop has been idle for quite
a while, but is now ready to go to
work on the black squares. Its
first threat is *31 B—R4*, attacking
the Rook which protects the Knight.
This would win the exchange at least.

30 ...	Q—Kt3

Prevents *31 B—R4* for the moment,
as *31 ... Q×Ktch* would be the
penalty.

31 Kt—B3

This forces the exchange of Queens,

as evading it by *31 ... Q—Kt1* loses
quickly after *32 B—R4.*

31 ...	Q×Q
32 R×Q	

This is how things look:

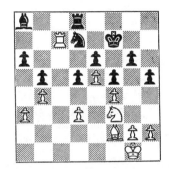

White controls the seventh rank
with his Rook, his Knight will have
the glorious square KKt5 as a base
for operations, and his Bishop has
black squares all over the board
at its disposal.

Let's look at Black's situation:

The Knight must not move—it's
pinned.

The Rook must not move—it
guards the Knight.

The Bishop must not move—it
will be captured if it does.

Meanwhile, Black must meet the
threat of *33 B—R4.*

32 ...	K—K1

The King moves over to protect
the Knight, as otherwise *33 B—R4*
drives away the Knight's present
defender.

33 Kt—Kt5	Kt—B1
34 B—B5!	

Threatens nothing less than *35
R—K7, mate on the move!*

34 ...   Kt—Q2

The other defenses are:

(1) *34 ...* R—Q2 *35* R—B8ch, R—Q1 *36* R×Rch, and White wins the Knight.

(2) *34 ...* R—Kt1 *35* R—K7ch, K—Q1 *36* Kt—B7ch, K—B1 *37* R—K8ch, and again the Knight is lost.

35 B—Q6!

Places Black in *Zugzwang* (the compulsion to move). And if one hasn't a decent move left, *zugzwang* can be quite embarrassing.

Let us look at the choice open to Black:

(1) The King may not move.

(2) The Bishop may move, only at the risk of instant capture.

(3) The Rook may move to Kt1, when *36* R×Kt, K×R *37* B×R wins a piece for White.

(4) The Knight may move to Kt3 (not to B1, as *36* R—K7ch is mate) when *36* R—K7ch, K—B1 *37* Kt—R7ch, K—Kt1 *38* Kt—B6ch, K—B1 *39* R—Q7 is discovered check and mate.

(5) Capitulation—upon which Black decides.

35 ...   Resigns

This is one of the earliest, and still one of the finest games to show how weaknesses on the black squares can be exploited properly.

It is a masterpiece—a genuine Steinitz.

Odyssey of an Isolated Pawn

A. Burn · Znosko-Borovsky

Ostend 1906, QUEEN'S GAMBIT DECLINED

An isolated Pawn looks anemic, and generally is a weakling. Tartakover used to say, "An isolated Pawn spreads gloom all over the chessboard." And this only confirmed what Philidor had said, many years before Tartakover was born, "A Pawn, when separated from his fellows, will seldom or never make a fortune."

That an isolated Pawn can become dangerous though (especially if it becomes a passed Pawn) is the theme of this fascinating game. As the number of pieces on the board diminishes, the power of the Pawn increases, and with every step it takes, its menace becomes greater. The entire army of the enemy may be tied up trying to halt its progress.

Znosko-Borovsky's masterly treatment of his isolated Pawn in the game that follows elicited Lasker's admiring comment, "It is a game of classic simplicity and beauty."

1 P—Q4	P—Q4
2 P—QB4	P—K3
3 Kt—QB3	P—QB4

Highly recommended by Dr. Tarrasch, who says, "This I hold to be the best, although I must add that I am almost completely alone in holding that opinion. The defense is based upon the undeniably correct idea that in the Queen's Gambit ... P—QB4 is the freeing move for Black, and must therefore be made as soon as possible. By this defense Black gets an isolated Pawn, but a fine free game for his pieces."

4 P × QP	KP × P
5 Kt—B3	Kt—QB3
6 B—Kt5	

This is not as strong as 6 ... P—KKt3, followed by 7 B—Kt2, the Rubinstein–Schlechter attack. The purpose of this fianchetto development is to exert pressure on the Queen Pawn, which eventually becomes an isolated Pawn.

6 ...	B—K2
7 B × B	KKt × B
8 P—K3	

On 8 P × P, the play might go:

8 ... P—Q5 *9* Kt—K4, O—O *10* P—K3, Q—Q4 *11* Kt—Kt3, P×P *12* Q×Q, Kt×Q *13* B—B4, and the game is fairly even.

8 ...	P×P
9 KKt×P	Q—Kt3!

Black seizes the initiative with this move. He attacks the Knight Pawn, and also threatens to give White an isolated Pawn by *10 ...* Kt×Kt.

10 Kt—Kt3

Parries both threats, but the Knight's retreat loses time for White—time which Black utilizes to speed his development.

10 ...	B—K3

Black, the second player in the opening, has four pieces in the field against two of White's. This would seem to indicate that Burn has not made the most of the opening.

11 B—Q3	O—O
12 O—O	KR—Q1
13 Kt—R4	

An aggressive move, which is completely unjustified. An attack should be initiated only after one has acquired a superiority in position. Otherwise it will be repulsed with severe loss of time.

A safer alternative was *13* Kt—K2, to strengthen the King-side.

13 ...	Q—B2
14 R—B1	Q—K4
15 Q—K2	QR—B1
16 P—B4	

This weakens the King Pawn, but good moves were getting scarce. If instead *16* Kt(R4)—B5, P—QKt3 *17* Kt×B, P×Kt, and Black's Pawn structure has been strengthened.

White's last move prompted Lasker to say ironically, "Attack at all cost!"

16 ...	Q—B3
17 P—B5	B—Q2

Obviously, not *17 ...* B×P *18* B×B, Kt×B *19* P—Kt4, and White wins a piece.

18 Kt(R4)—B5	P—QKt3
19 Kt×B	R×Kt
20 P—Kt4	

"Doing the work of protection twice and certainly overdoing it," says Lasker. "The Pawn at B5 is safe enough. The move would be strong if the aggressive intent, P—Kt5, could be realized, but on black points Black holds the sway."

20 ...	R(B1)—Q1

Black prepares for the advance of his Queen Pawn, the key to his strategy.

21 K—R1	R—Q3
22 R—KKt1	

Threatens to advance the Knight Pawn.

22 ...	Q—Kt4

Ruins that prospect at once!

23 QR—B1

This is the position, with Black to play:

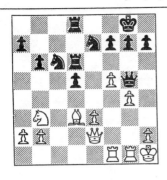

| 23 ... | P—Q5! |
| 24 P—K4 | |

Exchanging Pawns would lead to this: *24* P×P, Kt×P *25* Kt×Kt, R×Kt, and the doubled Rooks bear down heavily on the open file.

After White's actual move, the fragile isolated Pawn is suddenly transformed into a passed Pawn. And a passed Pawn is always potentially dangerous.

| 24 ... | Kt—K4 |
| 25 R—Kt3 | |

A better way to protect the Bishop (since retreating it would permit the Pawn to advance) was by *25* Kt—B1, in order to recapture with the Knight on *25* ... Kt×B. The Knight makes a better blockader of a passed Pawn than one of the heavy pieces (Queen or Rook) as it is not so easily driven away.

25 ...	Kt(K2)-B3
26 Kt—Q2	Kt×B
27 R×Kt	Kt—K4

The blockading Rook is easily driven away (as we see here) by a minor piece, after which the Pawn can take another step forward.

| 28 R—KKt3 | P—Q6! |
| 29 Q—Kt2 | R—QB3 |

A new advantage for Black! The Rook controls the Bishop file, and will penetrate into White's position by way of the seventh rank or the eighth.

30 Kt—B3	Kt×Kt
31 Q×Kt	R—B8
32 R(Kt3)—Kt1	R×R
33 R×R	Q—Q7

An excellent move! It clears the way for the Queen Pawn.

| 34 R—QKt1 |

Protects the Knight Pawn. Was there anything better? These are the alternatives:

(1) *34* R—B2, R×R *35* Q×R, P—Q7 and wins.

(2) *34* Q—B2, Q×Q *35* R×Q, P—Q7 and wins.

(3) *34* R—Q1, Q×P *35* R×P, Q—Kt8ch, and Black wins a Rook.

(4) *34* Q—Kt2, Q—B7 (threatens *35* ... P—Q7) *35* Q×Q, P×Q, and Black's next move *36* ... R—Q8 forces the Pawn through.

| 34 ... | Q—K7 |
| 35 Q—Kt2 | |

Clearly, *35* Q×Q loses after *35* ... P×Q followed by *36* ... R—Q8.

35 ...	Q—K6
36 R—Q1	P—Q7
37 P—KR3	Q—K8ch
38 Q—Kt1	Q—K7!

Capturing the King Pawn would be petty, in view of White's helpless position.

39 P—K5

White has nothing left but Pawn moves! If *39* Q—B1, Q×Qch *40* R×Q, P—Q8(Q) wins, or if *39* R—KB1, Q×R *40* Q×Q, P—Q8(Q) does likewise.

39 ...   R—Q6!
40 Resigns

This is the final position:

Rarely has the care and treatment of an isolated Pawn been shown in more elegant style.

Zugzwang, the Invincible Weapon

F. J. Marshall · E. Lasker

New York 1907, RUY LOPEZ

"The best way to learn endings, as well as openings," says Capablanca in *Chess Fundamentals*, "is from the games of the masters."

Here is a game that bears out the wisdom of this advice. It flares up, almost from the beginning, with exciting combination play—the kind that inspires you to exercise your own imagination in the opening. Then it plunges suddenly past the midgame right into the ending, one of the most remarkable ever seen on a chessboard. It is played with the care, thought and finesse that is characteristic of Lasker at his best.

And with Lasker at his best, we can always add to our understanding of the endgame.

1 P—K4	P—K4
2 Kt—KB3	Kt—QB3
3 B—Kt5	Kt—B3

A favorite defense with Lasker for many years, if only because it complies with the old rule, "*Sortez les pièces!*" (Get the pieces out!).

4 P—Q4

This is no improvement on *4 O—O*, the standard move, but Marshall wanted a wide-open game.

| 4 ... | P × P |

Preferable to *4 ... Kt × QP 5*

Kt × Kt, P × Kt *6* Q × P, and White's Queen is strongly placed in the center.

5 O—O	B—K2
6 P—K5	Kt—K5
7 Kt × P	O—O
8 Kt—B5	P—Q4!

Of course not *8 ... Kt × KP 9* Q—Q5, and one of the impetuous Knights is lost.

Black's actual move establishes a Pawn in the center, and clears the way for the debut of his Queen Bishop.

| 9 B × Kt |

A more promising line is *9 Kt × Bch, Kt × Kt 10 P—KB3, Kt— B4 11 P—QKt4, B—Q2* (on *11 ... Kt—K3, 12 P—KB4* is in White's favor) *12 B—K2, Kt—R5*, and the game is about even.

| 9 ... | P × B |
| 10 Kt × Bch | Q × Kt |

Whereas now, after ten moves of one of the most formidable openings, White does not have a single piece in active play!

11 R—K1

This indirect protection of the King Pawn (*11 ... Q × P 12 P— KB3*, winning a piece) is practically forced, since *11 P—KB3* instead succumbs to *11 ... Q—B4ch 12 K—R1, Kt—B7ch*, winning the exchange, while *11 B—B4* can be answered strongly by *11 ... P—B3* or *11 ... P—Kt4*.

11 ...   Q—R5

This sort of move is annoying to someone like Marshall, who likes to attack, and is uncomfortable on the defense.

12 B—K3   P—B3
13 P—KB3

This is the position, with Black to play:

13 ...   P × P!

Sacrifices a piece for the attack. As immediate return on the investment Lasker has an open file for his King Rook, and the prospect of maintaining a troublesome Pawn at Q5.

14 P × Kt

On *14 P—KKt3* instead, *14 ... Kt × P 15 P × Kt, Q × Pch 16 K—R1, R × P*, with (says Tartakover) ineluctable threats.

14 ...   P—Q5

After this move, White can find various ways to lose. For example:
(1) *15 B—B1, Q—B7ch 16 K—R1, B—Kt5 17 Q—Q2, Q—B8ch 18 R × Q, R × R* mate.
(2) *15 B—Q2* (additional protection for the Rook) *B—Kt5 16 Q—B1, R—B7* (threatens *17 ... B—B6*) *17 B—Kt5, R × Pch! 18 K × R, B—R6ch 19 K—R1* (if *19 K—B3, Q—Kt5ch 20 K—B2, Q—Kt7* mate) *Q—B7 20 Q—Q2, B—Kt7* mate.

15 P—KKt3

White should give up the Bishop at once by *15 Q—K2*, after which *15 ... P × B 16 Q × P* leaves a fairly even position.

15 ...   Q—B3
16 B × P

Marshall decides to return the piece, fearing that he might otherwise lose by something like this: *16 B—Q2, Q—B7ch 17 K—R1, B—R6 18 R—Kt1, P—KR4!* (threatens *19 ... B—Kt5* followed by *20 ... B—B6ch*) *19 Q × P, Q × Rch 20 K × Q, R—B8* mate.
Strangely enough, Marshall still had drawing chances, with this variation suggested by Tarrasch (after the game of course): *16 R—B1, Q × Rch 17 Q × Q, R × Qch 18 K × R, B—R3ch* (better than *18 ... P × B 19 K—K2*) *19 K—B2, R—B1ch 20 B—B4, P × B 21 Kt—Q2!, P × Pch 22 K × P, R—Kt1 23 Kt—Kt3, B—B5 24 R—Q1, B × Kt 25 RP × B, P—B4 26 R—QR1*.

16 ...	P × B
17 R—B1	

This is one move too late, as Marshall discovers to his sorrow.

17 ...	Q × Rch
18 Q × Q	R × Qch
19 K × R	

At this point, 99 out of 100 players (and this explains why there are so few Laskers) would "gain a tempo" by *19* ... B—R6ch or by *19* ... B—R3ch followed by *20* ... R—KB1. Lasker keeps the Bishop at home (where it still exerts force in two directions) and plays to weaken White's Pawn structure.

Foreseeing the possibility of White's Knight taking up a strong post at QKt3 (getting there by way of Q2) Lasker moves ...

19 ...	R—Kt1

to force ...

20 P—Kt3	

and the Knight is deprived of a fine square!

20 ...	R—Kt4!

Another subtle move! The Rook can swing over easily to either side of the board, and is thus in position to attack any of White's Pawns.

21 P—B4	

This allows Black a passed Queen Pawn, but the alternative is hardly any better: If *21* Kt—Q2, R—QB4 *22* R—B1 (or *22* Kt—B4, B—R3, and Black wins a Pawn) B—R3ch *23* K—K1, R—B6, and the King Pawn is not long for this world, the threat against it being *24* ... R—K6ch *25* K—Q1, B—K7ch *26* K—K1, B—Q6 dis ch *27* K—Q1, B × KP.

21 ...	R—KR4
22 K—Kt1	P—B4!

This little move accomplishes a great deal:

(1) It strengthens the Queen Pawn, transforming it into a protected passed Pawn.

(2) It clears the third rank completely, for the benefit of the Rook.

(3) It permits more scope to the Bishop, now that most of the Pawns stand on black squares.

23 Kt—Q2	K—B2

Otherwise the King, who is headed for the center, will be cut off by *24* R—KB1.

24 R—B1ch	

"Never miss a check!" is not always good advice. Here it wastes a move and helps Black, the enemy. The careful reader will note that Lasker had two plausible checks at his disposal at his 19th move, but wisely refrained from giving either one.

24 ...	K—K2
25 P—QR3	R—R3!

The Rook prepares to switch over to the Queen-side, to terrorize the Pawns in that area.

26 P—KR4

The attempt to stir up some counter-play by *26* P—QKt4 fails after *26* ... R—R3 *27* P×P, R×P *28* Kt—B3, B—R6, and Black wins the exchange, as *29* R—B2 allows *29* ... R—R8ch and quick mate.

26 ...	R—R3
27 R—R1	B—Kt5

A strong move, which fixes White's King-side.

28 K—B2	K—K3
29 P—R4	

To release the Rook from guard duty. If instead *29* Kt—B3, B×Kt *30* K×B, K—K4, and the threat of *31* R—B3ch wins a Pawn.

29 ...	K—K4
30 K—Kt2	R—KB3
31 R—K1	P—Q6!

The advance of the Pawn clears the square Q5. Now the King can penetrate with great effect into White's position.

32 R—KB1	K—Q5
33 R×R	

Marshall does not even try for the swindle *33* Kt—B3ch, K×P (on *33* ... K—K6 *34* R—K1 is mate!) *34* R—K1ch, K—B4 *35* R—K5ch, K—Kt3 *36* R—Kt5ch, followed by *37* R×B. The refuta-

tion (after *33* Kt—B3ch) would be simple: *33* ... B×Ktch *34* R×B, P—Q7, and it's all over.

33 ...	P×R
34 K—B2	P—B3

Lasker is playing to exhaust White's Pawn moves. After that, a move by White's King will permit further inroad by ... K—K6, while a move by the Knight loses the King Pawn.

35 P—QR5	P—QR3
36 Kt—B1	K×P
37 K—K1	B—K7
38 Kt—Q2ch	K—K6
39 Kt—Kt1	P—B4

Not at once *39* ... K—B6 *40* Kt—B3, K×P *41* Kt—K4ch, and White still needs subduing.

After Black's actual move, the Knight cannot get to K4.

40 Kt—Q2

Not of course *40* Kt—B3, P—Q7 mate.

40 ...	P—R4
41 Kt—Kt1	K—B6
42 Kt—B3	K×P
43 Kt—R4	P—B5
44 Kt×P	P—B6
45 Kt—K4ch	K—B5
46 Kt—Q6	P—B4

Ready to meet *47* Kt—Kt7 with *47* ... K—K6 and mate with either Pawn.

| 47 P—Kt4 | P×P |

48	P—B5	P—Kt6
49	Kt—B4	K—Kt6
50	Kt—K3	P—Kt7
51	Resigns	

"One of the most remarkable endgame combinations in the history of chess!" say Reinfeld and Fine of the latter part of this game.

Symphony of Combinations

E. Eliskases · E. Grunfeld

Mahrisch-Ostrau 1933, GIUOCO PIANO

What is it in a game that qualifies it to win a prize for brilliancy?

Is it the unexpected sacrifice of material? If so, this game features an offer of a Knight, followed later by the sacrifice of two Pawns on the seventh rank, just a step away from the Queening square.

Is it originality of ideas? Here, to give one instance, we see that a piece attacked only once may be in deadly danger, though protected by King, Queen and both Rooks.

Is it a finely-played ending? This one, with a magic Morphy move in it, is elegance itself.

Whatever it is that makes a game such as this worthy of the brilliancy prize, it holds us spellbound with its wealth of imaginative ideas.

1 P—K4	P—K4
2 Kt—KB3	Kt—QB3
3 B—B4	B—B4
4 P—B3	B—Kt3

Black wants to maintain a strong point at K4. On *4* ... P—Q3 instead, *5* P—Q4 in reply forces an exchange of Pawns (if *5* ... B—Kt3 *6* P×P, P×P *7* Q×Qch wins a Pawn for White) and the elimination of the strong point.

5 P—Q4	Q—K2

Black supports the King Pawn with another piece, as he does not want to yield the center by *5* ... P×P *6* P×P.

6 O—O	Kt—B3
7 P—Q5	Kt—Kt1

Practically forced, since *7* ... Kt—Q1 keeps the Knight out of play for a long time, while *7* ... Kt—QR4 is even worse. White would reply *8* B—Q3, threatening to win the Knight by *9* P—QKt4. If Black then tries to save the stranded Knight by *8* ... P—B4, the continuation *9* P—QKt4, P×P *10* P×P, Q×P *11* B—R3 suddenly springs a trap.

8 B—Q3	P—Q3
9 QKt—Q2	

With an eye to *10* Kt—B4 and *11* Kt×B, depriving Black of a stalwart Bishop.

9 ...	P—QR3

Gives the Bishop a flight-square, but *9* ... P—B3 serves the purpose better, as it strikes a blow at the center as well.

10 Kt—B4	B—R2
11 P—QR4	O—O

Disputing the center at this point by *11* ... P—B3 would be doubtful strategy, as after *12* P×P, P×P *13* B—B2, the Queen Pawn is rather weak.

12 P—QKt4

And now if Black plays *12* ... P—B3, there is this possibility: *13* P×P, P×P *14* P—Kt5, BP×P *15* P×P, P×P *16* Kt—Kt6, and White wins the exchange.

12 ...   Kt—K1

Prepares for *13* ... P—KB4, striking at the base of the Pawn chain, strategy recommended by Nimzovich.

13 Q—B2   P—KKt3

A further attempt to get in the freeing move *14* ... P—KB4, as well as making a square available to the Knight.

14 B—R6   Kt—Kt2
15 Kt—K3

Both sides concentrate their strength on the critical square KB5—White, to prevent the break by ... P—KB4, Black, to enforce it.

15 ...   P—KB3
16 QR—K1   R—B2
17 K—R1   Kt—Q2
18 P—Kt4

White has three pieces and two Pawns bearing down on the key square KB5. This would seem to put a definite stop to the threat of ... P—KB4, the vital move for the freeing of Black's pieces.

18 ...   Kt—B1
19 R—KKt1   B×Kt

Black decides to remove this Knight at once, in view of White's evident intention to open a file against his King by *20* Kt—B5, P×Kt *21* KtP×P. The continuation then could be *21* ... K—R1 (to unpin the Knight) *22* R—Kt2, Kt—K1 *23* QR—KKt1, and the threat of *24* R—Kt8 mate assures the return of the piece to White, and leaves him with a decisive advantage.

20 P×B!

The doubled Pawns are quite strong; they allow no point of entry to Black's pieces.

20 ...   B—Q2
21 R—Kt3   P—B3
22 B—B4

This is better than *22* P—B4, which permits *22* ... P×P *23* BP×P (if *23* KP×P, the pressure on KB5 is lessened, and Black might get in the thrust ... P—B4) R—B1, and Black controls an important open file.

22 ...   P×P
23 B×QP   B—K3
24 QR—KKt1   R—B1

If Black becomes impatient and tries to break through by *24* ... B×B *25* P×B, P—B4, then *26* B×Kt, K×B (*26* ... R×B *27* P×P does not help matters) *27* P×P wins a Pawn for White (*27* ... R×P *28* Q×R is of course unthinkable).

25 Kt—R4

The Knight is bound for B5, there to give up its life. Its capture will open the Knight file, uncovering attacks along the length of it.

| 25 ... | B × B |
| 26 P × B | R—B2 |

If the King moves out of the line of fire by 26 ... K—R1, the play would go 27 Kt—B5, P × Kt 28 P × P, and the Knight must submit to capture, since 28 ... Kt—K1 allows mate on the spot.

Black's actual move strengthens the square KKt2, so that it is guarded four times—but it's not enough!

This is the position, with White to play:

27 Kt—B5!

A sacrifice which Black must accept, or lose the exchange (after the Queen moves away) by 28 Kt × Kt, R × Kt 29 B × R.

| 27 ... | P × Kt |

The capture by 27 ... Kt × Kt is less favorable: 28 P × Kt, P—KKt4 (to keep the file closed), and White can continue the attack by 29 P—R4, or crash into the position immediately with 29 B × P, P × B 30 R × Pch, either of which lines should lead to victory.

| 28 P × P |

Now threatening 29 B × Kt, R × B 30 R × Rch, Q × R 31 R × Qch, and White has a decisive advantage in material.

28 ...	Q—K1
29 Q—KKt2	Q—Q2
30 R × Ktch	R × R
31 B × R	Q × B
32 Q—QB2	

A pin which forces Black to return some of his ill-gotten gains.

| 32 ... | Kt—Kt3 |
| 33 P × Kt | P—R3 |

The consequence of White's fine combination is that he has an extra Pawn and the better position. However, he must find a new way to break through, as the Knight file is closed once more.

34 Q—B5

Threatens to win the Queen Pawn by 35 Q—K6ch.

| 34 ... | Q—B1 |

If 34 ... R × P 35 Q—K6ch, K—B1 (on 35 ... K—R1 36 Q—K8ch, Q—Kt1 37 P—Kt7ch, K—R2 38 Q—Kt6 mates neatly) 36 R—KB1, Q—K2 37 P—Kt7ch, Q × P 38 R × Pch, and White wins the Queen and the game.

| 35 P—B4! | K—Kt2 |

Here too, capturing the Pawn is fatal. After 35 ... R × P 36 Q—K6ch, K—Kt2 (or 36 ... K—R1

37 P—Kt7ch winning the Queen)
37 Q—Q7ch, K—Kt1 *38* Q—R7 is mate.

    36 R—QB1

To support the advance *37* P—B5. If then *37* ... P×P *38* P×P, R×P, White wins nicely by *39* Q—Q7ch, K×P *40* R—Kt1ch, K—R4 *41* Q—R3 mate.

    36 ...   P—Kt3
    37 P—K4

This is meant to prevent Black from freeing himself by ... P—B4, in the event that White's Queen moves away.

    37 ...   Q—K2
    38 Q—B2   R—Kt2
    39 P—R4   P—QR4

Besides this move, Black must consider these alternatives:

(1) *39* ... P—KR4 (to prevent White from protecting his passed Pawn by *40* P—KR5) *40* Q—KB5, K—R3 *41* R—KKt1 (threatens *42* P—Kt7) Q—Kt2 *42* R—Kt5!, P×R *43* P×P mate.

(2) *39* ... K×P *40* R—Kt1ch, K—B2 *41* Q—B5 (threatens *42* Q—R7ch, K—K1 *43* R—Kt8ch, K—Q2 *44* Q×Qch, and the next check wins the Rook) K—B1 *42* Q—B8ch, K—B2 *43* Q—Kt8 mate.

    40 P—R5!   P×P

Against a waiting move, say *40* ... Q—B1, the breakthrough would come like this: *41* P×P, P×P *42* P—B5, P×P *43* Q×P, Q×Q *44* R×Q, R—R2 *45* P—Q6, and Black

is helpless.

    41 R—QKt1   P—Kt6
    42 R×P   Q—Q2
    43 Q—B5   Q—K2

If *43* ... Q×P *44* R—KB3 is decisive.

    44 Q—K6   Q—QB2

White now forces the game by clever combination play. He begins with an exchange of Queens, throwing in his passed Pawn as largesse. This is the position:

    45 Q—B7ch!   Q×Q

Black has no choice, as *45* ... K—R1 allows *46* Q—B8—mate on the move.

    46 P×Q   R—R2

On *46* ... K×P *47* P—R5 leads to an easy win.

    47 R×P

This begins an amazing clearance of Pawns. Nearly all of them disappear in the next few moves!

    47 ...   R×RP
    48 R×P   R×P
    49 R×P!

A little endgame trick, originally perpetrated by Morphy on Harrwitz in the third game of their match in 1858.

49 ...	K—B1
50 P—Q6	R × P
51 P—Q7	R—Q5

Now comes a beautiful conclusion! White gives up his splendid passed Pawns, for the sake of promoting an unlikely candidate—the innocent-looking Rook Pawn.

| 52 R × P! | K × P |

Or 52 ... R × P 53 R—R8ch, K × P 54 R—R7ch, K—K3 55 R × R, K × R 56 P—R6, and the Pawn cannot be headed off.

| 53 R—R8! | Resigns |

For after 53 ... R × P 54 R—R7ch, K—K3 55 R × R, K × R 56 P—R6, and the Pawn moves on to the coronation.

A delightful ending to a game beautifully played by Eliskases.

Escorting the Potential Queen

C. Schlechter · J. Mason

Monte Carlo 1903, PHILIDOR DEFENSE

"The winning of a Pawn among good players of even strength," says Capablanca, "often means the winning of the game."

The extra Pawn can be turned into a Queen, as the good player knows, and with a Queen ahead he can beat anybody in the world.

The technique of transforming a Pawn into a Queen is shown more simply, clearly and concisely in the following game than in any other game I know. Watch particularly how Schlechter makes use of his King to escort the passed Pawn up the board. Note how the King zig-zags alongside the Pawn, protecting it from attack, while himself evading checks by the Rook.

The method once learned is not easily forgotten.

1 P—K4	P—K4
2 Kt—KB3	P—Q3
3 P—Q4	P×P

Black should not give up the center, but play to maintain a strong point at K4, somewhat as follows: 3 ... Kt—Q2 *4* B—QB4, P—QB3 *5* Kt—B3, B—K2 *6* O—O, KKt—B3 *7* P—QR4, O—O *8* Q—K2, P—KR3 *9* B—Kt3, Q—B2, with a cramped but defensible game.

4 Kt×P	Kt—KB3
5 Kt—QB3	B—Q2
6 B—K2	Kt—B3
7 O—O	B—K2

The drawback to Black's unenterprising system of defense is that his pieces tend to get in each other's way. The Pawn position in the center (White Pawn at K4 against Black's at Q3) indicates White's pieces will have greater freedom of movement.

8 P—B4

Further restraint on Black's game! White's King Pawn and King Bishop Pawn prevent Black from occupying the center with his pieces. And without a say in the center, it will be difficult for Black to equalize.

8 ...	Kt×Kt

This attempt to get some freedom by exchanging pieces only helps White, whose Queen assumes a dominating position in the center.

9 Q×Kt	B—B3
10 P—QKt4!	

A good move! It helps White's development (his Bishop will come into the game at Kt2) and interferes with Black's (his Bishop will be driven back by P—Kt5).

| 10 ... | O—O |
| 11 B—Kt2 | Kt—K1 |

Normal development will not do, as 11 ... Q—Q2 cuts off the Bishop's retreat, and would cost the life of that piece after 12 P—Kt5.

Black therefore plays to get in the freeing move ... P—B4.

| 12 P—Kt5 | B—Q2 |

The interposition of 12 ... B—B3 (to drive the Queen off) would be a mistake, as the continuation 13 P—K5, P×P 14 Q×Q, R×Q 15 15 P×B wins a piece for White.

| 13 Kt—Q5 | P—KB4 |
| 14 B—Q3 | P—B3 |

The menacing Knight must be evicted, even though the Queen Pawn is weakened thereby.

15 P×QBP	P×BP
16 Kt×Bch	Q×Kt
17 QR—K1 !	

A strong developing move! The Rook comes into the game with a threat—18 P×P, winning a Pawn.

| 17 ... | P×P |

This capture must be made, if the Pawn is to be saved, even though it increases the range of White's pieces.

| 18 R×P | Q—B3 |

Just about the only move. On 18 ... Q—Q1 19 R×Kt, B×R 20 Q×KtP is mate, while if 18 ... Q—B2, there follows 19 KR—K1 (threatening 20 R—K7) Kt—B3 20

R—K7, Q—R4 (on 20 ... Q—Q4 21 B—B4 wins the Queen) 21 R×B, and White wins a piece.

| 19 Q—B4ch | Q—B2 |

Again the only move. On 19 ... P—Q4 instead, White wins in problem-like style by 20 B×Q, P×Q 21 B×BPch, K—R1 22 B—K7, R—B4 23 R—Q1, B—B1 24 P—Kt4, R—QR4 25 B—Q8, and the threats (26 R×Kt mate, as well as 26 B×R) are overwhelming.

This is the position, with White to play:

20 R—K7!

And the Rook comes in still further! Its control of the seventh rank will net at least a Pawn for White, while retaining the superior position. What more could anyone ask?

20 ...	Q×Q
21 B×Qch	P—Q4
22 B×Pch	P×B
23 R×B	

White has gained a Pawn in the mêlée. Now he must utilize his superiority in material by promoting the extra Pawn to a Queen.

23 ...	R—B1
24 R—B2	R—B5
25 R × QP	R(B5) × KBP
26 R × R	R × R
27 R—Q8	K—B1
28 B—R3ch	K—B2
29 R—Q7ch	K—Kt3

Of course not *29 ... K—K3 30 R—K7ch*, and the Knight goes.

30 R × RP	R—B5
31 R—K7!	Kt—B3
32 R—K2	

Saves the Bishop Pawn, but can he do the same for the Rook Pawn?

32 ...	R—QR5
33 B—Kt2	

Answer: He does not even try! White is willing to return one of the extra Pawns if he can thereby bring about another exchange of pieces.

One Pawn ahead, in a simple Rook and Pawn ending, is all he wants!

33 ...	R × P
34 B × Kt	K × B

Here is the position:

35 K—B2

The King starts out for the Queen-side, to give the Bishop Pawn protection as it moves up the board.

Black's King can take little or no part in the proceedings, as it is cut off from the Queen-side.

35 ...	P—R4

If Black plays to exchange Rooks, the win (for White) becomes elementary. This is how it could go: *35 ... R—R4 36 K—K1, R—R4 37 R × R, K × R 38 K—Q2, K—Q5 39 P—B3ch, K—B5 40 K—B2, K—B4 41 K—Q3, K—Q4 42 P—B4ch, K—B4 43 K—B3, K—-B3 44 K—Q4, K—Q3 45 P—B5ch, K—B3 46 K—B4, K—B2 47 K—Q5, K—Q2 48 P—B6ch, K—B2 49 K—K6*, and wins.

The idea, in this and similar cases, is simple: the passed Pawn keeps Black occupied, and allows White time to go after the deserted Pawns.

36 K—K1

Of course not *36 K—K3*, as it shuts off the action of the Rook and permits Black's King to cross over to the Queen-side.

36 ...	P—Kt4
37 K—Q2	K—B4
38 K—Q3	R—R1

Black hopes to make matters difficult for White's rather exposed King, who must stay near the passed Pawn, while evading checks by the Rook.

Here too, an exchange of Rooks loses quickly: *38 ... K—B5 39 P—B4, R × R 40 K × R, K—K5 41 P—B5* (forces Black to go after the Pawn, and gives White two spare moves) K—Q4 *42* K—K3, K×P *43* K—K4, and White captures the helpless Pawns.

| *39* P—B4 | R—Q1ch |
| *40* K—B3 | R—QB1 |

The Rook stops the advance of the Pawn, and is prepared to check the King whenever it emerges from behind the Pawn.

| *41* K—Kt4 | R—Kt1ch |

This puts up the most resistance, as a single wasted move simplifies the win for White. For instance, if *41* ... K—B5 *42* P—B5 (once the Pawn reaches B5, there are no problems) R—Kt1ch *43* K—R5, R—QB1 *44* K—Kt6, R—Kt1ch *45* K—B7, R—KR1 *46* P—B6, R—R2ch *47* K—Kt8, R—R1ch *48* K—Kt7, and it's all over.

| *42* K—R5 |

Note how the King zig-zags. It is the key to the win in this type of ending.

| *42* ... | R—QB1 |

If *42* ... R—R1ch *43* K—Kt6, R—Kt1ch (if *43* ... R—QB1 *44*

P—B5) *44* K—B7, and White's next move is *45* P—B5.

43 K—Kt5	R—Kt1ch
44 K—R6	R—QB1
45 R—QB2!	

Threatens to advance the Pawn. Black's King can now approach, but it's too late.

| *45* ... | K—K4 |

Rook moves are met as follows:

(1) *45* ... R—R1ch *46* K—Kt7, followed by *47* P—B5.

(2) *45* ... R—B2 *46* K—Kt6, R—B1 *47* P—B5.

(3) *45* ... R—B4 *46* K—Kt6, R—B1 *47* P—B5.

| *46* K—Kt7 | R—B4 |
| *47* K—Kt6 | Resigns |

For if *47* ... R—B1 (not *47* ... K—Q3 *48* R—Q3ch, and White wins the Rook) *48* P—B5, K—K3 *49* P—B6, K—Q3 *50* P—B7, K—Q2 *51* R—Q2ch, K—K2 *52* K—Kt7, and White wins.

The strategy may be relatively simple, but Schlechter's clear and concise play makes the game a fine piece of instruction.

The Pillsbury Bind

V. Chekhover · I. Rudakovsky

Moscow 1945, QUEEN'S GAMBIT DECLINED

"The scheme of a game," says Réti, "is played on positional lines, the decision of it, is as a rule, effected by combinations."

The following game, one of the unknown masterpieces of chess, illustrates this principle of strategy beautifully.

Early in the play, White gets a grip on the Queen-side (known as the Pillsbury Bind) which keeps his opponent busy on that wing. Then he conjures up threats of mate to harass him on the other. Rendered desperate by trying to prevent the collapse of his Queen-side, while at the same time warding off checkmate on the King-side, Black falls victim to the inevitable combination —in this case a pretty one.

1 P—Q4	P—Q4
2 P—QB4	P—K3
3 Kt—KB3	Kt—KB3
4 B—Kt5	B—K2
5 P—K3	O—O
6 Kt—B3	QKt—Q2
7 Q—B2	

Quite strong, though *7* R—B1, played several times in the Capablanca–Alekhine Championship Match, is more popular.

7 ...	P—B3

Black should get in the freeing move *7* ... P—B4 instead, before White plays his Rook to Q1.

8 B—Q3	

More to the point is *8* R—Q1, to make it difficult for Black to advance his Queen Bishop Pawn. A plausible continuation would be: *8* ... P—QR3 *9* P—QR3, R—K1 *10* B—Q3, P×P *11* B×P, P—Kt4 *12* B—R2, B—Kt2, and the freeing of this Bishop is still not assured.

8 ...	P×P
9 B×BP	Kt—Q4

Anxious to get some elbow-room, Black offers an exchange of Bishops.

10 B×B	Q×B
11 O—O	P—QKt4

This looks promising, since Black seems to gain time for the development of his Bishop. It creates a weakness though at his QB4 square, that will cost him dear.

A safer line of play, even though it hurts to give up the centralized Knight, would be *11* ... Kt×Kt *12* P×Kt, P—QKt3, followed by

13 ... B—Kt2.

12 B—K2   P—QR3

Protects the Knight Pawn, so that he can get in the advance *13 ... P—QB4.*

But never a chance does White give him to make that freeing move!

13 Kt—K4

Uncovers an attack on the Bishop Pawn, and a threat to control the key square QB5.

13 ...   B—Kt2

This is the position, with White to play:

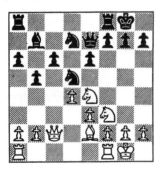

14 Kt—K5!

Good strategy! Before seizing the outpost QB5 with his Knight, White plays to remove one of the pieces guarding that square—Black's Knight at Q2.

Playing *14* Kt—B5 would be premature at this point, as after *14 ...* Kt×Kt *15* Q×Kt, Q×Q *16* P×Q, the square QB5 would be occupied by a Pawn (which has no mobility) instead of a piece (which does have freedom of movement, and exerts pressure on the surrounding

area).

14 ...   QR—B1

Necessary, as the Bishop Pawn was attacked by Knight and Queen. There was no relief in *14 ...* Kt×Kt, as after *15* P×Kt White obtains a fine outpost at Q6 for his remaining Knight.

15 Kt×Kt   Q×Kt

At one stroke White disposes of two pieces that guarded the vital QB5 square!

16 Kt—B5!

Another powerful stroke! The Knight dominates a great deal of the board from this outpost, and makes it difficult for Black's pieces to move about freely. The fact that the Knight cannot be driven off by Pawns must add to Black's frustration.

The paralyzing power of the Knight at the outpost QB5 was first realized by Pillsbury, who used it to great effect in some famous games, notably Pillsbury–Tarrasch, Vienna 1898 (see *Chess Strategy and Tactics* by Reinfeld and Chernev).

16 ...   Q—B2
17 KR—Q1   QR—Q1
18 QR—B1

Strategically, to intensify the pressure on the Bishop file.

Tactically, to win a Pawn by *19* Kt×B, Q×Kt *20* Q×P. But this is incidental, as the position is worth more than a Pawn.

18 ...   B—B1
19 Q—K4!

Just in time to stop *19 ... P—K4!*
This would free the Bishop, and also
open a file for the King Rook after
20 ... P×P 21 P×P.

19 ...	Kt—B3
20 Q—R4	Q—R4

Black tries to get some counter-
play on the Queen-side. The advance *20 ... P—K4* instead would
be risky, as White's *21 Q—Kt3* in
reply pins, and then probably wins
the impetuous Pawn.

21 P—QR3

Just to keep the Queen from getting closer.

21 ...	P—Kt5
22 P—R4	Kt—Q2
23 P—QKt3	

By which the Pawn position on
the Queen-side is stabilized.

23 ...	Kt × Kt

The advance of the King Pawn is
still premature as after *23 ... P—K4
24 Kt×Kt, B×Kt 25 R—B5* wins
the Pawn for White.

24 R × Kt	Q—Kt3
25 R(Q1)—QB1	

Doubles the pressure on the file—
and on the opponent.

25 ...	B—Kt2
26 P—R5	

An effective move! Black's Knight
Pawn is isolated, and his Queen
driven back to the second rank.

26 ...	Q—R2

This is the position, with White to
play:

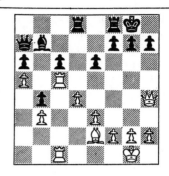

27 B—Q3!

Black's Queen-side is fixed, so
White turns his attention to the King-
side.

The threat is *28 Q×P* mate, a
threat which is easily parried by
moving one of the Pawns near
the King. Any Pawn move though,
creates a permanent weakness in
the Pawn structure, one that can be
exploited, in one way or another.

For instance, if Black replies *27
... P—R3*, then the continuation *28
Q—K4, P—Kt3 29 R—R5, K—Kt2
30 Q—K5ch, K—R2 31 Q—KKt5* is
decisive.

27 ...	P—Kt3
28 Q—B6!	

The Queen plants herself securely
in one of the holes created by Black's
last move. A hole is a square (such
as KB6 or KR6 in the present
position) brought into being by the
advance of a nearby Pawn. It is a
weak square, because it is no longer
under the surveillance of a Pawn,
and is vulnerable to invasion by an
enemy piece. Such a piece can
settle itself comfortably in one of
these holes, secure in the knowledge
that no enemy Pawn can disturb it.

White's plan is classical in its simplicity. He will advance the King Rook Pawn to R4, R5 and R6, and then play Q—Kt7 mate. If the Pawn is captured en route, say when it reaches R5, mate by the Rook is the instant penalty.

28 ...   R—Q3

Black vacates the square Q1 for his Queen, the only piece that can hope to dislodge White's Queen. Now if 29 P—R4, the intended defense is 29 ... Q—R1 30 P—R5, Q—Q1, and the threat of mate is parried.

29 Q—K7

An attack on the exposed Rook, so that Black will have his hands full warding off the accumulating threats. Black has three problems, each on a different part of the board:

(1) On the King-side, he must guard against being mated.

(2) On the Queen-side, he must try to break loose from White's stranglehold.

(3) In the middle, he must rescue any pieces that are exposed.

29 ...   R(B1)—Q1

Or 29 ... Q—Kt1 30 B—K4, R—B1 31 P—R4, Q—B2 32 Q—B6, Q—Q1 33 Q×Q, R(either one) ×Q 34 B×BP or 34 R(B1)—B4, with an easy, routine win.

30 P—R4   R(Q1)—Q2

The Queen must be evicted from the premises! Black does not play 30 ... R(Q3)—Q2, as he wants the first rank and the square Q1 available to his own Queen.

31 Q—B6   Q—R1

Only by retreat can Black's Queen rush to the rescue!

32 B—K4!

Not at once 32 P—R5, on account of 32 ... Q—Q1 in reply.

After the text (which incidentally prevents 32 ... R—Q4), if Black plays 32 ... Q—Q1, White exchanges Queens, captures the Bishop Pawn, and wins easily if prosaically.

32 ...   Q—K1
33 P—R5!

Each step the Pawn makes increases the danger to Black's King. The Pawn is headed for R6, where it will settle itself firmly in the other hole in Black's position.

The capture 33 B×BP would be premature, as 33 ... B×B 34 R×B, R×R 35 R×R, R×P regains the Pawn and allows Black fighting chances.

33 ...   R—Q1

The Rook withdraws, so that the Bishop Pawn may have the added protection of the Queen.

The fact that Black is kept busy warding off threats on both sides of the board is the clue to the next move, which presents Black with an insoluble problem (the hardest kind to face).

34 B×BP!

One of the beauties of chess is the fact that moves are often made which look irrational at first glance.

The Bishop Pawn is apparently adequately protected. As will be seen though, one of its defenders is overworked. The Queen not only has to guard this point (QB3) and the Rook at Q1, but must keep an eye out for mate threats against the King.

34 ...	B × B
35 P—R6!	

A *Zwischenzug*, an in-between move instead of the expected recapture. This one, which threatens mate, requires instant attention.

35 ...	K—B1

On the alternative defense 35 ... Q—B1, the win is forced by 36 R × B (threatens 37 R × R, R × R 38 R—B8, Q × R 39 Q—Kt7 mate) Q × P 37 R × R, R × R 38 R—B8ch, and Black must give up his Queen.

This is the position, with White to play:

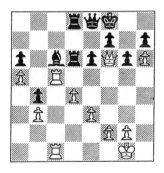

36 R × B

White regains his piece, is a Pawn ahead, and threatens 37 R × R, R × R 38 R—B8, Q × R 39 Q—R8ch, winning the Queen.

36 ...	R × R

There is not much choice. If Black plays 36 ... Q—Q2 (to reply

to 37 R × R with 37 ... Q × R), there follows 37 R—B7, Q—K1 38 Q—Kt7 mate.

37 R × R	

White gets his Rook back and prepares to seize the seventh rank by 38 R—B7. This would keep the King from escaping, and again threaten him with mate by the Queen.

37 ...	R—Q2

There is no relief in 37 ... Q × R, White forcing a winning ending by 38 Q × Rch, Q—K1 39 Q—Q6ch, K—Kt1 40 Q × RP, Q—K2 (otherwise 41 Q—Kt7 wins at once) 41 Q—Kt6, and the passed Pawn cannot be stopped.

38 R—B8!	

Attacks the Queen with his unprotected Rook. A pretty enough conclusion, but precisians and pedants may point out that White missed a brilliancy in 38 Q—Kt7ch, K—K2 39 R × KPch!, K × R (39 ... K—Q1 40 R × Qch is of course hopeless) 40 Q—K5 mate. Many a player has had quicker wins or more artistic ones than actually occurred pointed out to him by lesser lights, who revel in the fact that they found something overlooked by the master. The reason the master didn't see the shorter line is that he was not looking for it in the first place! The move with which he wins is the one whose effects he saw earlier and analyzed thoroughly *before starting his final combination.* Once the series of forcing moves clicks, there is no reason at all for him to waste time looking for other moves that might win. It takes time to analyze combinations, and the shorter way, ventured on hurriedly, might turn out to have a hole in it.

The moral is: *Play the move that forces the win in the simplest way. Leave the brilliancies to Alekhine, Keres and Tal.*

38 ...   Q × R

Naturally, *38* R—Q1 *39* R × R does not help matters.

40 Q—R8ch

White wins the Queen and the game.

Magnificent play by White, who never once relaxed his iron control of the game. A remarkable circumstance is that none of Black's pieces or Pawns, with the exception of the brave little Pawn at Kt5, ever crossed the fourth rank—Black's side of the board!

The Galloping Knight

S. Tarrasch · S. Vogel

Nuremberg 1910, RUY LOPEZ

One piece wins this game practically single-handed! Tarrasch's Queen Knight makes 13 of the 37 moves in the game, holds the enemy Rooks at bay, captures Pawns here and there, and as a final touch, clears the way for a passed Pawn to become a Queen.

From the technical standpoint, the game offers a valuable lesson in the art of getting the most out of a minute advantage. Especially interesting is the way the Knight provokes a weakness which enables it to gain complete possession of Q6—a square the Knight visits three times!

1 P—K4	P—K4
2 Kt—KB3	Kt—QB3
3 B—Kt5	P—Q3

The authorities do not recommend this line, the Steinitz defense, since it leads to a cramped game for Black, with little opportunity for counterplay.

Any defense though, which has been favored by World Champions Steinitz, Lasker and Capablanca can not be all bad.

4 P—Q4	B—Q2
5 Kt—B3	Kt—B3
6 O—O	B—K2
7 R—K1	P×P

Black must give up the center, and that is the chief drawback to the Steinitz defense.

Delay may lead him in the following trap, discovered by Tarrasch: *7 ... O—O* (the most natural move on the board, but it loses) *8 B×Kt, B×B 9 P×P, P×P 10 Q×Q, QR×Q 11 Kt×P, B×P* (if *11 ... Kt×P 12 Kt×B* wins a piece for White) *12 Kt×B, Kt×Kt 13 Kt—Q3* (not *13 R×Kt, R—K8ch,* and mate next), *P—KB4 14 P—KB3, B—B4ch 15 Kt×B, Kt×Kt 16 B—Kt5, R—Q4* (on *16 ... QR—K1 17 B—K7* wins the exchange) *17 P—QB4, R—Q2 18 B—K7,* and White wins the exchange.

8 Kt×P	Kt×Kt
9 Q×Kt	B×B
10 Kt×B	O—O
11 B—Kt5	

A strong move, but Capablanca found a better one, which led to a brilliant finish against Fonaroff. Capa played *11 Q—B3,* and the game continued as follows: *11 ... P—B3 12 Kt—Q4, Kt—Q2 13 Kt—B5, B—B3 14 Q—KKt3, Kt—K4 15 B—B4, Q—B2 16 QR—Q1, QR—Q1 17 R×P!, R×R 18 B×Kt, R—Q8* (if *18 ... B×B 19 Q×B* regains the Rook by the threat of mate, leaving White a Pawn ahead) *19 R×R, B×B 20 Kt—R6ch!,*

K—R1 *21* Q×B!, Q×Q *22* Kt×Pch, and the Knight fork wins a piece nicely.

11 ...   Kt—Kt5

Black aims to simplify the position by exchanging pieces whenever he can do so.

12 B×B   Q×B
13 P—QB4

This will strengthen the position of the Knight when it eventually reaches Q5.

13 ...   P—QR3
14 Kt—B3   Q—K4

Now the threat of *15* ... Q×Pch forces White to exchange Queens.

15 Q×Q   P×Q

On *15* ... Kt×Q instead (to centralize the Knight), White protects the Bishop Pawn by *16* P—QKt3, and then plays *17* P—B4, driving the Knight back and out of play.

This is the position, with White to play:

16 Kt—Q5!

Simple and strong! The chief threat is not *17* Kt×P, as the reply

17 ... QR—B1 regains the Pawn for Black, but *17* P—KR3, to which the retreat *17* ... Kt—R3 renders the Knight *hors de combat*, while the alternative *17* ... Kt—B3 allows an exchange by *18* Kt×Ktch, which breaks up Black's Pawn position.

16 ...   P—QB3

Plausible, but not the best way to evict the Knight from its fine outpost. Black should play *16* ... Kt—B3, after which *17* Kt×Ktch, P×Kt *18* QR—Q1, QR—Q1 left White with only a minimal advantage.

After his actual move, Black's Q3 square is slightly weakened. It is remarkable that this imperceptible weakness is enough to cost him the game.

17 Kt—K7ch   K—R1

Now White must guard against *18* ... P—KKt3, which might leave his Knight stranded.

18 Kt—B5   QR—Q1
19 QR—Q1

There is only one open file, so both sides dispute its possession.

19 ...   P—KKt3
20 Kt—Q6

Driven out from the outpost Q5, the Knight establishes a more effective one at Q6.

The immediate threat is *21* Kt× Pch, winning the exchange.

20 ...   R—Q2

Protecting the Knight Pawn (which also was attacked) by *20* ... R—QKt1 would be inferior, as that surrenders the Queen file to White.

21 P—B5!

Very strong! The advance of the Pawn supports the outpost, provides a useful square (QB4) for the convenience of the Knight, and fixes Black's Pawns on the Queen-side.

This is the position, with Black to play:

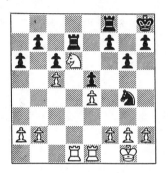

21 ...   K—Kt1

Doubling Rooks by *21 ... R(B1)—Q1* would be penalized by *22 Kt × Pch*, and White wins the exchange.

22 Kt—B4!

Discovers an attack on the Rook, and also threatens to win the King Pawn by driving off its defender with *23 P—B3*.

22 ...   KR—Q1

Black decides to give up the King Pawn for the sake of establishing a Rook on the seventh rank.

Protecting the Pawn by *22 ... R—K2* would leave him with the inferior game after *23 R—Q6* followed by *24 KR—Q1*.

23 R × R   R × R
24 P—B3

Finally this move comes in, and with great effect. The Knight is forced to retreat.

24 ...   Kt—R3

Black gives up the Pawn at once, in return for which his Rook will be enabled to seize the seventh rank.

The alternative *24 ... Kt—B3* leads to this: *25 R—K2, R—K2 26 R—Q2, R—Q2* (necessary, to prevent an invasion by the White Rook) *27 R × R, Kt × R 28 P—QKt4*, and White threatens to win the Knight Pawn by *29 Kt—R5*.

25 Kt × P

There is no time to keep the enemy Rook out by *25 R—K2*, as Black then saves his Pawn by *25 ... P—B3*.

25 ...   R—Q7
26 Kt—B4   R—QB7
27 P—QKt3   R × RP
28 R—Q1!

Black has regained his Pawn, but now White has had time to improve his position. His Rook commands the all-important Queen-file, and can not be hindered from getting behind the black Pawns.

28 ...   P—R4

Hoping to undermine White's Queen-side position by *29 ... P—R5*.

29 R—Q8ch   K—Kt2
30 R—QR8   P—R5
31 R × P   R × R
32 P × R   Kt—Kt1

The Knight is home again, "the sad result," says Tarrasch, "of the expedition to Kt5."

33 Kt—Q6	K—B3

The King and Knight must hurry over to head off the potential passed Pawn.

34 Kt×KtP	K—K4
35 P—R5	Kt—K2

Prepares to meet *36* P—R6 with *36* ... Kt—B1, and the Pawn is halted—for the time being.

But White prevents the Knight move with a little Knight move of his own.

36 Kt—Q6!

For the third time, the Knight returns to this key square!

36 ...	K—Q5
37 P—R6	Resigns

Superb position play by a master in that domain.

The Roving Rook

H. N. Pillsbury · J. W. Showalter

Brooklyn 1897, QUEEN'S GAMBIT DECLINED

One of the most beautiful Rook endings ever played (and that qualifies it to be instructive as well as entertaining) is from a little-known game of Pillsbury's.

It is characterized by fierce energy, the sort with which Pillsbury so often demolished his opponent's position "root and branch" in the midgame. Despite its typical vigor, the ending is not lacking in finesse, and a study of its fine points will add polish to anyone's play.

1 P—Q4	P—Q4
2 P—QB4	P—K3
3 Kt—QB3	Kt—KB3
4 B—Kt5	

Pillsbury was the first master to realize the strength of this opening, which he once described as "a Ruy Lopez on the King-side."

4 ...	B—K2
5 P—K3	QKt—Q2
6 Kt—B3	O—O
7 R—B1	

A strong line of play. The Rook bears down on the Queen Bishop file, which will be opened, sooner or later, by an exchange of Pawns.

7 ...	P—QR3

Clearly in order to meet *8* B—Q3 with *8* ... P×P *9* B×P, P—QKt4 *10* B—Q3, B—Kt2, followed by *11* ... P—B4. By this means, the Queen Bishop would be developed, generally a problem in this opening.

8 P×P	P×P
9 B—Q3	P—B3

Better than *9* ... P—Kt4 *10* O—O, B—Kt2, and the Bishop has very little scope, the diagonal being blocked by one of Black's own Pawns.

10 O—O	R—K1
11 B—Kt1	Kt—K5

Superficially attractive, this attempt to free the position is not as good as it looks. More to the point is *11* ... Kt—B1, followed by ... B—KKt5 and ... Kt—K3 in due course.

12 B—B4	Kt(Q2)—B3

Opposing Bishops by *12* ... B—Q3 loses a Pawn by *13* B×Kt, B×B (if *13* ... P×B *14* B×B, P×Kt *15* Q×P wins a Pawn), *14* B×Pch, K×B *15* P×B.

13 Kt—K5	

White's pieces are strongly placed,

in a formation favored by Pillsbury.

13 ...	B—KB4
14 P—B3	Kt × Kt
15 P × Kt	B × B
16 R × B	R—R2

An awkward move, but how else protect the Knight Pawn? If *16 ... R—Kt1 17 Kt × QBP* wins the exchange for White, while *16 ... Q—B1* is not an attractive move to make, the Queen being relegated to the defense of a Pawn.

| 17 Q—Q3 | B—Q3 |

Black is anxious to drive off the annoying Knight, but finds (after White's next move) that the Knight is not ready to leave. A better try might have been *17 ... Kt—Q2* instead.

| 18 B—Kt5! | P—KR3 |

If Black captures the Knight, there is some pretty play, viz: *18 ... B × Kt 19 P × B, R × P 20 Q—Q4* (attacks both Rooks) Q—Kt1 (protects both Rooks) *21 B—B4*, and White wins the exchange.

| 19 B—R4 | P—KKt4 |

Desperate measures, but White was threatening to increase the pressure by *20 Q—B5*, followed by *21 P—Kt4* and *22 P—Kt5*.

| 20 B—Kt3 | Kt—R4 |
| 21 Q—B5 | |

Threatens mate in two by *22 Q × BPch*, and mate by the Knight.

| 21 ... | Q—B3 |

A natural move, but it meets with a surprising refutation.

This is the position, with White to play:

| 22 Kt—Kt4! |

This pretty move wins a Pawn against any defense. For instance, if *22 ... Q—K3 23 B × B, Q × B 24 P—KB4*, and White threatens *25 P × P*, winning a Pawn. If then:

(1) *24 ... P—B3 25 Q—Kt6ch, Kt—Kt2 26 Kt × RPch*, and White either mates next move or wins the Queen.

(2) *24 ... Kt—Kt2 25 Kt—B6ch, K—B1 26 Kt × R*, and White wins the exchange.

(3) *24 ... Q—K2 25 Kt × Pch, K—Kt2 26 Q × KtPch, Q × Q 27 P × Q*, and Black is threatened with *28 R × Pch* as well as loss of the Knight by *29 P—Kt4*.

22 ...	Q × Q
23 Kt × Pch	K—R2
24 Kt × Q	B × B
25 P × B	P—Kt4
26 K—B2!	

A fine move! This guarding of the Pawns at Kt3 and K3 frees the

Knight for active duty. It also makes it possible for one of the Rooks to utilize the King Rook file for attack.

| 26 ... | K—Kt3 |
| 27 R—KR1 | |

This is better than defending the Knight by 27 P—Kt4.

White is willing to exchange pieces, being a Pawn ahead.

| 27 ... | K × Kt |

On 27 ... Kt—Kt2, White forces mate in problem-like style by 28 R—R6ch, K × Kt 29 P—Kt4 mate—a pure mate!

| 28 R × Kt | R(R2)—K2 |
| 29 R—R6! | |

Taking the King Pawn now would be fatal for Black, as after 29 ... R × P, there follows 30 P—Kt4ch, K—B5 31 P—Kt3 mate.

| 29 ... | P—B3 |
| 30 R—K1 | |

A subtle move, which shortly brings about an exchange of Rooks.

30 ...	P—R4
31 P—Kt4ch	K—K3
32 P—B4	P × P
33 P × P dis ch	K—Q2
34 R × Rch	K × R
35 R—R7ch	

Seizes the seventh rank, the road to happiness for a Rook.

| 35 ... | K—Q3 |
| 36 R—KB7 | K—K3 |

Forced, as 36 ... R—K3 loses the Pawn after 37 P—B5.

| 37 R—QR7 | |

"Notice the scope of White's Rook," says the Reverend Cunnington, "moving freely along Black's second rank and attacking the Pawns, while White's King (strongly placed) debars Black's Rook from his K6, K7 and K8; and if the Rook went to K5, P—Kt3 defends the Bishop Pawn."

| 37 ... | P—Kt5 |

On 37 ... P—R5 instead, White wins a Pawn by 38 P—B5ch, K—Q3 39 R—KB7.

38 R × P	P × P
39 R—B5	K—Q3
40 R × P(B3)	R—K5!

Black defends well. Using his Rook actively offers the best chance of saving the game.

| 41 P—Kt5! | |

A brilliant move! It deserves a diagram:

Black must consider these possibilities:

(1) 41 ... R × BPch 42 R—B3, R × Rch 43 K × R, P × P 44 K—Kt4,

P—B4 *45* K×P!, P×P (*45* ...
P—B5 *46* K—B4 offers Black no
chance) *46* K—B4, K—B4 *47* K—
B3!, K—B5 *48* K—K2, K—B6
49 K—Q1, and White wins.

(2) *41* ... R×BPch *42* R—B3,
P×P *43* R×R, P×R *44* P—R4!,
P—B4 *45* K—B3, P×P *46* K×P,
K—B4 *47* K—B3!, K—Kt5 *48*
K—K2! (but not the natural *48*
P—Kt4, as then Black does not
take the Pawn, but plays *48* ...
K—B6 and wins!), K—B6 *49* K—
Q1, and White wins.

(3) *41* ... R×QP *42* P—Kt6,
R×Pch *43* R—B3, R—K5 (if *43*
... R—KKt5 *44* R—KKt3 wins,
or if *43* ... R×Rch *44* K×R, K—
K2 *45* P—R4, and Black cannot
stop both passed Pawns) *44* P—Kt7,
R—K1 *45* R×Pch, K—K2 *46* R—
B8, R×Rch *47* P×R(Q)ch, K×Q *48*
P—R4, and again Black is helpless
against the passed Pawns.

(Note to the reader: If you have
skipped the variations above, go
back to the diagram and play them
over. They are not difficult, and
they are interesting, even if they do
look at first glance like some more of
those confounded instructive things.)

41 ...	P×P
42 P×P	R×P
43 R—K3!	

Cuts the King off from the King-
side. Black will have to depend on
his Rook to do all the work.

43 ...	P—B4

There was no point in attacking
the Pawn by *43* ... R—KKt5, as
44 R—KKt3 forces the Rook back,
after which the Pawn takes another
step forward.

44 P—Kt6	R—QR5
45 P—R3	P—Q5
46 R—KKt3	R—R1

The Rook must return before it's
too late.

47 P—Kt7	R—KKt1
48 R—Kt5!	

This prevents the King from com-
ing down the board to escort his
Pawns. If Black should play *48*
... K—B3 (to get to Kt4 and B5)
the continuation would be: *49* P—
R4!, P—B5 *50* K—K2, P—B6 *51*
K—Q3, K—Kt3 *52* P—R5ch, K—
R3 *53* K×P, P—B7 *54* R—QB5,
R×P *55* R×P, and White wins, as
Black's King is cut off.

48 ...	P—B5
49 K—K2	K—K3
50 P—R4	K—B3
51 R—Kt3	K—B4

Taking the Pawn loses on the
spot, e.g. *51* ... R×P *52* R×R,
K×R *53* P—R5, and the Pawn
cannot be headed off, while Black's
Pawns present no danger.

52 P—R5	K—B5
53 R—B3ch	K—K5

This puts up more of a fight than
53 ... K—Kt5, after which *54*
R—B7 separates Black's King from
his Pawns.

54 R—B7	P—Q6ch
55 K—Q2	K—Q5
56 R—Q7ch	K—B4
57 P—R6	R—K1

An attempt at counter-attack.
Against less active play, White
advances P—R7, then moves his
Rook to KB7 and KB8, which

assures his Rook Pawn of Queening.

58	P—R7	K—Kt5
59	R—Kt7ch	K—B4
60	R—Kt8	R—K7ch
61	K—Q1	P—B6
62	R—B8ch	

But not *62* P—R8(Q), P—B7ch *63* K—B1, R—K8ch *64* K—Kt2, P—B8(Q)ch, and Black mates in two.

62	...	K—Q5
63	R—B4ch	

"A splendid move," says the Reverend Cunnington, but of course White can also win by Queening either Pawn.

63	...	K—K6
64	P—R8(Q)	P—B7ch
65	R × P	R—K8ch
66	K × R	Resigns

Web of Black Squares

K. Schlechter · W. John

Barmen 1905, QUEEN'S GAMBIT DECLINED

Certain squares on the chessboard seem to be vital nerve centers. Control of them gives a player a tremendous positional advantage—nearly always a decisive one.

In the following game, Schlechter's over-all strategy is impressive, but never more so than in the way he utilizes the key squares K5, KB6 and KR6. He occupies the latter two with his pieces, and gets a powerful grip on the King-side. As for K5, not only does Schlechter secure possession of that square, but he makes use of it as a convenient jumping-off place for his pieces. It is occupied in turn by a Knight, the Queen, a Pawn, and then the other Knight. When the King himself threatens to assume command from there, it is an indication to the opponent that it's time to resign.

The game is a large-scale masterpiece, with the action taking place over the full range of the board—the King-side, the center, and the Queen-side. It is undoubtedly the greatest game Schlechter ever played, and for that matter, one of the greatest games anybody ever played.

1	P—Q4	P—Q4
2	P—QB4	P—K3
3	Kt—QB3	P—KB4

Black's arrangement of Pawns is known as the Stonewall Formation. Its purpose is to create a strong Pawn support for a Knight at K5, and with the center made secure, to play for an attack on the King-side.

There are two drawbacks to the Stonewall. One is that the square K4 is weakened: an enemy piece posted there could not be driven away by Pawns. The second is the weakening of Black's Queen Bishop, whose range of action is restricted by the Pawns standing on white squares.

4	Kt—B3	P—B3
5	B—B4	B—Q3
6	P—K3!	

This is stronger than the immediate exchange of Bishops. After 6 B×B, Q×B, Black continues by ... Kt—Q2 and ... P—K4, freeing his Queen Bishop.

6 ...		Kt—B3

Black in turn does not care to exchange Bishops, as after 6 ... B×B 7 P×B, White's grip on K5 could not be shaken off.

7	B—Q3	Q—B2

Hopes, with his threat of winning a Pawn by 8 ... B×B 9 P×B,

Q × P, to induce White to exchange Bishops.

8 P—KKt3!

White is not to be tempted. Instead, he re-enforces the position of his Bishop.

8 ...	O—O
9 O—O	Kt—K5

A fine outpost for the Knight, if the beast can manage to stay there. But White has P—B3 in reserve, whenever he chooses to dislodge the Knight.

10 Q—Kt3

The Queen develops with a threat: *11* P × P, KP × P *12* B × Kt, BP × B *13* Kt × KP, and White wins a Pawn, the Knight being immune to capture.

10 ...	K—R1
11 QR—B1	B × B

Rendered impatient by the menacing aspect of the position (one threat being *12* P × P, KP × P *13* Kt × P), Black decides to clear away a couple of pieces.

12 KP × B

The result though, is that Black is saddled with a backward King Pawn on an open file (and the mortality rate on backward Pawns is high).

12 ...	Q—B2
13 Kt—K5	

This Knight, which cannot be driven away by Pawns, is powerfully placed at K5—one of the vital nerve centers of the chessboard.

Black's position is the inferior one at this point, for two reasons:

(1) His black squares are weak, greatly due to the absence of the Bishop controlling those squares.

(2) His Queen Bishop has little freedom of movement, since it is hemmed in by Pawns occupying white squares—the color on which the Bishop travels.

13 ...	Q—K2

At this point, one would expect White to play something like *14* Q—B2 (not at once *14* P—B3, as *14 ...* Kt—Q7 wins the exchange) followed by *15* P—B3, evicting the Knight from its outpost, but Schlechter has a more effective continuation.

14 B × Kt!

Surprising—he closes the King file!

14 ...	BP × B
15 P—B3	

But this move will not only pry it open, but rid White of his doubled Pawn as well!

15 ...	KP × P

Otherwise Black loses a Pawn after *16* P × KP, P × KP *17* Kt × KP.

16 QR—K1!

This is stronger than recapturing the Pawn. Black must lose a move now to avoid the threat of *17* P × P, BP × P *18* Kt × QP, P × Kt *19* Kt—Kt6ch, and White wins the Queen by discovered attack.

16 ...	Q—QB2
17 Q—R3	

Another restraining move. If Black replies *17 ...* Kt—Q2, *18*

Q—K7 is practically fatal.

17 ...	K—Kt1
18 R×P	Kt—R3
19 P—Kt3	Q—Q1
20 P—QB5	

Increases the pressure on the black squares. The square Q6 (from White's side) is now inaccessible to Black's pieces.

20 ...	Kt—B2
21 Q—Kt2	B—Q2
22 Q—QB2	Q—K2
23 R(K1)—KB1	QR—K1
24 P—KKt4	B—B1
25 R—R3	

Threatens mate on the move, and forces a loosening of the Pawn position around Black's King.

| 25 ... | P—Kt3 |

The only move, since 25 ... P—KR3 loses the exchange after the reply 26 Kt—Kt6. But the advance of the Knight Pawn irreparably weakens Black's KB3 and KR3 squares. Eventually, White will plant pieces firmly on those squares.

26 P—Kt4

"It is surprising" says Réti, "that White suddenly begins to attack on the Queen-side. But that is the epic of Schlechter's game. He carries out operations apparently not concerted on different parts of the board, so that one has the impression that a game with no clear preconceived objective is in progress. And it is only at the end that one perceives for the first time the connection of things seemingly disconnected, with the result that the game is rounded off into one great homogeneous whole."

| 26 ... | Q—B3 |
| 27 R(R3)—B3 | R—K2 |

Black defends patiently. An attempt to open the position would be disastrous. For example: If 27 ... P—KKt4 28 P×P, Q×P 29 R×Rch, R×R 30 R×Rch, K×R 31 Q—B2ch, K—Kt2 (or 31 ... K—K2 32 Q—B7ch, K—Q1 33 Q—B8ch, Kt—K1 34 Kt—B7ch, and Black loses his Queen) 32 Q—B7ch, K—R3 (here if 32 ... K—R1 33 Q—B8ch, Q—Kt1 34 Kt—B7 is mate) 33 Q—B8ch, Q—Kt2 34 P—Kt5ch, and Black must abandon his Queen.

| 28 P—QR4 | P—QR3 |

This is the position, with White to play:

The next few moves need a bit of explanation. Schlechter wants to post his Queen Knight at KR6, supported by a Pawn at Kt5. If he plays 29 P—KKt5 at once, the reply would be 29 ... Q—B4. To prevent even this much counter-play, Schlechter will swing the Queen Knight over to K3 (by way of Q1), *then* play 29 P—KKt5, and follow that with 30 Kt—Kt4 and 31 Kt—R6ch.

29 Kt—Q1!	R—Kt2
30 Kt—K3	Q—K2

If *30 ...* P—R3 instead (to discourage *31* P—KKt5) White plays *31* P—KKt5 anyway, and after *31 ...* P×P continues by *32* Kt(K3)—Kt4, Q—K2 (if *32 ...* Q—B4 *33* Kt—R6ch wins the Queen) *33* Kt—R6ch, K—R1 *34* R—KR3, and there is no defense to the threats *35* Kt(R6)—B7 dble ch, K—Kt1 *36* R—R8 mate, and *35* Kt—B5 dis ch, winning the Queen, the only try *34 ...* R—R2 being refuted by *35* Kt×Pch, an attack on King, Queen and Rook.

31 P—KKt5

The encirclement continues, leaving Black with less and less moves.

31 ...	B—Q2
32 Kt(K3)—Kt4	B—K1
33 Kt—R6ch	K—R1
34 Q—K2	Q—Q1
35 Kt(K5)—Kt4	B—Q2
36 Q—K5	Kt—K1
37 R—KR3	Q—B2

This is the position:

Black is confined to the first two ranks, and tries to get some freedom by exchanging Queens.

Against passive play, White could prepare a mating combination by *38* R—R4, *39* R—B3, *40* R(B3)—R3, *41* Kt—B7ch, R×Kt *42* R×Pch, K—Kt1 *43* R—R8 mate.

38 Kt—B6!

White is now in full control of the key squares.

38 ...   Q×Q

Black must go through with this exchange, as avoiding it by *38 ...* Q—Q1 succumbs to *39* Kt×RP (threatens *40* Kt×R) K×Kt *40* Kt—B7 dis ch, and Black loses his Queen.

39 BP×Q

And now White has an open Bishop file on which to double his Rooks.

39 ...	R—K2
40 R(R3)—KB3	Kt×Kt

Practically forced, in view of the various threats, one for example being *41* Kt×B, R×R *42* R×R, R×Kt *43* R—B8ch, K—Kt2 *44* R—Kt8 mate.

41 R×Kt	R×R
42 KP×R!	

The proper way to take the Rook. Now the key square K5 is available to the Knight, and finally the King.

42 ...	R—K1
43 Kt—B7ch	K—Kt1
44 Kt—K5	R—Q1

Forced, to save the Bishop and to prevent loss of the Rook by *45* P—B7ch.

45 K—Kt2

The King is to be brought closer to the center before White breaks through decisively.

| *45* ... | K—B1 |
| *46* P—R4 | B—K1 |

On *46* ... B—B1 *47* P—KR5, P×P *48* R—KR1 lets the Rook become more active.

47 K—B3	B—B2
48 K—B4	K—K1
49 R—QKt1!	

The maneuvering was all on the King-side of the board, but the breakthrough comes on the Queen-side!

| *49* ... | K—B1 |
| *50* P—Kt5 | Resigns |

The continuation could be *50* ... RP×P *51* P×P, B—K1 *52* P×P, B×P (if *52* ... P×P *53* R—Kt7 wins instantly) *53* Kt×B, P×Kt *54* K—K5 (the King finally occupies the key square) R—K1 *55* R—Kt7, and Black can cease his struggles.

A strategical masterpiece! Outwardly the game may offer little glamour or excitement, but to the connoisseur it is a complete delight.

Endgame Arithmetic

J. Mieses · S. Reshevsky

Margate 1935, CARO-KANN DEFENSE

In an innocent-looking position, Reshevsky, alert as a cat, pounces on a Pawn (something he has done a thousand times before).

As suddenly as he won the Pawn, Reshevsky hastens to return it, and bring the position to an ending where Pawns are even. The rest (though a master might consider it just a matter of counting up moves) is a bit of endgame artistry.

1 P—K4	P—QB3
2 P—Q4	P—Q4
3 Kt—QB3	P×P
4 Kt×P	Kt—B3
5 Kt—Kt3	

The more aggressive line is *5* Kt×Ktch, after which *5* ... Kt P× Kt in reply weakens Black's Pawn position on the King-side, while *5* ... KP×Kt lets White have four Pawns to three on the Queen-side.

5 ...	P—K4

Disputes the center at once! Another way of doing so (in order to get rid of the Queen Pawn) is *5* ... P—B4 *6* Kt—B3, P—K3 *7* B—Q3, Kt—B3 *8* P×P, B×P *9* P—QR3, O—O *10* O—O, P—QKt3 *11* P—QKt4, B—K2 *12* B—Kt2, B—Kt2, and Black has equalized.

6 B—K3

Clearly, if *6* P×P, Q×Qch *7* K×Q, Kt—Kt5, and Black regains his Pawn.

Somewhat stronger than Mieses's *6* B—K3 move is *6* Kt—B3 (Knights before Bishops!) a line of play with which Alekhine beat Tartakover brilliantly at Kecskemet in 1927 (but then Alekhine always beat Tartakover brilliantly!).

6 ...	P×P
7 Q×P	Q—R4ch
8 Q—Q2	

A better interposition is *8* B—Q2, after which *8* ... Q—Q4 *9* Q×Q, Kt×Q *10* B—QB4, leaves White with a slightly superior game.

8 ...	B—QKt5!

Forces *9* P—QB3, and the resultant weakening of White's Q3 square.

9 P—QB3	B—K2
10 B—Q3	O—O
11 KKt—K2	P—B4!

This permits the Queen Knight to develop at B3, the ideal square.

12 Kt—B5

This looks attractive, since it assures White of the two Bishops, but ...

(1) He cannot keep the Bishops very long, and,

(2) It allows Black time to get his Queen-side pieces into play quickly.

12 ...	B × Kt
13 B × B	Kt—B3
14 O—O	QR—Q1

An attack on the Queen which compels White to lose a move.

15 Q—B2	P—KKt3

After this, White must either allow the exchange of the Bishop, or move it to R3, where it is awkwardly placed.

16 B—K4

The retreat to Q3 is no better, as 16 ... Kt—K4 attacks the Bishop again.

16 ...	Kt × B
17 Q × Kt	KR—K1

The Rook develops with gain of time. The threat is 18 ... B—Kt4 19 Q—B3, B × B 20 P × B, P—B4, and White has to fend off an invasion by 21 ... R—Q7, as well as an attack on the isolated Pawn by 21 ... R—Q6.

18 Q—B2	P—B5!

Very good, since it brings pressure to bear on the square Q6, which was weakened by White's ninth move.

There is now the possibility of posting a piece at Q6, where it has the strong support of the Bishop Pawn.

19 P—QKt4

An impatient move, which weakens the Bishop Pawn. The position is not a happy one, but 19 Kt—Q4 might have put up more fight.

19 ...	Q—B2
20 KR—Q1	Kt—K4
21 B—B4	

Pins the Knight, which was on its way to Q6.

21 ...	B—Q3

Intending 22 ... Kt—B6ch 23 P × Kt, B × B, and White's Pawn weaknesses may turn out to be fatal.

22 Kt—Q4

Instead of this, Mieses could have lost gloriously by 22 B—Kt3, Kt—Q6 23 B × B, R × B 24 Kt—B1 (to get rid of the unwelcome Knight) Kt—K8 25 Q—R4, P—QKt4! 26 Q × KtP, R × R! 27 Q × Rch, K—Kt2 28 Q—K2, Kt—B6 dble ch and mate!

22 ...	Kt—B6ch
23 Kt × Kt	B × B
24 P—Kt3	

This is usually a bad formation in Castled positions, since the white squares are weakened by the Pawn's advance. This weakening contributes to White's downfall, although it is difficult to see at this stage how Black can exploit his advantages.

24 ...	B—R3

The Bishop prepares to retreat to Kt2, where it commands the long diagonal, and has a target in the Bishop Pawn.

25 P—QR4	B—Kt2
26 P—Kt5	

This only helps Black, who now gets his Queen into more active play.

26 ...	Q—B4!
27 QR—B1	R—Q4!

Indicating that he intends to double Rooks on the Queen-file. To prevent this, White must exchange Rooks.

28 R × R	Q × R

Now the Knight is attacked, and there is a threat of invading the position by 29 ... R—Q1, followed by 30 ... Q—Q6.

This is the position, with White to play:

29 Kt—Q4

This loses a Pawn, but the alternatives are not satisfactory:

(1) 29 Kt—Q2, R—K7 30 R—Q1, B—R3, and Black wins a piece (if 31 P—B4, Q—Kt7 is mate).

(2) 29 K—Kt2, R—Q1 30 R—K1, Q—Q6 31 Q × Q, P × Q 32 P—B4, R—QB1 33 R—Q1, R × P 34 R × P, R × P, and the extra Pawn should win for Black.

29 ...	B × Kt
30 P × B	

Mieses must have counted on Black to continue with 30 ... Q × QP, whereupon 31 Q × BP, R—K8ch 32 K—Kt2!, gets him out of the woods.

But Reshevsky has a little *zwischenzug* up his sleeve!

30 ...	R—K5!

Attacks the Queen Pawn twice, and cleverly prevents the capture of his Bishop Pawn.

Now if 31 Q × P, the reply 31 ... R—K8ch *forces* 32 R × R, and White loses his Queen.

31 R—Q1	R × P
32 R × R	Q × R
33 K—B1	K—B1
34 P—R5	

On 34 K—K1 instead, there follows 34 ... K—K2 35 Q—K2ch, K—Q3, and the threat of exchanging Queens, or of advancing further with the King, assures an easy win for Black.

After White's actual move, it looks as though we were in for a long, dreary ending, with Black's King facing countless checks as soon as he comes into the open, but Reshevsky finds an artistic way to simplify matters and finish off his opponent.

He forces an exchange of Queens, and throws in his precious passed Pawn as a bonus. Such is the power of a superior position!

| 34 ... | Q—Q6ch! |
| 35 Q—K2 | |

White can win a Pawn by *35* Q×Q, P×Q *36* K—K1, K—K2 *37* K—Q2, K—Q3 *38* K×P, but after *38* ... K—B4 by Black, his Queen-side Pawns are doomed.

35 ...	Q×Qch!
36 K×Q	K—K2
37 K—K3	K—Q3
38 K—Q4	P—B6!

The point! The Pawn must be captured, and Black gains time to pounce on the helpless Queen-side Pawns.

| 39 K×P | K—B4 |
| 40 P—Kt6 | P×P! |

Simpler than trying to gain two Pawns by *40* ... P—QR3. After *41* K—Q3, K—Kt5 *42* K—Q4, K×P *43* K—B5, it would require all of Black's skill to avoid losing!

One Pawn ahead (preferably an outside passed Pawn) is enough to assure the win!

| 41 P×P | K×P |
| 42 Resigns | |

If White chose to play on, the next few moves could be *42* K—Kt4, K—B3 *43* K—B4, P—Kt4ch *44* K—Kt4, giving us this position:

Black has two methods of winning, both of which should be familiar to the student:

(1) He advances King and passed Pawn, forcing White to retreat. When his own King is far enough in enemy territory, he abandons the passed Pawn, and goes after the unprotected Pawns of his opponent. The moves would be: *44* ... K—Kt3 *45* K—Kt3, K—B4 *46* K—B3, P—Kt5ch *47* K—Kt3, K—Kt4 *48* K—Kt2, K—B5 *49* K—B2, P—Kt6ch *50* K—Kt2, K—Q6, and wins.

(2) He can count moves—the master method! From the position on the diagram, simply count how many moves it would take Black to capture all the Pawns. Since the total is seven moves, see what White can do in seven moves. He would capture the passed Pawn, then the Bishop and Rook Pawns. White's King would then be behind the King Knight Pawn, which could freely go on to become a Queen.

The procedure would be: *44* ... K—Q4 *45* K×P, K—K5 *46* K—B6, K—B6 *47* K—Q7, K×P *48* K—K7, K—Kt7 *49* K×P, K×P *50* K—Kt7, K×P *51* K×P, P—Kt4, and Black wins.

In the Grand Manner

D. Janowsky · J. R. Capablanca

New York 1916, QUEEN'S GAMBIT DECLINED

In the book of the New York 1924 Tournament, Alekhine says of the game between Capablanca and Yates, "Capablanca's planning of the game is so full of that freshness of his genius for position play that every hypermodern player can only envy him."

In the game that follows, Capablanca shows his consummate mastery of all styles of play!

The subtle strategy initiated by his 10th move could have been a profound concept of Lasker's; the powerful restraining moves by the Pawns are worthy of a Philidor; the switch attack from one side of the board to the other is reminiscent of a Bogolyubov attack; the sacrifice of a Pawn on the Queen-side in order to win a piece on the King-side is in the style of Spielmann, while the mate threat by the two Rooks on an open board might have been the inspiration for the finish of the Nimzovich–Bernstein game at Carlsbad in 1923.

The whole game might have been a breathtaking brilliancy of Alekhine's—except that it was played by Capablanca!

1	P—Q4	Kt—KB3
2	Kt—KB3	P—Q4
3	P—B4	P—B3

The purpose of this, the Slav Defense, is to support the center Pawn without locking in the Queen Bishop, as occurs after *3 ... P—K3.*

The drawback to this line is that an early development of the Bishop weakens the Queen-side.

| 4 | Kt—B3 | B—B4 |
| 5 | Q—Kt3 | |

A stronger continuation is *5 P×P, P×P 6 Q—Kt3, Q—Kt3 7 Kt×P, Kt×Kt 8 Q×Kt, P—K3 9 Q—Kt3, Q×Q 10 P×Q, B—B7 11 B—Q2, B×P 12 P—K4,* as in the classical 23-mover won by Torre from Gotthilf in 1925.

5 ...		Q—Kt3
6	Q×Q	P×Q
7	P×P	Kt×P
8	Kt×Kt	P×Kt

Black's Queen-side Pawns are weak, but in return for this two open files are available to his Rooks.

| 9 | P—K3 | Kt—B3 |
| 10 | B—Q2 | B—Q2!! |

One of the most profound moves ever played—easily surpassing the highly-praised *19 QR—Q1* in the celebrated Andersssen–Dufresne game, and equalling in subtlety the *36 R—Q5* move in the Alekhine–

Tartakover masterpiece, played at Vienna in 1922.

Not only does Capablanca *un-develop* the Bishop, but he locks it in next move by *11* ... P—K3!

Capablanca intends to continue by ... Kt—R4, ... P—QKt4 (the Pawn being protected by the Bishop) and ... Kt—B5. The Knight would then occupy an important outpost and be strongly supported by Pawns. It is true that White could capture the Knight, but the recapture would not only undouble Black's Knight Pawns, but leave him with the advantage of the two Bishops. In the consequent play, Black could bring a great deal of pressure to bear on his opponent's Queen-side Pawns.

11 B—K2	P—K3
12 O—O	B—Q3
13 KR—B1	K—K2!

Capablanca prepares for the ending (even at this early stage!) by bringing his King to the center, instead of Castling.

| 14 B—B3 | KR—QB1 |
| 15 P—QR3 | |

This frees White's Queen Rook from the defense of the Rook Pawn, but it creates a hole at QKt3, an organic weakness which is irremediable. The energetic *15 Kt—K5* was preferable.

| 15 ... | Kt—R4! |

Black proceeds with his plan of posting the Knight at QB5. White can prevent this by playing *16*

B × Kt, but the recapture by *16 ... P × B* straightens out Black's Pawns, and leaves him with the two Bishops.

| 16 Kt—Q2 | |

Guards against loss of the exchange by *16 ... Kt—Kt6*, and also prepares for *17 P—K4*, an advance in the center which offers hope of counter-play.

| 16 ... | P—B4! |

"Not through the Iron Duke!" as the bridge players say.

| 17 P—KKt3 | P—QKt4! |
| 18 P—B3 | |

This is the position, with Black to play:

| 18 ... | Kt—B5 |

"Black's first plan is completed," says Capablanca. "White will now have to take the Knight, and Black's only weakness, the doubled Queen Knight Pawn, will become a source of great strength at QB5. Now for two or three moves Black will devote his time to improving the general strategic position of his pieces before evolving a new plan, this time a plan of attack against White's position."

19 B×Kt

Janowsky would rather capture with the Knight, but after *19 ...* KtP×Kt in reply, his Bishops would have very little scope.

19 ...	KtP×B
20 P—K4	K—B2

Clears a good square for the Bishop, in the event of an attack on it by *21* P—K5.

21 P—K5

This move, and White's next, are anti-positional, if only for the fact that placing Pawns on black squares reduces the mobility of his Bishop— that can travel on black squares only!

A far better plan (since we must be constructive) was *21* P×QP, P×P *22* P—B4 followed by *23* Kt—B3 and *24* Kt—K5. The Knight would then be strongly placed, while its removal would cost Black one of his Bishops, and leave White with a protected passed Pawn.

21 ...	B—K2
22 P—B4	P—QKt4

The threat of breaking through, after suitable preparation, by ... P—Kt5 will fix White's pieces on the Queen-side. Black could then switch suddenly to the King-side, break up that wing by ... P—KKt4, and attack on the open Knight file with his Rooks.

23 K—B2

If White plays *23* B—Kt4 instead (to prevent the potential break-through by ... P—Kt5) the con-

tinuation *23* ... B×B *24* P×B, R—R5 *25* R×R, P×R, followed by *26* ... R—QKt1 wins a Pawn for Black.

23 ...	R—R5
24 K—K3	KR—QR1

Threatens to win a piece by *25* ... P—Kt5.

25 R(R1)—Kt1	P—R3
26 Kt—B3	P—Kt4
27 Kt—K1	R—KKt1
28 K—B3	

More tenacious resistance might have been offered by *28* Kt—Kt2, in order to recapture with the Knight on *28* ... P×Pch.

28 ...	P×P
29 P×P	R(R5)—R1
30 Kt—Kt2	R—Kt5
31 R—Kt1	QR—KKt1

"Black is now ready to reap the reward for his well developed plan," says Capablanca. "All that is now needed to incline the balance in his favor is to bring the Bishop at Q2 to bear pressure against White's position."

32 B—K1

Janowsky fights hard to escape from the pin.

He plans to rescue the Knight from the attack threatened on it by Black's Rook Pawn, with this line of play: *32* ... P—R4 *33* B—B2, P—R5 *34* P—R3, R(Kt5)—Kt2 *35* Kt—K3, and he can breathe again.

But Capablanca crosses him up by switching the action to the Queen-side!

This is the position, with Black to play:

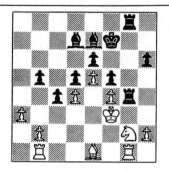

32 ...   **P—Kt5!**

A brilliant sacrifice! It clears a diagonal for the Queen Bishop, whose next few moves practically decide the game. This Bishop has had to wait in the wings since its memorable 10th move.

33 P×P

The alternative is *33 B×P, B×B 34 P×B*, and Black can pursue the attack by *34 ... P—R4* or *34 ... R—QKt1*, either of which should be good enough to win.

33 ...   **B—QR5!**

The Bishop is on its way to B7 (gaining time there by attacking the Rook) and then to K5, where it will strike at the Knight behind the King.

34 R—QR1

If White plays *34 R—B1*, to prevent the Bishop from coming in, the reply *34 ... R×Pch!* wins for Black.

Capablanca's games are studded with these little tactical finesses.

34 ...   **B—B7**
35 B—Kt3

This saves the Knight from the effects of *35 ... B—K5ch*, by cutting off the pressure of the Rooks on the file. But the pin is still effective, as Capablanca quickly demonstrates.

35 ...   **B—K5ch**
36 K—B2   **P—R4!**

Threatens to win a piece by *37 ... P—R5 38 Kt×P, B×Kt 39 B×B, R×B*.

37 R—R7

White tries to work up some kind of attack, since *37 Kt—K3* offers no hope after *37 ... P—R5 38 Kt×R, P×Kt*, and Black wins two pieces for a Rook.

37 ...   **B×Kt**
38 R×B   **P—R5**
39 B×P   **R×Rch**
40 K—B3   **R×RP**
41 B×B

On *41 R×Bch* instead, Black wins by *41 ... K—B1 42 B—B6, R(Kt1)—R1!* (the threat of mate on the move cleverly forces a reduction of pieces) *43 B×R, K×R*, and the rest is child's play.

41 ...   **R—R6ch**
42 K—B2   **R—QKt6**

There isn't a discovered check on the board that can hurt Black; every one of his pieces and Pawns stands on a white square!

43 B—Kt5 dis ch   **K—Kt3**
44 R—K7   **R×Pch**
45 K—B3   **R—QR1**

Threatens *46* ... R—R6 mate.

46 R × Pch

A spite check. Janowsky must realize there isn't one chance in a million that Capablanca will move *46* ... K—R4, and allow himself to be mated.

46 ...   K—R2

47 Resigns

Janowsky's checks run out. If *47* R—K7ch, K—-Kt1 ends them, or if *47* R—R6ch, K—Kt2 *48* K—Kt3, R—R6ch *49* K—R4, R—KR7 is checkmate.

March of the Little Pawns

H. N. Pillsbury · I. Gunsberg

Hastings 1895, QUEEN'S GAMBIT DECLINED

Almost every tournament brings its share of exciting moments, but none I venture to say contributed more than the one played at Hastings in 1895.

To begin with, it brought together the strongest field since the institution of International Chess Tournaments in 1851. Add to this the fact that the world's leading masters had not met previously in tournament play, and you will have an idea of the interest stirred up by this occasion. Neither Lasker, Champion of the World, nor Steinitz, the Grandmaster who was previous holder of the title, had met each other in tournament play. Nor had either of them ever encountered the mighty Dr. Tarrasch, winner of four International Tournaments in succession. There were other powerful entries too, such as Tschigorin, who had recently drawn a bitterly-fought match with Tarrasch, young Schlechter, whose reputation as a formidable antagonist had preceded him, and the rising stars Janowsky and Mieses, who were known and feared for the vigor of their attacking play. There was the contingent from England, headed by Blackburne and Teichmann, both dangerous obstacles to any aspiring master. Should these be cleared, there were others—Schiffers, Bardeleben, Walbrodt, Gunsberg, Marco and Burn.

By no stretch of the imagination could the chess-playing public picture the unknown Pillsbury as a possible winner of the highest honors. Imagine then the keen interest that arose when this youngster proceeded to win game after game with astonishing ease and accuracy. Imagine if you can the excitement of the spectators when the final round began with Pillsbury leading the field. Three players were in the running for first prize—Pillsbury with 15½ points, Tschigorin with 15, and Lasker with 14½.

Lasker, as befitted a World's Champion, made short work of his opponent, disposing of Burn in 20 moves. Tschigorin had some trouble subduing Schlechter, but eventually won a long game.

Pillsbury, meanwhile, thinking that a draw would be sufficient to win the tournament, played the opening of his game against Gunsberg tamely, allowing most of the pieces to be exchanged. Suddenly aware of the danger of being overtaken, Pillsbury began to play with the energy and brilliance with which he had previously mowed down Tarrasch, Steinitz, Janowsky, Pollock and Burn. His admirable handling of the endgame has been well described by Reinfeld:

"Suddenly things began to happen at Pillsbury's board: the colorless King and Pawn ending came to life. Pillsbury sacrificed a precious Pawn— or did he lose it? He allowed Guns-berg menacing passed Pawns on both sides, rushing down to Queen. It seemed impossible that Pillsbury's King could hold back the Pawns on both wings. The excitement in the tournament room mounted un-bearably as the realization of Pills-bury's predicament became clear to the spectators. Only one man was calm—perhaps deceptively calm: Pillsbury. He had calculated every-thing down to the most delicate detail. With the white-hot inspira-tion of unique genius, he had in-tuitively sensed the possibilities of a seemingly sterile position; with inexorable accuracy he had worked out the subtly timed win. In a few moves, the ending wound up as Pillsbury had foreseen: Gunsberg resigned."

So beautifully did Pillsbury con-duct this ending as to render it a classic in the field of Knight endings as well as in King and Pawn endings.

1	P—Q4	P—Q4
2	P—QB4	P—QB3
3	P—K3	P—KKt3
4	Kt—QB3	B—Kt2

Lasker says of this, "Black chooses a peculiar, but not altogether sound

manner of development. The objec-tion to this mode of bringing the Bishop out is that it costs two moves, brings the Bishop on a line that is blocked, and allows the first player possibilities of a King-side attack beginning with P—KR4."

Tartakover, on the other hand, approves of this formation, saying, "A profound conception, a combina-tion of the Queen's Gambit and the King's Fianchetto."

5	Kt—B3	Kt—B3
6	B—Q3	O—O
7	Kt—K5	P × P
8	B × BP	Kt—Q4
9	P—B4	B—K3

Whenever a piece lacks Pawn protection, it is in danger. Here, for example, White's King Bishop is threatened with capture by *10* ... B × Kt *11* BP × B, Kt × Kt (attacks the Queen) *12* P × Kt, B × B, and Black has won a piece.

10 Q—Kt3

Lasker recommends *10* Q—B3 instead, to be followed soon by P—KR4.

10	...	P—QKt4
11	B × Kt	

White must exchange, as the re-treat *11* B—Q3 loses a Pawn by *11* ... Kt × KP or *11* ... Kt × BP.

11	...	B × B
12	Kt × B	Q × Kt
13	Q × Q	P × Q
14	Kt—Q3	

The Knight would like to settle

down at QB5.

14 ...   Kt—Q2

But Black will have none of that!

15 B—Q2   KR—B1
16 K—K2

The position looks drawish, as the open Bishop file foreshadows an early exchange of all the Rooks.

White might be said to have a trifle the better of it, his King being nearer the center for the endgame.

16 ...   P—K3
17 KR—QB1   B—B1
18 R × R   R × R
19 R—QB1   R × R
20 B × R   B—Q3

This is rather lifeless. The energetic *20* ... P—Kt5, followed by *21* ... P—QR4 would have made things more difficult for Pillsbury.

21 B—Q2   K—B1
22 B—Kt4   K—K2
23 B—B5!   P—QR3

A far better move was *23* ... P—QR4, if only to prevent White from giving his strongly-placed Bishop additional support by *24* P—QKt4.

The play, if White persisted, could go as follows: *24* P—QKt4, P × P *25* B × P, B × B *26* Kt × B, K—Q3 *27* P—Kt4, P—B3, and after *28* ... P—K4 the position is perfectly even.

24 P—QKt4   P—B3
25 P—Kt4   B × B

Gunsberg becomes impatient, probably considering the position an easy draw. But the recapture of the Bishop gives White a passed Pawn, always a dangerous weapon in an ending.

26 KtP × B   Kt—Kt1

Black hopes to consolidate his position by posting his Knight at B3, but the timorous defense gives Pillsbury an opportunity to effect one of his characteristic breakthroughs.

A more spirited line is this, suggested by Lasker: *26* ... P—QR4 *27* P—B5, P—Kt4 *28* P—B6, Kt—Kt3 *29* Kt—B5, P × P *30* P × P, K—Q3 *31* Kt—Kt7ch, K × P *32* Kt × Pch, K—B2, and Black has, if anything, the better chance, as he threatens ... Kt—B5 and ... Kt—Q3.

This is the position on the board, before lightning struck it:

27 P—B5!

The first surprise, and more will follow! White's threat is *28* P × KP, K × P *29* Kt—B4ch, and the vital Queen Pawn falls.

If Black accepts the offer of a Pawn by *27* ... KtP × P *28* P × P, P × P, then *29* Kt—B4 wins the

Queen Pawn and leaves White with the great advantage of having two connected passed Pawns in the center. Or if Black tries 27 ... KP×P, there follows 28 P×P, and 28 ... P—Kt4 is met by 29 Kt—Kt4, and again White wins the Queen Pawn, and acquires two connected passed Pawns.

> 27 ...   P—Kt4

This keeps the Knight from moving to KB4.

> 28 Kt—Kt4!

The Knight leaps in, and threatens to remove most of the Pawns by 29 P×P, K×P 30 P—B6, K—Q3 31 P—B7, K×P 32 Kt×Pch, K—Q3 33 Kt×P, P—R3 34 Kt—Kt8.

> 28 ...   P—QR4
> 29 P—B6!

Another surprise! If the Knight is taken, 30 P—B7 wins at once.

> 29 ...   K—Q3
> 30 P×P!

And still another! Now if 30 ... P×Kt, there follows 31 P—K7, K×KP 32 P—B7, and the Pawn will become a Queen.
"*Alles hochst pikant!*" says the *Deutsche Schachzeitung* admiringly.

> 30 ...   Kt×P
> 31 Kt×Kt   K×Kt

Now look at the position!

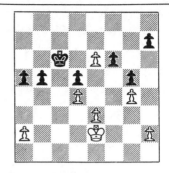

Has Pillsbury overplayed his hand? Will he lose the King Pawn that seems beyond help? Or will he find a magical saving move?

> 32 P—K4!

Beautiful! This brilliant move (and the next!) will assure White of obtaining two connected passed Pawns.

> 32 ...   P×P
> 33 P—Q5ch!   K—Q3

Obviously the impudent Pawn may not be captured.

> 34 K—K3   P—Kt5

Or 34 ... P—B4 35 P×P, P—QKt5 36 P—B6, P—R5 37 P—B7, K—K2 38 P—Q6ch, K—B1 39 P—Q7, K—K2 P—B8(Q)ch, and White wins easily.

> 35 K×P   P—R5
> 36 K—Q4   P—R4

This loses supinely, whereas 36 ... K—K2 instead would have led to this exciting finish: *37* K—B4, P—Kt6 *38* P×P, P—R6 *39* K—B3, P—B4 (to create a passed Pawn on the King-side) *40* P×P, P—R4 *41* P—Kt4!, P—R7 *42* K—Kt2, P—R8(Q)ch (forces the King to the last rank, where he will be subject to check upon the Queening of another Pawn) *43* K×Q, P—Kt5 *44* P—Kt5, P—R5 *45* P—Kt6, P—Kt6 *46* P×P, P×P *47* P—Q6ch!, K×P *48* P—Kt7, K—B2 *49* P—K7, P—Kt7 *50* P—Kt8(Q)ch, K×Q *51* P—K8(Q)ch, and White wins by one move!

37 P×P   P—R6

38 K—B4

Of course not the hasty *38* P—R6, when Black makes a last-minute escape by *38* ... P—Kt6 *39* P—R7 (if *37* K—B3, P×P wins for Black) P×P, and Black draws by virtue of Queening with check.

38 ...	P—B4
39 P—R6	P—B5
40 P—R7	Resigns

Exquisite endgame play by Pillsbury, and a fitting climax to a great tournament victory.

Irresistible Pawn-Roller

F. J. Marshall · J. R. Capablanca

New York 1909, QUEEN'S GAMBIT DECLINED

Capablanca demonstrates the process of winning, in his usual effortless style. Though Marshall makes no conspicuous errors, Capablanca manages to obtain a Queen-side majority of Pawns in only fifteen moves. This slight positional advantage is enough, in the hands of Capablanca, to be decisive.

The Pawns advance at every opportunity, and their steady progress eventually compels Marshall to give up a piece to prevent one of them from Queening. The continuation from that point on is unusually interesting. In only fourteen more moves, Capablanca who has won a Bishop for two Pawns, weaves an air-tight mating net around Marshall's King.

Commenting on the game, Lasker (who was not given to uninhibited praise of his peers) said, "Capablanca's play is an example of how slight advantages should be utilized."

1 P—Q4	P—Q4
2 P—QB4	P—K3
3 Kt—QB3	P—QB4

Impressed by the way Mieses beat Rubinstein in the second game of their match, Capablanca adopts the former's defense.

4 BP×P	KP×P
5 Kt—B3	Kt—QB3
6 P—KKt3	B—K3

Criticizing Capablanca may be *lèse-majesté*, but I would suggest the development of the King-side by *6* ... Kt—B3 *7* B—Kt2, B—K2 *8* O—O, O—O, as preferable.

7 B—Kt2	B—K2
8 O—O	Kt—B3
9 B—Kt5	

The stronger line, discovered years later, is *9* P×P, B×P *10* Kt—QR4, B—K2 *11* B—K3, O—O *12* Kt—Q4, and White's position is superior.

9 ...   Kt—K5!

A good move, which frees Black's game.

10 B×B   Q×B

"Would anyone defending against the Queen's Gambit want a better position than this after ten moves?" says Tarrasch proudly in justification of his pet line, the Tarrasch Defense.

11 Kt—K5

But not *11* P×P, Kt×Kt *12* P×Kt, Q×P, and White's Queen-side is broken up.

In the Rubinstein–Mieses game, White's *11 R—B1* at this point led to play which enabled Mieses to exploit his positional advantages— pressure on the open file, and a Pawn majority on the Queen-side. I give the continuation here, not only because it is interesting, but because it is rare that Rubinstein the Giant-killer is beaten so quickly and effectively.

The game went on (after *11 R—B1*) as follows: *11 ... Kt×Kt 12 R×Kt, P—B5 13 Kt—K5, O—O 14 P—Kt3, Q—Kt5! 15 Q—Q2, QR—B1 16 R—Q1, P—QKt4 17 P—B4, Kt×Kt 18 BP×Kt, P—QR4 19 P×P, R×P! 20 R—Kt3* (if *20 R×R, Q×Q 21 R×Q, QP×R*, and Black will soon have two connected passed Pawns) *Q—R5 21 P—K3, KR—B1! 22 B—B1, R—B7* (the almighty seventh rank!) *23 Q—K1, P—Kt5 24 B—Q3, Q×P!*, and White resigned in view of what might follow: *25 B×R, R×B 26 R—Kt1* (either Rook) *R—Kt7ch 27 K—B1, B—R6* (or simply *27 ... R×RP*), and White is helpless to ward off the threats of mate.

11 ...	Kt×QP!

This is better than trying to break up White's Pawns by *11 ... Kt× Kt(B6) 12 P×Kt, Kt×Kt 13 P×Kt, Q—Q2 14 P—KB4, O—O 15 Q—B2*, and White has a respectable game.

12 Kt×Kt	P×Kt
13 P—K3	

But not *13 B×P, B—R6*, and suddenly three of White's pieces are in danger.

13 ...	Kt—B6ch
14 Kt×Kt	P×Kt
15 Q×P	O—O
16 KR—B1	

Marshall avoids *16 Q×P*, as after *16 ... Q×Q 17 B×Q, QR—Kt1 18 B—K4, R×P*, Black has a passed Pawn, and a Rook on the seventh, but the move he selects is no great improvement, since his Rook "bites on granite."

Marshall should have started the Pawns rolling on the King-side, where he has the preponderance of Pawns, say by *16 P—K4*, followed by *Q—K3, P—B4* and *P—B5*. He would then have the makings of a King-side attack.

Capablanca's comment on Marshall's move is illuminating from the psychological standpoint: "White's inactivity on his stronger wing took away all the chances he had of drawing the game."

There is no mention of a possibility that Marshall might *win* the game!

16 ...	QR—Kt1
17 Q—K4	

Threatening *18 B—R3*, which would either bring about an exchange of Bishops, or induce a weakening of Black's Pawn structure by *18 ... P—B4*.

17 ...	Q—B2
18 R—B3	

This is the position, with Black to play:

18 ...   P—QKt4!

Capablanca starts playing out his trumps—the Queen-side Pawn majority. From now on the Pawns will push on every chance they get.

19 P—QR3   P—B5
20 B—B3

On *20* P—Kt3 instead, *20 ...* Q—R4 attacks the Rook, and also threatens *21 ...* P×P. This practically compels the reply *21* P—QKt4 which leaves Black with a powerful passed Pawn.

20 ...   KR—Q1

Capablanca never misses a trick! He seizes the only open file.

21 R—Q1   R×Rch
22 B×R   R—Q1
23 B—B3   P—Kt3!

It is not the purpose of this move to threaten *24 ...* B—Q4 *25* Q—Kt4, P—KR4, winning a piece, as the critics (Tarrasch, Schlechter, Panov, Golombek, Reinfeld, Goetz and others) suggest, since White could now confound all the critics by playing *26* Q—B4, and if *26 ...* Q×Q, capture by *27* KP×Q, thereby

protecting his Bishop.

The purpose of Black's move is to provide an outlet for the King, and free the Rook from guarding the last rank. It is the prelude to an invasion (by Black's Rook) of the seventh rank.

Note please that White cannot now prevent the Rook's coming in by playing *24* R—B2, as *24 ...* B—B4 in reply would cost him a whole Rook.

24 Q—B6   Q—K4!

This is better than *24 ...* Q×Q *25* B×Q, as then Black's Knight Pawn is attacked.

25 Q—K4   Q×Q
26 B×Q   R—Q8ch!

An important move which prevents White from bringing his King to the center.

27 K—Kt2   P—QR4

The key to Black's strategy: he will advance the Queen-side Pawns, and also institute an attack on White's Queen Knight Pawn—a weak point.

28 R—B2   P—Kt5
29 P×P   P×P
30 B—B3

If White tries to get the King into play by *30* K—B3, he might fall into this embarrassing loss: *30 ...* P—Kt6 *31* R—K2, B—R6!, and suddenly White's Rook is surrounded, and threatened with capture by *32 ...* B—B8.

30 ...	R—QKt8
31 B—K2	

Marshall defends stubbornly. Not only does he threaten the Bishop Pawn, but he is prepared to punish precipitous play. On *31* ... P—B6, he rescues his game by *32* P×P, P—Kt6 *33* R—Q2, P—Kt7 *34* B—Q3, and the Pawn will fall.

31 ...	P—Kt6!
32 R—Q2	

If *32* R—B3, R×P *33* B×P, R—B7, and Black wins a piece.

32 ...	R—QB8

With the powerful threat of *33* ... R—B7. White prevents this, but must still sacrifice a piece to halt the Pawns.

33 B—Q1	P—B6
34 P×P	P—Kt7
35 R×P	

Clearly, not *35* B—B2, as Black wins instantly by *35* ... R×B!

35 ...	R×B
36 R—B2	

This is the position, with Black to play:

From now on, Capablanca shows how to make the most out of a slight advantage in material. He brings the game to a conclusion with simple, vigorous moves. For the student it is a marvellous lesson, as so many games are given up as lost, at a stage when to all except the expert, there seems to be a good deal of fight left.

36 ...	B—B4

Rooks belong behind passed Pawns—which is why Capablanca drives this one away from where it is!

37 R—Kt2	R—QB8

And to add insult to injury, Capablanca moves *his* Rook behind the dangerous Pawn.

38 R—Kt3	

Marshall's Rook has little mobility, being tied down to the defense of a Pawn.

38 ...	B—K5ch

Forces the King to the side of the board, as *39* P—B3 loses the King Bishop Pawn after the reply *39* ... R—B7ch.

39 K—R3	R—B7
40 P—KB4	P—R4

This initiates a threat of mate which wins a Pawn immediately. White must guard against *41* ... B—B4ch *42* K—R4, R×Pch *43* K—Kt5, K—Kt2 *44* R—Kt7, R—R6 *45* P—Kt4, P×P, and Black mates quickly.

41 P—Kt4	P × Pch
42 K × P	R × RP
43 R—Kt4	P—B4ch
44 K—Kt3	

Or *44* K—Kt5, K—Kt2, and mate can be delayed for one move only.

44 ...	R—K7
45 R—B4	R × Pch
46 K—R4	K—Kt2
47 R—B7ch	K—B3

48 R—Q7	B—Kt7
49 R—Q6ch	K—Kt2

Now if *50* R—Q7 ch, K—R3 followed by *51* ... R—R6 mate. Or if *50* K—Kt5, R—Kt6ch *51* K—R4, R—Kt5 mate.

50 Resigns

Capablanca himself considers this game one of the most accurate he ever played.

Quiet, Like a Tiger

M. Botvinnik · I. Kann

Moscow 1931, DUTCH DEFENSE

One of America's leading players once said to me that he liked games where nothing happens. This one of Botvinnik's, I am sure, would please him. There *are* little combinations in the game, but they appear only in the notes.

Botvinnik wins the game purely by strength of position. Control of the Queen file, with emphasis on the key square Q5, enables his pieces to penetrate the adverse position. The exchanges which take place about the 30th move clear off some of the heavy pieces, and leave Botvinnik a Pawn ahead in a Rook and Pawn ending.

He wins it in a breeze.

1 P—Q4	P—K3

If Black embarks on the Dutch Defense with *1* ... P—KB4, he must be prepared to face the perils of the Staunton Gambit. In this, White sacrifices a Pawn for the sake of rapid development, and the possibility of working up an attack. Two typical lines are:

(1) P—Q4, P—KB4 *2* P—K4, P×P *3* Kt—QB3, Kt—KB3 *4* B—KKt5, P—KKt3 *5* P—KR4, B—Kt2 *6* P—R5, Kt×P *7* R×Kt, P×R *8* Q×Pch, K—B1 *9* Kt—Q5, Kt—B3 *10* B—QB4, and White has

good winning chances.

(2) *1* P—Q4, P—KB4 *2* P—K4, P×P *3* Kt—QB3 Kt—KB3 *4* B—KKt5, P—KKt3 *5* P—B3, P×P *6* Kt×P, P—Q4 *7* Kt—K5, B—Kt2 *8* Q—Q2, O—O *9* O—O—O, and White has the initiative (*9* ... Kt— Kt5 *10* Kt×QP!). Black has an extra Pawn as consolation, and as Steinitz once mentioned, "A Pawn ahead is worth a little trouble."

2 P—QB4	P—KB4
3 P—KKt3	Kt—KB3
4 B—Kt2	B—K2
5 Kt—KB3	P—Q3
6 O—O	O—O
7 P—Kt3!	

Apparently the Queen Bishop is to be posted at Kt2, where it will bear down on the long diagonal, and make it difficult for Black to get in the freeing move ... P—K4.

But Botvinnik's plans for the Bishop are more subtle than the indicated fianchetto. The Bishop is to be developed at QR3, where its influence will be stronger than at Kt2.

This arrangement will also permit the posting of the Queen Knight at B3, a more aggressive square than Q2 for this piece.

7 ...	Q—K1
8 Q—B2	Q—R4
9 Kt—B3 !	

This prevents Black from even starting the counter-attack characteristic of the Dutch—*9* ... Kt—K5, followed by ... P—KKt4, ... R—B3 and ... R—R3.

9 ...	Kt—B3
10 B—QR3 !	

White is ready to meet *10* ... P—K4 with *11* P×P, P×P *12* B×B, Kt×B *13* Kt×P, and he nets a Pawn.

10 ...	B—Q2

Instead of this, Botvinnik suggests *10* ... P—R4 followed by *11* ... Kt—QKt5. The Knight then obstructs the Bishop, and deprives it of any influence on the diagonal.

11 P—Q5 !	

Of course not *11* P—K4, tempting though it looks, as after *11* ... P×P *12* Kt×P, Kt×Kt *13* Q×Kt, P—Q4 is a simultaneous attack on Queen and Bishop, which wins a piece for Black.

11 ...	Kt—Q1

Practically forced, as *11* ... Kt—K4 loses a piece by *12* Kt×Kt, P×Kt *13* B×B.

12 Kt—K5	

"Attracted by the superiority of two Bishops over Knight and Bishop," says Botvinnik, "White allows his opponent breathing space. He should have continued *12* QR—Q1, increasing the pressure."

12 ...	P×Kt
13 B×B	R—B2
14 B—QR3	P×P

This move and Black's next, clear a path for his Bishop.

15 Kt×P	P—B5 !

Things begin to look brighter! Black has visions of playing *16* ... B—R6 followed by *17* ... Kt—Kt5.

16 QR—Q1 !	

This move, seizing control of the Queen-file, is the first step in the process of centralization.

Botvinnik is as familiar with the benefits that accrue from controlling the center as Nimzovich, whether or not he has read that famous strategist's formula governing situations of this sort, "An attack on a wing should be met by play in the center."

16 ...	Kt×Kt

This exchange does not help matters for Black. The recapture will bring another of White's pieces to the center. A preferable line of play was *16* ... B—R6 *17* Kt×Ktch, R×Kt *18* B—B3, Q—B2 *19* KR—K1.

17 B×Kt	B—K3
18 Q—Q3 !	

Stronger than the likely *18* Q—K4, the move Black probably expected. The reply to that would be *18* ... P—B3, forcing an exchange to Black's advantage, as after *19* B×B, Kt×B, his Knight becomes active again.

After White's actual move, the response *18* ... P—B3 would be fatal, as then *19* B—B3 attacks the Queen, and also threatens the life of the King by *20* Q×Ktch, R×Q *21* R×Rch, and mate next move.

18 ...   B×B

There was little choice, as *19* B—B3 was still in the air.

19 Q×B

Far superior to *19* P×B, which shuts off the action of White's Queen and Rook on the Queen file. It would also permit Black counter-play, by *19* ... R—B3, followed either by *20* ... R—R3, or by the entrance of the Knight into the game (*20* ... Kt—B2 and *21* ... Kt—Kt4).

After *19* Q×B on the other hand, White dominates the Queen file, his Queen is centralized, his Bishop casts a death-ray along the diagonal leading to B8, and he still threatens mate by *20* Q×Kt! What more could a man want?

19 ...   Kt—B3

This is the position, and it requires a bit of consideration:

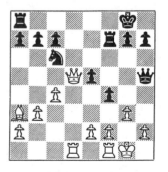

The Knight guards the square Q1, protects the King Pawn, and stands ready to meet the invasion *20* Q—K6 with *20* ... Kt—Q5.

Clearly, this troublesome Knight must be driven off if White is to make further progress. But how? If *20* P—QKt4 at once, the Bishop is blocked, and Black has time to get in the move *20* ... R—Q1. If after that, White persists in being aggressive, and plays *21* Q—K6, he meets with disaster as follows: *21* ... Kt—Q5 *22* P—Kt4, Q—Kt4 *23* P—R4, Q×RP *24* Q×P, Q× KtPch *25* K—R2, R—B4 *26* Q×R, Q×Q *27* P—K3 (hoping to win the pinned Knight) Kt—B6ch *28* K— Kt2, Q—Kt5ch *29* K—R1, Q—R6, and White is mated.

20 B—B5!

This is the star move, and one that was not easy to discover, according to Botvinnik. The Bishop keeps up the pressure without obstructing the Knight Pawn. This Pawn is bound for Kt5, where it will attempt to dislodge the Knight from its fine post.

20 ...   R—K1
21 P—QKt4   P—QR3

Sets the stage for a brilliant finale. Black should have played *21* ... P—KR3 (to give the King some air) and then if *22* P—Kt5, Kt—Q1 still holds the fort.

22 P—Kt5   P×P
23 P×P   Kt—R4

Not a happy spot for the Knight, but the alternative *23* ... Kt—Q1 was worse, as then White simply snaps up the luckless piece with his Queen.

This is the position, with White to play:

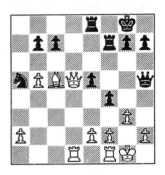

24 Q—K6!

A spectacular entrance into enemy territory! This move, and the following invasion of the seventh rank by the Rook, are reminiscent of a similar maneuver in the masterpiece that Rubinstein won from Maroczy in 1920 (the score of which with complete notes appears in my *Logical Chess Move by Move*).

24 ...	R—R1
25 R—Q7	Q—Kt3
26 Q—Q5	

Once again White threatens mate on the last rank! Black can avert this, but only at the cost of a Pawn.

26 ...	P—R3
27 R×P	R—K1
28 B—Kt4	

"Our life is frittered away by detail," says Thoreau, "Simplify! Simplify!"

Botvinnik intends to exchange Bishop for Knight, obtaining a passed Pawn thereby. This Pawn will advance at every available opportunity.

28 ...	P—Kt3
29 B×Kt	P×B
30 P—Kt6	Q—K3

It may seem strange to have Black offer an exchange of Queens, but how else can he free his pinned Rook, and the pieces tied down to its defense?

| 31 Q×Q | R×Q |
| 32 R—Kt1 | R—K1 |

The alternatives are easily disposed of: If 32 ... R×P 33 R—B8ch wins a Rook for White. Or if 32 ... R×R 33 P×R, R—B3 (on 33 ... R—K1, 34 R—Kt8 wins) 34 R—Kt8ch, and the Pawn becomes a Queen next move.

33 R×R	K×R
34 P—Kt7	R—QKt1
35 P×P	P×P
36 K—Kt2	K—K3
37 K—B3	P—Kt4
38 K—K4	Resigns

Black is in *zugzwang;* he must make a move, and any move he makes loses quickly.

If his King goes to the King-side, White attacks on the Queen-side, thus: 38 ... K—B3 39 K—Q5, K—K2 40 K—B6, K—Q1 41 R—Q1ch, K—K2 42 K—B7, and White wins.

If his King goes to the Queen-side, White attacks on the King-side, thus: 38 ... K—Q3 39 K—B5, K—B2 40 K—Kt6, R—KR1 41

P—Kt8(Q)ch, R × Q *42* R × R, and White gathers up the King-side Pawns.

If his King retreats, White maintains the opposition and forces Black to step to one side or the other, thus: *38* ... K—K2 *39* K—K5, K—K1 *40* K—K6, K—Q1 (if *40* ... K—B1 *41* K—Q7 followed by *42* K—B7 wins) *41* K—Q6, K—K1 *42* K—B7, and White wins.

Moves by the Pawns are meaningless and quickly exhausted, White waiting them out by simply moving his Rook up and down the Knight file.

Botvinnik's play throughout has been simple, clear and logical.

Cornucopia of Ideas

E. Zagoryansky · P. Romanovsky

Moscow 1943, NIMZO-INDIAN DEFENSE

This is one of those unknown masterpieces that bubbles over with good things. Among the strategic ideas you will see is a position held in complete restraint by virtue of control of the white squares, permitting the King to wander casually over to the Queen-side as a prelude to the decisive combination. After a tactical interlude, involving a sacrifice of the exchange, there follows a vivid demonstration of the power of a Rook on the seventh rank. And, since chess is cruel, there is a massacre of the innocents—the hapless Pawns being the victims.

1 P—Q4	Kt—KB3
2 P—QB4	P—K3
3 Kt—QB3	B—Kt5

Restraint is the essence of the Nimzo-Indian—a sound, fighting defense to the Queen Pawn Opening. Black plays to prevent P—K4 by White, first by pinning the Queen Knight, and second by bearing down on K5 with his Queen Bishop, from the square QKt2.

Black also retains the possibility of saddling his opponent with a doubled Pawn by ... B×Kt, thus providing him with a good object of attack.

4 P—K3	P—QKt3
5 B—K2	B—Kt2
6 B—B3	

A strategic error, since the exchange of Bishops is to Black's advantage. He can now play to gain control of K5 and QB5, squares which have lost the protection of the white-squared Bishop.

6 ...	B×B
7 Kt×B	O—O
8 O—O	P—Q4

The beginning of Black's long-range plan to get a grip on K5 and QB5. He intends to remove both of White's Knights, and leave him with a Bishop hampered by Pawns standing on black squares.

9 Q—Kt3	B×Kt
10 P×B	

Somewhat better was *10* Q×B, even though it allows Black to gain time with *10* ... Kt—K5.

10 ...	Kt—B3!

The Knight's ultimate aim is to occupy the square QB5. For the moment its threat is to win a Pawn by *11* ... Kt—QR4.

11 B—R3	R—K1
12 Q—R4	Q—Q2!

Another developing move with gain of time! The tactical threat is *13 ... Kt×QP 14* Q×Q, Kt×Ktch *15* P×Kt, Kt×Q, winning a Pawn. The strategic threat is *13 ...* Kt—QR4, in order to seize the outpost QB5.

13 P×P	P×P
14 KR—Q1	

Blissfully unaware of any danger, White makes a normal developing move. It turns out to be the decisive mistake, since it enables Black to carry out his object (which I have indicated several times before) of getting a grip on QB5, one of the weakened white squares.

14 ...	Kt—QR4!
15 Q×Q	Kt×Q
16 B—Kt4	Kt—B5

Threatens to steal the Bishop by *17 ...* P—QR4.

17 P—QR4	P—QR4
18 B—R3	R—K3!

A strange move, the purpose of which will become evident in a move or two.

19 Kt—Q2	Kt×Kt
20 R×Kt	R—QB3

Now we see what the Rook is up to—restraint! White is not to be allowed to free his game by means of P—QB4 or P—K4.

One may ask why the power of a Rook is to be spent on preventing a Pawn from moving. The answer is that the Rook is doing this only temporarily. The Knight will work its way over to Q3, and relieve the Rook of that duty.

21 B—Kt2

White would rather keep the Bishop at R3, in order to capture the Knight on its arrival at Q3, but the Bishop must retreat. On *21* R—B2 instead (to protect the Bishop Pawn), *21 ...* R—B5 in reply attacks the Rook Pawn, and forces the Bishop to retreat anyway if White is to save the Pawn.

21 ...	R—K1
22 K—B1	Kt—B3
23 R—B2	Kt—K5
24 K—K2	Kt—Q3
25 K—Q3	P—B4

Tightens the grip on the squares K5 and QB5. On the former, Black bears down with Rook, Knight and two Pawns, on the latter with Rook, Knight and Pawn.

26 P—B3	Kt—B5

Attacks the King Pawn once more, and ties White's pieces down to its defense.

27 B—B1	R(B3)—K3
28 R—K2	K—B2
29 R—K1	P—B3
30 R—QKt1	R(K1)—K2!

This makes it possible for the King to move behind the Rook on its journey to QR3. Once the King reaches that square, the plan is to advance ... P—QKt4, and after P×P, P×P, to create a passed Pawn on the Queen Rook file.

31 R—K2	K—K1
32 P—R3	P—R4
33 R—Kt3	K—Q2
34 R—K1	K—B2
35 P—Kt3	K—Kt2

36 B—Q2   K—R3
37 R(K1)—QKt1

This is intended to hinder Black from advancing his Queen Knight Pawn. That Black can do so though, with favorable chances for himself, may be seen from this analysis: *37 ... P—QKt4 38 P×P, P×P 39 B—B1* (on *39 R×P, R×Pch! 40 B×R, R×Bch 41 K—B2, Kt—R6ch 42 K—Q2, Kt×Rch 43 R×Kt, R×KBP,* and Black should win) *R×Pch! 40 B×R, R×Bch 41 K—B2, P—QR5 42 R—Kt4, R×KBP,* and Black has the better of it.

There is a combination in the position though—an effective one. And Black finds it!

This is the position, with Black to play:

37 ...	R×Pch!
38 B×R	R×Bch
39 K—B2	R—K7ch
40 K—Q1	

Clearly, *40 K—Q3, R—Q7* mate is unthinkable, while if *40 K—B1, R—Q8ch 41 K—B2, R×R 42 R×R* (on *42 K×R, Kt—Q7ch* regains the Rook), *Kt—R6ch* followed by *43 ... Kt×R* leads to a pure Pawn ending with Black a Pawn ahead—and that's the easiest kind of ending to win.

| 40 ... | R—QR7 |

This leaves White curiously helpless. If he tries *41 R—B1* (to dislodge Black's Rook from the seventh rank), Black simply plays *41 ... R×P.* If then *42 R—B2, Kt—K6ch* wins the exchange, or if *42 K—K2, R—R7ch* compels the King to return to the first rank.

41 P—Kt4	BP×P
42 BP×P	P—R5
43 P—Kt5	R×P

A pleasant alternative was *43 ... R—R7.*

| 44 K—K2 |

This results in loss of the exchange, but other moves permit *44 ... R—R7* followed by *45 ... R—KR7* and *46 ... R×P,* securing Black a passed Pawn on each side of the board.

| 44 ... | R—R7ch |
| 45 K—B3 |

This is not a blunder, as everything else is hopeless. White's only chance lies in getting over to the King-side, to acquire a passed Pawn of his own.

This is the position, with Black to play:

45 ...	Kt—Q7ch

A family check, with so few pieces on the board!

46 K—Kt4	Kt × R(Kt6)
47 R × Kt	P—R5
48 R—Kt1	R—QB7
49 K × P	R × P

The removal of this Pawn secures Black two connected passed Pawns, with one ready to protect the other.

50 P—Kt6	P—R6
51 K—Kt4	R—Q6
52 P—R4	R × Pch
53 K—Kt5	R—Q7

54 R—QR1	P—R7
55 P—R5	P—Kt4
56 P—R6	P × Pch
57 K × P	R—R7ch
58 K—Kt5	R—Kt7ch
59 K—B6	P—Kt5
60 P—Kt7	P—Kt6
61 K—B7	R × Pch
62 K × R	K—Kt4

Not the hasty 62 ... P—Kt7, when 63 R × Pch, K—Kt4 64 R × Pch might result in Black's giving up chess!

63 K—B6	P—Kt7
64 Resigns	

Endgame Duel— Knight against Rook

M. Botvinnik · M. Vidmar

Groningen 1946, CATALAN SYSTEM

This is a glorious game of Botvinnik's, worthy to rank with his famous victory over Capablanca at Avro in 1938.

The game is fascinating throughout its length, from the opening that Botvinnik conducts in original style, through the midgame where the sacrifice of the exchange permits his Rook to dominate the board, to the ending where his agile Knight dances rings around the opposing Rook.

A great deal may be learned from this game, but more than that, it is a game that one plays over and over again with renewed pleasure each time, as one takes delight in reading over and over again a fantastic tale of John Collier's or a priceless pastiche by Perelman.

1 P—Q4	P—Q4
2 Kt—KB3	Kt—KB3
3 P—QB4	P—K3
4 P—KKt3	P × P
5 Q—R4ch	Q—Q2
6 Q × BP	Q—B3

Black insists on exchanging Queens! White must comply, his Queen Bishop being unprotected.

7 QKt—Q2	Q × Q

8 Kt × Q	B—Kt5ch

Black wants to exchange Bishops too, but a preferable alternative was *8* ... B—K2 (simple development) or *8* ... P—B4 (attack on the center).

9 B—Q2	B × Bch
10 KKt × B!	

Clever play! The long diagonal is cleared for the Bishop, and there are prospects of setting up a strong Pawn center with P—K4.

10 ...	Kt—B3
11 P—K3	Kt—QKt5
12 K—K2!	

Simple and strong! The King meets the threat of *12* ... Kt—B7ch by coming to the center. This is perfectly safe now that Queens are off the board, and there is little danger of running into a mating attack.

12 ...	B—Q2
13 B—Kt2	B—B3
14 P—B3	

The Bishop is blocked temporarily, for the sake of building up a Pawn center.

14 ...	Kt—Q2
15 P—QR3	Kt—Q4
16 P—K4	Kt(Q4)—Kt3
17 Kt—R5	

Threatens to ruin Black's Pawn position by playing *18 Kt × B*.

| 17 ... | B—Kt4ch |
| 18 K—K3 | O—O—O |

The Knight Pawn is now protected, and Black prepares to drive off the annoying Knight at R5 by *19 ... Kt—Kt1* and *20 ... Kt—B3*.

19 KR—QB1!

Far superior to the natural *19 QR—B1*. The action will be on the Queen-side, and the Queen Rook is needed where it is, to support an advance of the Queen Rook Pawn. This Pawn has an important role to play in the plan to disorganize Black's forces.

| 19 ... | Kt—Kt1 |
| 20 P—QKt3 | B—Q2 |

A prudent retreat. Vidmar is aware of the danger inherent in a cramped position, and would very much like to free his game by bringing about an exchange of pieces. But if he plays *20 ... Kt—B3*, there follows *21 P—QR4, Kt×Kt 22 P×B*, and his Knight at R4 is doomed.

At this point, the dilettante, who is always on the lookout for brilliancies, might say to himself, "Wouldn't it be nice if I could play *21 Kt(Q2)—B4* and then *22 Kt—Q6* mate?"

The master player, I assure you, gives this possibility little more than a passing thought. What concerns him, at this and other stages, is that all his pieces be in active play. If they are not effectively placed, he moves them (by retreat if necessary) to squares where they can exert some influence. He gives more thought to this, which is the substance of position play, than to the planning of intricate combinations.

Botvinnik's next move brings the Bishop into more active play, though all it seems to do is keep a long diagonal under observation.

| 21 B—B1 | Kt—B3 |
| 22 Kt×Kt | B×Kt |

This is the position, with White to play:

23 P—QR4!

Initiates the threat *24 P—R5, Kt—R1 25 P—R6*, followed by *26 P×Pch*. This would split up Black's Pawns, making them vulnerable to attack, and at the same time open a file for White's Queen Rook.

| 23 ... | B—K1 |
| 24 P—R5 | Kt—R1 |

An unhappy retreat, but the Knight guards the Bishop Pawn from the corner. On *24 ... Kt—Q2* instead, the sequel, according to Botvinnik, would be *25* P—R6, P—QKt3 *26* R—B3, K—Kt1 *27* QR—B1, R—QB1 *28* Kt—B4 (threatens *29* Kt—Q6) R—Q1 *29* Kt—R3, R—QB1 *30* Kt—Kt5, and White wins.

Black's pieces are now all on the first rank, and while the position might have pleased Steinitz, it would take the patience and defensive skill of a Steinitz to keep it intact.

| 25 P—R6 | P—QKt3 |
| 26 P—QKt4 | K—Kt1 |

Black prepares to advance the Bishop Pawn so that the Knight can get back into the game. If at once *26 ...* P—QB3, there follows *27* B—Kt5, K—B2 (blocks the Knight, but how else save the Pawn?) *28* R—R3, R—Q3 *29* QR—B3, and after *30* P—K5 the Pawn will fall.

| 27 R—B3 | P—QB3 |
| 28 QR—B1 | P—B3! |

A preventive measure against *29* Kt—B4 followed by *30* Kt—K5.

The attempt to mobilize his own Knight would be premature, as after *28 ...* Kt—B2 *29* P—Kt5, Kt×KtP *30* B×Kt, P×B *31* R—B7, B—Q2 *32* R—Kt7ch, K—R1 *33* R(B1)—B7 establishes both of White's Rooks on the seventh rank, with a winning position.

| 29 Kt—Kt1! | B—Q2 |
| 30 Kt—R3 | |

Intending to break in by *31* P—Kt5, P×P *32* B×P, B×B *33* Kt×B, with unremitting pressure.

Black could avoid this by playing *30 ...* P—QKt4, but then comes *31* Kt—Kt1, Kt—B2 *32* R—R3, followed by a tour of the Knight to Q2, Kt3, and B5. Once the Knight is established on this strong outpost, the position would be definitely won for White.

| 30 ... | Kt—B2 |
| 31 P—Kt5! | |

"It is worth giving up a Pawn," says Fine, "to get a Rook on the seventh rank."

31 ...	Kt×KtP
32 B×Kt	P×B
33 R—B7!	

This is the position, with **Black** to play:

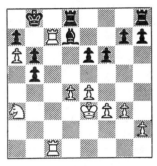

The situation is critical, and could lead to checkmate for Black. For example, if *33 ...* P—Kt5 *34* R—Kt7ch, K—R1 *35* R(B1)—B7 (threatens *36* R×Pch, K—Kt1 *37* R(B7)—Kt7ch, K—B1 *38* R—R8 mate) B—B1 *36* R×Pch, K—Kt1 *37* Kt—Kt5, and Black must give up a piece to prevent *38* R(B7)—Kt7ch, B×R *39* R×Bch, K—B1 *40* Kt—R7 mate.

| 33 ... | R—QB1 |

Black misses his chance! Instead of this, 33 ... B—B1 34 Kt×P, R—Q2! 35 R×R, B×R 36 Kt×P, K×Kt 37 R—B7ch, K×P 38 R×B, R—QB1! probably draws, since he dominates the open file, and has a dangerous passed Pawn.

34 R—Kt7ch	K—R1
35 R×B	

Fine play! Botvinnik sacrifices the exchange for the sake of maintaining a Rook on the seventh rank.

35 ...	R×R
36 Kt×P	KR—QB1

The only move. If Black tries to save his King-side Pawns by 36 ... R—KKt1, there follows 37 R×Pch, K—Kt1 38 R—Kt7ch, K—B1 (on 38 ... K—R1, 39 Kt—B7ch regains the exchange, with a winning position for White) 39 Kt—Q6ch, K—Q1 40 P—R7, R—QR8 41 R—Kt8ch, K—B2 (if 41 ... K—Q2 or 41 ... K—K2 42 R×R, R×P 43 R×Pch wins the other Rook) 42 R×R, R×P 43 Kt—Kt5ch, and White removes the second Rook and wins.

After Black's actual move, both of his Rooks are tied down to the Bishop file.

37 R×KtP	P—R3
38 R×Pch	K—Kt1
39 R—Kt7ch	K—R1
40 R—R7ch	

This gains time on the clock, and also demonstrates the opponent's helplessness to him—a favorite device of Tarrasch's.

40 ...	K—Kt1

41 R—Kt7ch	K—R1
42 P—Kt4	

Preparing to fix Black's Rook Pawn by P—R4 and R5.

42 ...	P—K4

A desperate move, since it affords White the opportunity to get a passed Pawn, but Black wants the square QB4 for one of his Rooks.

He intends either to drive the Knight away, or force an exchange of Rooks.

43 P—Q5	R(B8)—B4
44 R—R7ch	K—Kt1
45 R—Kt7ch	K—R1
46 R×P	R—QKt1

This will end the white Rook's career.

47 R×Rch	K×R
48 P—R7ch	K—Kt2!

Vidmar puts up a hard fight. If instead 48 ... K—R1 49 P—Q6, R—B1 (forced, as getting behind the Pawn by 49 ... R—B8 loses at once by 50 P—Q7, R—Q8 51 Kt—B7ch, K×P 52 Kt—Q5, and the Rook is cut off from the Pawn) 50 K—Q3!, K—Kt2 (on 50 ... R—B8, 51 Kt—B3 wins instantly) 51 Kt—B7, K×P 52 K—B4, K—Kt3 53 K—Q5, and wins, a plausible continuation being 53 ... R—Q1 54 Kt—K6, R—Q2 (other Rook moves permit 55 P—Q7 and Q8) 55 Kt—B5, R—Q1 56 P—Q7, K—B2 57 Kt—K6ch, etc.

This is the position, with White to play:

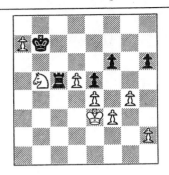

49 Kt—Q6ch!

This is much better than *49 P—Q6, R—B1 50 K—Q3, R—B8 51 Kt—B3, R—QR8*, and Black still needs subduing.

49 ...	K × P
50 Kt—K8	K—Kt3
51 Kt × P	R—B6ch
52 K—B2	R—B2

To guard against loss of the King Pawn by *53 Kt—Q7ch*, or of the Rook Pawn by *53 Kt—Kt8*.

53 P—R4	R—B2
54 Kt—R5	K—B2
55 P—Kt5!	P × P
56 P × P	R—R2

57 Kt—B6	R—R7ch

On *57 ... R—B2* (of course not *57 ... R—Kt2 58 Kt—K8ch* winning the Rook) *58 P—B4, P × P 59 P—K5* wins quickly.

58 K—Kt3	R—R8

Hoping to get behind the Pawn, but White puts an end to that aspiration.

59 K—Kt2!

Domination! The Rook has only one decent square open to it on the Rook file.

59 ...	R—R1

The last chance to stop the Pawn. On *59 ... R—R8* instead, the continuation *60 P—Kt6, R—R1 61 P—Kt7, K—Q3 62 P—Kt8(Q)* forces Black to give up his Rook.

60 P—Kt6	Resigns

For if *60 ... R—R3 61 P—Kt7, R—Kt3ch 62 K—B2, R × P 63 Kt—K8ch* and White wins the Rook neatly by a Knight fork.

Perennial Favorite

E. Bogolyubov · R. Réti

Mahrisch-Ostrau 1923, FRENCH DEFENSE

Back in 1933, when Fred Reinfeld and I were enthusiastically analyzing thousands of master games to find *The Fifty Greatest Chess Games Ever Played*, one of the undisputed choices on any of the lists (and we made many of them) was the magnificent game won by Réti from Bogolyubov in 1923.

In our introduction to the game, we had this to say of it:

"It is well known that an attack undertaken without adequate means must result in loss of the initiative, if parried properly. This is demonstrated most convincingly in the present game—the chief interest of which lies in the harmonious simplicity of Réti's beautifully-timed play. The unusual movements of the Knight add a certain piquancy to Black's artistic conduct of the game.

Réti's play is versatile: he performs many tasks here, and performs them well. He thrusts back a premature attack, he demonstrates the power of a compact center, he steadily cuts down his opponent's mobility, he maneuvers his Knights with exquisite skill, he obtains and exploits a passed Pawn according to plan."

Today, having played through and analyzed thousands of games in the thirty-year interval, the game between Bogolyubov and Réti is still, in my opinion, one of the most beautiful and instructive ever played.

1 P—K4	P—K3
2 P—Q4	P—Q4
3 Kt—QB3	Kt—KB3
4 P—K5	

One would expect Bogolyubov to adopt the Alekhine attack, with which he has won some brilliant games: *4* B—Kt5, B—K2 *5* P—K5, KKt—Q2 *6* P—KR4, B×B *7* P×B, Q×P *8* Kt—R3, Q—K2 *9* Q—Kt4, P—KKt3 *10* Kt—B4, P—QR3 *11* O—O—O, being the start of one of them.

4 ...	KKt—Q2
5 Q—Kt4	P—QB4!

Black *must* attack the center in this line of the French Defense.

The immediate threat is 6 ... P×P *7* Q×QP, Kt—QB3, winning the King Pawn.

6 Kt—Kt5

In his anxiety to attack, Bogolyubov violates opening principles. Having developed the Queen prematurely, he now moves the Knight twice in the opening.

6 ...	P×P!

Now if 7 Kt—Q6ch, B×Kt 8 Q×KtP, B×P protects the Rook, and wins a piece for Black.

7 Kt—KB3	Kt—QB3
8 Kt—Q6ch	B×Kt
9 Q×KtP	

Repulsing the attack

9 ...	B×P!
10 Kt×B	Q—B3!

Saves the Rook, forces an exchange of Queens, and puts an end to the demonstration.

11 Q×Q	Kt×Q
12 B—QKt5	

White must devote a few moves now to regaining the Pawn he lost.

12 ...	B—Q2
13 Kt—B3	Kt—K5!
14 O—O	

Building up a powerful center

14 ...	P—B3

Threatens to hold on to the extra Pawn by *15 ... P—K4*.

15 B×Kt	P×B
16 Kt×P	P—QB4

The four black Pawns now constitute a compact and powerful center, the Rooks have open files on which to operate, and the King is well posted for the ending—all a consequence of White's faulty strategy in embarking on an attack without sufficient means.

Réti's play from this point on is as delightful as it is convincing.

17 Kt—K2	

Centralizing the King for the ending

17 ...	K—B2

With Queens off the board, the King need not seek safety in Castling, as there is little danger of his being mated. At B2, the King supports the center Pawns, and is ready to take active part in the ending.

18 P—KB3	Kt—Q3
19 P—QKt3	

The Bishop is to be developed on the Queen-side. An attempt to bring it into play on the King-side would be rebuffed with loss of time, viz:

(1) *19 B—Q2, Kt—B5*, and the Bishop must return.

(2) *19 B—K3, P—Q5*, and the Bishop is driven off.

(3) *19 B—B4, P—K4*, and the Bishop must retreat.

19 ...	P—K4

The Pawns begin to look formidable.

20 B—R3	QR—QB1
21 QR—Q1	

Cutting down the scope of the Bishop

21 ...	P—Q5

Placing the Pawns on black squares limits the action of White's Bishop, while it increases the mobility of Black's (which travels on white squares).

22 Kt—B1	

The Knight is bound for Q3, to get some counter-play by the attack on the Bishop Pawn.

This is the position, with Black to play:

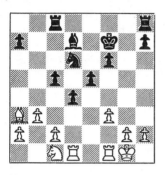

22 ...   Kt—B4

The Knight gains time by its threat of winning the exchange with 23 ... Kt—K6.

The Knight's move also unpins the Queen Bishop Pawn, making the advance ... P—B5 now possible.

23 R—B2

Establishing an outpost at K6

23 ...   Kt—K6

A fine spot for the Knight. It can either settle down at this advanced outpost, or use it as a jumping-off place for further invasion into enemy territory.

24 R—K1   P—B5!

A powerful move! The immediate threat is 25 ... P×P 26 BP×P, Kt—B7, and the attack on Rook and Bishop will force White to give up the exchange.

25 P—QKt4

If *25* P×P instead, *25 ... R×P 26* R(K1)—K2, KR—QB1, and Black wins the Bishop Pawn.

25 ...   B—R5!
26 R(K1)—K2

White cannot save the Pawn by *26* P—B3, as then *26 ...* Kt—B7 wins the exchange.

This is the position, with Black to play:

The galloping Knight

26 ...   Kt—Q8!

The beginning of some fancy stepping by the Knight.

27 R—B1   Kt—B6
28 R(K2)—B2   Kt—Kt8!

Réti notes that the Knight took ten moves to pay a visit to the home of White's Knight.

29 B—Kt2

The Pawn chain

29 ...   P—B6!

A thrust at the Bishop, to relegate it to the back rank.

30 Kt—Kt3

The alternative is not appetizing: *30 B—R1, Kt—Q7 31 R—K1, B×P,* and Black is not only a Pawn ahead, but has two wicked-looking connected passed Pawns.

30 ...   B×Kt
31 RP×B

If *31 R×Kt, B×RP, 32 R—R1, P×B,* and Black wins, or if *31 BP×B, P—B7 32 B—B1, P—Q6,* and there is no defense to the threat of *33 ... P—Q7 34 B×P, Kt×B 35 R×Kt, P—B8(Q),* and White must give up his Rook for the newly-crowned Queen.

31 ...   Kt—Q7
32 R—K1

Control of the vital files

32 ...   KR—Q1!
33 B—B1

Breakthrough to obtain a passed Pawn

33 ...   P—Q6!

If now *34 B×Kt, P×B 35 R×QP, P×P 36 R×R, R×R,* and White can do nothing to prevent *37 ... R—Q8,* forcing the promotion of the passed Pawn.

34 P×P   R×P
35 B×Kt   R×B!

If now *36 R×R, P×R 37 R—Q1, R—B8,* and the passed Pawn will become a Queen.

36 R—R1   K—K3!

Ready to meet *37 R×P* with *37 ... R×R 38 K×R, P—B7,*

and White must give up his Rook for the Pawn.

37 K—B1

With the hope of being allowed to play *38 R×R, P×R 39 R—Q1, R—B8 40 K—K2,* with good drawing chances.

37 ...   R × Rch

But this rudely dispels any fond hopes!

38 K×R   P—B7
39 R—QB1

The power of the King in the ending

39 ...   K—Q4
40 K—K3   R—B6ch!

Drives back White's King, so that his own King may advance.

41 K—Q2   K—Q5!

The aggressive position of Black's King is decisive!
If White removes the dangerous Pawn, he loses quickly, e.g. *42 R×P, R×Rch 43 K×R, K—K6 44 K—B3, K—B7,* and White's King-side Pawns are doomed.

42 P—R4

Simplifying to a won ending

42 ...   R—Q6ch!

The Knock-out punch! If *42 K—K2, K—B6,* followed by *43 ... R—Q1* and *44 ... K—Kt7,* when White must give up the Rook for the Pawn.
Or if *43 K×P, R—B6ch 44 K—*

Q2, R × R *45* K × R, and now, *so strong is the position of Black's King, that he can win on either side of the board!*

Black can move to B6, capture both Knight Pawns, and win as he pleases, or he can move to K6 and B7, and capture the King-side Pawns to win.

43 Resigns

Command of the Board

A. Rubinstein · K. Schlechter

San Sebastian 1912, QUEEN'S GAMBIT DECLINED

Rubinstein's games flow along so smoothly and easily, and are so pleasant to play over, that one is apt to forget that they also offer valuable instruction.

The importance of centralizing the pieces, for instance, is something the chess writers keep on stressing in their chapters on strategy. That centralization should of itself confer enough advantage to be decisive seems almost incredible, and yet Rubinstein asks for nothing more. In the midgame, with his King and Bishop close to the center, his Knight standing on K5, and a Rook dominating the seventh rank, Rubinstein is complete master of the situation. Given such superiority in the midgame, it is no wonder he plays the ending in exquisite style!

The whole game, including as *bonne-bouche* a journey by the King to the stronghold of the enemy, is a treat. It is one of Rubinstein's finest efforts.

1	P—Q4	P—Q4
2	Kt—KB3	Kt—KB3
3	P—B4	P—K3
4	Kt—B3	P—B4

This is the Semi-Tarrasch Defense. It offers more freedom for Black's pieces than the Orthodox

Defense, but it requires careful handling to achieve equality.

5	BP×P	Kt×P
6	P—K4	Kt×Kt
7	P×Kt	P×P
8	P×P	B—Kt5ch

Black has a good alternative in 8 ... B—K2 the sequel to which could be 9 B—K2, O—O 10 O—O, P—QKt3 11 Q—Q2, B—Kt2 12 Q—K3, Kt—Q2 13 B—Kt2, Kt—B3 14 B—Q3, R—QB1 15 QR—B1, R×R 16 R×R, Q—R1, as in the game Lilienthal–Flohr, Moscow, 1935.

| 9 | B—Q2 | Q—R4 |

This is where Black goes wrong. The exchanges which now follow bring White's King closer to the center, where it is well placed for the ending. The subsequent pressure of White's Rooks on the open files will also make it difficult for Black to develop his Queen-side normally.

A safer continuation was 9 ... B×Bch 10 Q×B, O—O 11 B—B4, Kt—B3 12 O—O, P—QKt3 13 KR—Q1, Kt—R4 14 B—Q3, B—Kt2, with an even game.

| 10 | R—QKt1! | B×Bch |

Black avoids the plausible 10 ...

Kt—B3, which loses by *11* R × B, Kt × R *12* Q—Kt3, Q × P *13* Q × Q, Kt × Q *14* B—B4, and the Knight is trapped.

| *11* | Q × B | Q × Qch |
| *12* | K × Q | O—O |

Black has an opportunity to go wrong—and grasps it! The right move is *12* ... K—K2, centralizing the King. With Queens off the board, and the game approaching the end-game stage, the King belongs near the center, where he can take part in the action.

13 B—Kt5!

A powerful move, whose object is two-fold: to impede Black's development, and to provoke a weakness in his position.

13 ...   P—QR3

This weakens Black's QKt3 square, but what else is there? If

(1) *13* ... B—Q2 *14* B × B, Kt × B *15* R × P, and White wins a Pawn.

(2) *13* ... Kt—Q2 *14* B × Kt, B × B *15* R × P wins a Pawn.

(3) *13* ... Kt—B3 *14* B × Kt, P × B *15* KR—QB1, B—Q2 *16* Kt—K5, and White wins a Pawn.

(4) *13* ... P—QKt3 *14* KR—QB1, B—Kt2 *15* K—K3, R—B1 *16* R × Rch, B × R *17* R—QB1, B—Q2 (if *17* ... B—Kt2 *18* R—B7 should win) *18* B × B, Kt × B *19* R—B7, Kt—B3 *20* Kt—K5, and White has a winning position.

| *14* | B—Q3 | R—Q1 |
| *15* | KR—QB1 | P—QKt4 |

On *15* ... Kt—B3 *16* K—K3 leaves Black without a reasonable continuation.

16 R—B7!

The Rook's domination of the seventh rank should be enough by itself to win the game.

16 ...		Kt—Q2
17	K—K3	Kt—B3
18	Kt—K5	B—Q2

This is the position, with White to play:

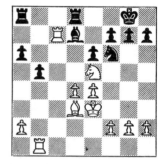

White commands a good deal of the board. The next step is to make things difficult for Black, say by dislodging his Knight from its present strong post.

19 P—Kt4!

Obviously threatening to win a piece by *20* P—Kt5, Kt—K1 *21* R × B. If Black meets this threat by *19* ... B—K1, there follows *20* P—Kt5, Kt—R4 (on *20* ... Kt—Q2 *21* Kt—B6, KR—B1 *22* Kt—K7ch wins a Rook) *21* QR—QB1, and Black's prospects are dreary.

19 ...		P—R3
20	P—B4	B—K1
21	P—Kt5	P × P
22	P × P	Kt—R2

The least of the evils, since *22* ... Kt—Q2 loses in a trice (if not sooner) by *23* Kt—B6.

At this point in his notes, Capablanca comments admiringly on the precision with which Rubinstein conducts this game.

23 P—KR4	KR—B1
24 QR—QB1	R × R
25 R × R	R—Q1

Black might have put up more resistance with *25 ... P—B3* at this point, instead of a move later.

26 R—R7	P—B3
27 P × P	P × P
28 Kt—Kt4	B—R4
29 Kt—R6ch	K—R1
30 B—K2!	

Profiting by the fact that *30 ... B × B* would cost Black the exchange by *31 Kt—B7ch*.

30 ...	B—K1
31 R × P	K—Kt2
32 Kt—Kt4	P—B4

This is the position, with White to play:

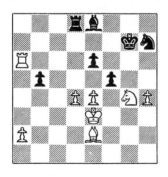

33 R—R7ch!

Forces the King to retreat, to prevent loss of a piece, or even mate itself. For instance, if *33 ...*

K—Kt3 *34* P—R5ch, K—Kt4 *35* R—Kt7ch, K × P *36* Kt—B6 dble ch, K—R3 *37* R × Ktch, K—Kt3 *38* P—K5, and White has won a piece.

Or if *33 ...* K—Kt3 *34* P—R5ch, K—Kt4 *35* R—Kt7ch, K—R5 *36* P × P, P × P *37* Kt—R6!, Kt—B1 *38* Kt × Pch, K—R6 *39* B—B1ch, K—R7 *40* R—Kt2ch, K—R6 (if *40 ...* K—R8 *41* Kt—Kt3 mate) *41* K—B2, and there is no escape from *42* R—Kt3 dble ch and *43* R—R3 mate.

33 ...	K—R1
34 Kt—K5	P × P
35 B × P!	Kt—B3

Here too, Black cannot afford *35 ... B × B*, on account of *36* Kt—B7ch in reply, winning the Rook.

36 B × B	R × B
37 K—B4	K—Kt1
38 K—Kt5	R—KB1

There is no hope in *38 ...* Kt—R2ch *39* K—R6, and the threats (*40* R—Kt7ch, followed by mate with the Knight, or *40* Kt—Kt6, and mate by the Rook at Kt7) are too much to cope with.

39 K—Kt6

Threatens this problem-like finish: *40* R—Kt7ch, K—R1 *41* Kt—B7ch, R × Kt *42* R × R, Kt—Kt1 *43* R—R7 mate!

39 ... Resigns

If *39 ...* Kt—K1 *40* Kt—B7!, with the threat of *41* Kt—R6ch, K—R1 *42* R—R7 mate, should resolve any lingering doubts.

The King Takes a Walk

M. Botvinnik · I. Kann

Sverdlovsk 1943, SICILIAN DEFENSE

In a midgame position with all the pieces still on the board, Botvinnik makes a few deft moves—and magically the scene is transformed! The midgame has suddenly become an endgame, with two of Botvinnik's Pawns close to the Queening square. Some pretty play follows in which the King takes an important part, when once again there is a sudden change. The passed Pawns disappear—both of them given away to simplify the position—and Botvinnik can win in any way he pleases.

1 P—K4	P—QB4
2 Kt—KB3	P—K3
3 P—Q4	P×P
4 Kt×P	Kt—KB3
5 Kt—QB3	P—Q3

The Sicilian is a fighting defense, and in the opinion of most masters, the best way to meet *1* P—K4. It is especially effective against an impetuous opponent, who may be tempted into attacking prematurely.

6 B—K2	P—QR3

The Scheveningen Variation, in which Black tries to set up this sort of formation:

Pawns at QR3, QKt4, Q3 and K3.
Queen at QB2.
Bishops at QKt2 and K2.
King Knight at KB3.

Queen Knight at QB3 or Q2.
Queen Rook at QB1.
King Rook (after Castling) at Q1.

Black plays to control the Queen Bishop file, and to occupy the outpost QB5 with his Queen Knight. Once the Knight reaches that square, it dominates a good deal of the board from there, or forces White to give up a Bishop (that could be troublesome) for the Knight.

7 P—QR4	

This prevents Black from getting in the thrust 7 ... P—QKt4, one of the objectives in the ideal formation.

The observant reader will note that the master chess player is as much concerned with the prevention of his opponent's development as he is with the completion of his own.

7 ...	Q—B2
8 P—B4	QKt—Q2
9 O—O	P—QKt3
10 B—B3	

Ready to dispute control of the long diagonal.

10 ...	B—Kt2
11 P—B5!	

An alert move, which offers Black a choice of evils.

11 ...	P—K4

This weakens the square Q4, and makes a backward Pawn of the Queen Pawn, but the alternative *11 ... P×P 12 P×P*, opening the King-file against his King, was not more palatable.

12 Kt—Kt3	Kt—B4
13 Q—K2!	B—K2

Black would like to exchange pieces and ease his defense, but if *13 ... Kt×Kt, 14 P×Kt* opens the Queen Bishop file to White's advantage.

14 K—R1	P—R3

This prevents an annoying pin by *15 B—Kt5*, as well as a troublesome attack by *15 P—Kt4* and *16 P—Kt5*.

15 B—Q2	R—Q1
16 B—K1	

The Bishop was doing little at Q2, moving there only because it was deprived of the opportunity to develop aggressively at KKt5. The retreat to K1 will enable it to swing over to Kt3 or R4, where it can take a more active role.

16 ...	Q—B1

The Queen is bound for QR1, to add weight to the pressure on White's King Pawn—which then would be attacked by four pieces.

17 R—Q1	Q—R1

With the hope that the four-fold attack on the Pawn will induce White to exchange Knights.

18 Kt×Kt!	

White falls in with this idea, since the exchange turns out to his advantage—no matter how the

Knight is recaptured!

18 ...	QP×Kt

No better is *18 ... KtP×Kt*, to which the reply is *19 B—R4* followed by *20 B×Kt*. The removal of this Knight would allow White to occupy the outpost Q5 permanently with a piece.

19 B—Kt3!	R×R
20 R×R	Q—Kt1
21 Kt—Q5!	

The Knight leaps in of course!

21 ...	Kt×Kt
22 P×Kt	

All of a sudden White has a passed Pawn, his Queen has come to life, and he threatens to win a Pawn!

22 ...	B—Q3

This is probably best, and if let alone, Black will play *23 ... P—B3*, and make a breakthrough difficult.

The alternatives are: *22 ... B—B3 23 P—Q6, B×B 24 Q×B*, with a winning position for White, and *22 ... P—B3 23 P—Q6, B×B* (if *23 ... B×P 24 B×B* wins a piece) *24 P—Q7ch* followed by *25 Q×B*, again with a probable win for White.

This is the position, with White to play:

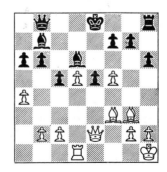

23 P—B6!   P—Kt3

This is better than *23* ... P×P, when White can blockade the position by *24* B—K4, and then regain his Pawn with advantage by *25* B—R4 and *26* R—KB1.

24 B×P!

This wins an important Pawn. Black cannot afford to capture the Bishop, the sequel to *24* ... B×B being *25* P—Q6, K—Q1 *26* Q×B, R—K1 *27* Q—K7ch!, R×Q *28* QP×Rch, K—B2 (if *28* ... K—K1 *29* B×B wins nicely) *29* R—Q8, and White wins a piece and the game.

24 ...   K—Q1
25 B×B   Q×B

This is the position, with White to play:

26 Q—K7ch!

This must have come as a shock to Kann!

26 ...   Q×Q
27 P×Qch   K—Q2

Unfortunately, Black may not take the Pawn, as then *28* P—Q6ch uncovers an attack on his Bishop.

28 P—Q6

And now White has two formidable connected passed Pawns, one of them only a step away from Queening.

28 ...   B×B
29 P×B   R—QB1
30 K—Kt2   P—KKt4
31 R—Q5!

The Rook is unprotected, but in no danger, as an attack on it by *31* ... K—K3 or *31* ... K—B3 loses instantly by *32* P—Q7.

31 ...   R—KKt1

The Rook is tied down to the first rank, an attack on the Queen Pawn being meaningless: *31* ... R—B3 *32* K—Kt3, R×P *33* P—K8(Q)ch, and Black loses his Rook.

32 K—Kt3   P—B3
33 K—Kt4   K—K3

To prevent further inroad by *34* K—B5 and *35* K×BP—but White has two strings to his bow, as the early novelists used to say.

34 K—R5!

The King wanders nonchalantly up the board, to pick up a Pawn or two before forcing the decisive simplification.

It might not be inappropriate to stop the play for a while, and listen to the advice of the great masters on the role of the King in the endings.

Steinitz: In the ending the King is a powerful piece for assisting his own Pawns, or stopping the adverse Pawns.

Tarrasch: It cannot be too greatly emphasized that the most important role in Pawn endings is played by the King.

Capablanca: The King, which during the opening and middle-game stage is often a burden because it has to be defended, becomes in the end game a very important and aggressive piece, and the beginner should realize this, and utilize his King as much as possible.

Nimzovich: The great mobility of the King forms one of the chief characteristics of all endgame strategy. In the middle game the King is a mere "super," in the endgame on the other hand—one of the "principals." We must therefore develop him, bring him nearer the fighting line.

Znosko–Borovsky: The King plays a most important part in the endgame, and gains in power and activity as the number of pieces on the board diminishes. Acting in eight different directions, he becomes, instead of the weakest piece, one of the most formidable units.

Fine: The King is a strong piece; use it!

Now back to the game. This is the position:

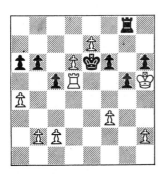

White threatens to capture the Rook Pawn. The Pawn cannot be saved by *34 ... R—KR1*, as White simply replies *35 K—Kt6*, followed by *36 K—Kt7*, winning easily.

34 ...	P—QR4
35 K × P	K—B2

Threatens mate—a momentary thrill for Black.

36 K—R5	R—R1ch
37 K—Kt4	R—R5ch
38 K—Kt3	

Definitely not *38 K—B5, R—B5* mate!

38 ...	R—R1

The Rook must hurry back, as otherwise *39 P—Q7* wins for White.

39 P—KB4	P × Pch
40 K × P	K—K3
41 P—Q7!	

This effects the denouement. Botvinnik gives away the beautiful passed Pawns—but he remains with an easily-won ending.

41 ...	K × P
42 P—Q8(Q)ch	R × Q
43 R × R	K × R
44 K—B5	Resigns

On *44 ... K—K2*, White can win by *45 P—R4* (the outside passed Pawn is usually a trump in endings with even Pawns) K—B2 *46 P—R5*, K—Kt2 *47 P—R6ch, K × P 48*

K × P, and Black's remaining Pawns are helpless.

White can also win neatly, as Botvinnik points out, by *45* K—Kt6!, K—K3 *46* P—R4, P—B4 *47* K—Kt5!, K—K4 *48* P—R5, P—KB5 *49* P—R6, P—B6 *50* P—R7, P—B7 *51* P—R8(Q)ch!

Surprise! Surprise!

T. Petrosian · L. Pachman

Bled 1961, SICILIAN DEFENSE

More than 400 years ago, the great player Ruy Lopez (after whom the strongest King-side opening was named) recommended as good tactics placing the board so that the sun shone in the opponent's eyes!

The chess masters of today have no need of such devices. There are subtler ways to distract an opponent.

Here, the wily Petrosian conjures up various threats against a Pawn on the Queen-side of the board. Pachman is kept busy defending that area, when suddenly there comes a blazing Queen sacrifice on the King-side which catches Pachman completely off-balance. This startling move is followed by a quiet move, and out of nowhere there appears a threat of mate—a threat which cannot be staved off.

When so eminent a theoretician as Pachman can be caught by surprise almost in the opening, there is reason to believe that the rest of us can also learn something from Petrosian's ideas in this game.

1 Kt—KB3	P—QB4
2 P—KKt3	Kt—QB3
3 B—Kt2	P—KKt3
4 O—O	B—Kt2
5 P—Q3	P—K3

This leads to an almost imperceptible weakening of the black squares, but it is enough for the profound strategist Petrosian, who likes nothing better than working on almost imperceptible weaknesses.

6 P—K4

Now, by a transposition of moves, we have a Sicilian Defense.

6 ...	KKt—K2
7 R—K1	O—O

Strangely enough, this natural move might be the decisive mistake! Instead of this, Black should play 7 ... P—Q4, and fight for a share of the center.

8 P—K5!

A fine move! It cramps Black's game, and at the same time makes the square K4 available to White's pieces.

8 ... P—Q3

An understandable attempt to eliminate White's annoying King Pawn.

9 P×P!	Q×P
10 QKt—Q2!	

White gains time by developing with a threat—*11 Kt—K4*, an attack on the Queen and the Queen Bishop Pawn.

There are some pretty combinations in the air. If Black counter-attacks by *10 ...* Kt—Q5, the sequel could be *11* Kt—K4, Q—B2 *12* B—B4, P—K4 *13* Kt×KP!, B×Kt *14* Kt—B6ch, K—Kt2 *15* B×B, Q—Q1 *16* Kt—Q5ch, P—B3 (if *16 ...* K—Kt1 *17* Kt×Ktch, Q×Kt *18* B×Kt, and White wins a piece) *17* B—B7, Q—Q2 *18* R× Ktch, and White wins the Queen.

Or (after *10 ...* Kt—Q5) *11* Kt—K4, Q—B2 *12* B—B4, Kt× Ktch *13* Q×Kt, Q—Kt3 *14* B—Q6, R—K1 *15* B×P, Q×P *16* Kt—Q6 (attacks the Rook, and also threatens *17* Q×Pch) R—B1 *17* Kt×B, Kt×Kt *18* B×R, and White has won the exchange.

10 ...   Q—B2

Indicating that he proposes to consolidate his position by *11 ...* P—K4, if let alone.

11 Kt—Kt3!   Kt—Q5

Plausible enough, but Black might have put up a better defense with *11 ...* P—Kt3, and if *12* B—B4, Q—Q1.

This is the position, with White to play:

12 B—B4

Chess players dream of making this sort of move—developing a piece with gain of time!

12 ...   Q—Kt3

This is preferable to *12 ...* Kt×Ktch *13* Q×Kt, Q—Kt3 *14* B—K3, B—Q5 *15* B×B, P×B *16* Q—KB6, Kt—B3 *17* B×Kt, and the Queen Pawn falls.

13 Kt—K5!

With this pretty threat: *14* Kt—B4, Q—Kt4 (not *14 ...* Q—Kt5, when *15* P—QB3 wins a piece for White) *15* P—QR4, and the Queen must abandon the Bishop Pawn, or lose her own life by refusal to do so (*15 ...* Q—Kt5 *16* B—Q2).

13 ...   Kt×Kt
14 Kt—B4!

An important interpolation.

14 ...   Q—Kt4
15 RP×Kt

The opening of the file furnishes White with new means of attack. The threat is now *16* R—R5, an attack on the Queen, and the Pawn behind the Queen.

15 ...   P—QR4
16 B—Q6!

A cunning move! If at once *16* B—B7, Kt—B3 guards the Rook Pawn. After the actual move, the Knight is pinned, and protecting it by *16 ...* R—K1 sets the Rook up as a target. White then plays *17* B—B7, and if Black tries to save the Rook Pawn by *17 ...* Kt—B3, *18* Kt—Q6 is a decisive Knight fork.

16 ...	B—B3
17 Q—B3!	K—Kt2

The subtlety of Petrosian's strategy can be seen in the way he has reduced his opponent to a state of passivity in a mere *17* moves!

Let's compare the two positions:

Black's Queen Rook and Queen Bishop are undeveloped, while his Queen is tied down to the defense of two weak Pawns. On the Kingside, Black's Knight is pinned, his Bishop must guard the Knight, and the King must guard the Bishop which guards the Knight.

White, on the other hand, bears down on two semi-open files with his Rooks, has two strongly-centralized pieces in his Knight and Bishop, and dominates the long diagonal with his Queen and King Bishop.

This is position play *par excellence*.

18 R—K4	R—Q1

Black does not suspect anything! He could have held out longer (if there is any particular merit in prolonging a lost game) by *18 ...* Kt—B4, giving up the exchange.

This is how things stood before the blow fell:

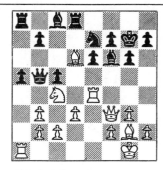

19 Q × Bch!

A brilliant sacrifice, which must have jolted Pachman out of his chair.

19 ...	K × Q
20 B—K5ch	K—Kt4

On *20 ...* K—B4 instead, there is a mate in three by *21* R—B4ch, K—Kt4 *22* B—B6ch, K—R3 *23* R—R4 mate.

21 B—Kt7!

A quiet little move!

21 ...	Resigns

If *21 ...* P—K4 *22* P—R4ch, K—R4 (or *22 ...* K—B4 *23* B—R3 mate) *23* B—B3ch, B—Kt5 *24* B × B mate. Or if *21 ...* Kt—B4 *22* P—B4ch, K—Kt5 *23* Kt—K5ch, K—R4 *24* B—B3 mate.

Bolt from the Blue

D. Andric · Daja

Belgrade 1949, QUEEN'S INDIAN DEFENSE

For the connoisseur of combination play, this game is a sheer delight. From the lightning-like sacrifice which initiates a threat of mate, and the further sacrifice which leads to the imprisonment of Black's Royal Family, and finally to the triumphant march of a passed Pawn, it sizzles with brilliant ideas.

For the player who is anxious to increase his strength, this game is enlightening. The principles of chess strategy come to life in the course of the game, and make its outcome almost inevitable.

In the opening, White acquires a clear advantage in position before striking the first blow. In the midgame, superiority in position enables White's lesser forces to hold the enemy in complete restraint. In the ending, White's clever simplification sweeps away all the pieces, leaving a position with Pawns only on the board—the easiest sort of ending to win.

The whole of this is effected with the consummate artistry of a master player.

1 P—Q4	Kt—KB3
2 P—QB4	P—K3
3 Kt—KB3	P—QKt3
4 P—KKt3	B—Kt2
5 B—Kt2	

The Bishops view each other at long range, prepared to fight for control of the long diagonal.

5 ...	B—K2
6 O—O	O—O
7 Kt—B3	

White now threatens to dominate the center by *8* Q—B2 followed by *9* P—K4, and this practically forces Black's next move.

7 ...	Kt—K5
8 Q—B2	Kt×Kt

At this point, White might think that his opponent has fallen into the Monticelli trap, and play the tempting-looking *9* Kt—Kt5, which threatens *10* Q×P mate as well as *10* B×B followed by *11* B×R. He would quickly be disillusioned though by the reply *9* ... Kt×Pch *10* Q×Kt (if *10* K—R1, B×Bch wins) B×B, which wins for Black, as O'Sullivan found out when he lost it this way against Rossolimo at Hilversum in 1947.

The Monticelli trap, which has claimed some notable victims, goes like this: *1* P—Q4, Kt—KB3 *2* P—QB4, P—K3 *3* Kt—KB3, P—QKt3 *4* P—KKt3, B—Kt2 *5* B—Kt2, B—Kt5ch *6* B—Q2, B×Bch *7* Q×B, O—O *8* Kt—B3, Kt—K5 *9* Q—B2, Kt×Kt *10* Kt—Kt5, and

White wins (or should!). So mighty a player as Capablanca fell into the Monticelli trap against Euwe in the eighth game of their match in 1931. Capablanca lost the exchange, but drew the game. Then, as though to show his contempt for the trap, or perhaps to demonstrate that the King of Chess could not fall into a trap unwittingly, Capablanca deliberately made the same opening moves in the tenth game of the match, allowed Euwe to win the exchange, and again drew the game!

9 P×Kt

White now has a strategic threat in *10* P—K4, control of the center, and a tactical threat in *10* Kt—Kt5, gain of the exchange.

| *9* ... | Q—B1 |
| *10* P—QR4 | |

This move requires a bit of explanation. If at once *10* P—K4, the reply *10* ... P—QB4 followed by *11* ... Kt—B3 and *12* ... Kt—R4 offers Black good counter-play. After White's actual move (which threatens further expansion by *11* P—R5) Black is intimidated into making a response that shuts off the square QR4 from his Knight.

10 ...	P—QR4
11 P—K4	P—Q3
12 Kt—Q2	

Clears the way for *13* P—B4, the customary advance in this type of position.

| *12* ... | P—K4 |

Black tries to get a grip on the black squares, as a means of securing a fair share of the center.

| *13* P—B4 | Kt—B3 |

Develops a piece with a threat—to win a Pawn by *14* ... P×QP *15* P×P, Kt×P.

Black hopes to induce *14* P—Q5, to which he would reply *14* ... Kt—Kt1, followed by *15* ... Kt—Q2 and *16* ... Kt—B4. The Knight would then stand like a rock on this square, safe from any attack by a Pawn.

Black does manage to induce P—Q5, but not at a time when the consequences are favorable for him.

| *14* B—Kt2 | B—B3 |

Another piece attacks the Queen Pawn, provoking its advance.

| *15* BP×P | P×P |
| *16* P—Q5 | Kt—Kt1 |

Black sticks to his plan. A better defense was *16* ... Kt—K2, but it was difficult to see that his King was in danger, and that a combination was in the air.

| *17* B—QR3 | R—Q1 |

This is the position, with White to play:

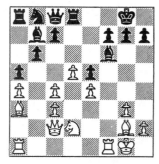

A glance at the board shows that Black has only one piece in the neighborhood of his King.

This one protector must be destroyed!

18 R×B!   P×R
19 Q—Q1

This is much stronger than the inviting *19* B—K7, which allows Black counter-play after *19* ... R—K1 *20* B×P, by *20* ... Q—Kt5 followed by *21* ... Kt—Q2.

White now has a terrible threat in *20* Q—R5, followed by *21* B—R3 and *22* B—KB5.

19 ...   P—QB4

The only move. This cuts off the action of the Bishop, and enables Black's Queen to reach KB1, to help defend the King.

20 Q—R5   R—Q3
21 B—R3   Q—B1
22 B—B5

Threatens mate on the move.

22 ...   Q—Kt2
23 Kt—B3   Kt—Q2

Obviously, Black hopes to consolidate his position with *24* ... Kt—B1 and *25* ... Kt—Kt3, but he isn't given time for this.

24 B—B1

Menaces the life of the Queen by *25* B—R6. The Queen could not then retreat to R1, as mate in two would be the consequence.

24 ...   K—R1

On *24* ... Kt—B1, the continuation *25* B—R6, Q—R1 *26* Q—Kt4ch, Kt—Kt3 *27* P—R4 followed by *28* P—R5, *29* K—Kt2 and *30* R—R1 wins for White.

25 B—R6   Q—Kt1

White must act quickly, before Black has time to regroup his forces by *26* ... Kt—B1 and *27* ... Kt—Kt3.

Bearing in mind Pillsbury's injunction, "So set up your attacks that when the fire is out, it isn't out!" Andric strikes once more.

This is the position, with White to play:

26 B×Kt!   R×B
27 Kt×P!

The point! White gives up a Knight, and the sacrifice must be accepted. The alternatives are:

(1) *27* ... R—B2 *28* P—Q6!, and Black must lose a Rook, or allow the ruinous *29* Kt×Pch.

(2) *27* ... R—K2 *28* Q—R4!, and *29* Q×Pch will be fatal.

(3) *27* ... QR—Q1 *28* Kt×R, R×Kt *29* Q—B5, R—Q3 (If *29* ... Q—Q1 *30* Q—Kt4, Q—KKt1 *31* Q × R wins) *30* P—K5!, P×P *31* Q×KPch, P—B3 *32* Q×R, and White wins.

27 ...   P×Kt
28 Q×KPch   P—B3
29 Q×Pch   R—Kt2

White is a Rook down, and hasty play (say *30* P—K5 or *30* P—Q6) would allow Black time to drive the Queen off by *30* ... R—KB1 or *30* ... Q—B2.

30	R—KB1!		B—R3
31	P—Q6		B × P

Black's only chance lies in capturing all the material he can.

32	P—Q7!		B × R
33	B × Rch		

Begins a liquidation which clears away all the pieces, leaving an ending which White wins by just one move!

33	...		Q × B
34	P—Q8(Q)ch		R × Q
35	Q × Rch		Q—Kt1
36	Q × Qch		K × Q
37	K × B		Resigns

For after *37* ... P—Kt4 *38* P × P, P—R5 *39* P—Kt6, P—R6 *40* P—Kt7, and White will Queen his Pawn with check!

A brilliant game with a sparkling finish.

Lured into Zugzwang

F. J. Marshall · J. R. Capablanca

New York 1918, QUEEN'S GAMBIT DECLINED

It would be an exaggeration to say that the master strategist is always more than a match for the attacking player. But how the latter can be made to look helpless!

For example, *out of all the tournament and match games*, 69 in total, played by Capablanca against such great masters of attack as Janowsky, Marshall, Yates, Colle, Bogolyubov, Mieses and Tartakover, he lost only two games!

Here is the complete box score:

Opponent	Capa's wins	Draws	Capa's losses
Janowsky	9	1	1
Marshall	10	13	1
Yates	8	1	0
Colle	4	0	0
Bogolyubov	5	2	0
Mieses	2	0	0
Tartakover	5	7	0
	—	—	—
Totals	43	24	2

In the game that follows, Capablanca sacrifices a Pawn in the early middle game to secure an advantage in position. In a short while (such is the efficacy of this strategy) Marshall's pieces are completely tied up. A Knight that is under attack must stay where it is, while neither of the two Rooks protecting the Knight dares move away from the file it occupies. The King—well, the King by himself can do very little. All that is left to Marshall are some feeble moves by his Pawns. When these die out, Marshall tries a swindle or two. The swindles come to nothing, and Marshall must turn down his King in surrender.

Capablanca's conduct of the game is truly impressive. It is as fine an illustration of *The Power of Position Play* as you will ever see.

1	P—Q4	P—Q4
2	Kt—KB3	Kt—KB3
3	P—B4	P—K3
4	Kt—B3	QKt—Q2
5	B—Kt5	B—K2
6	P—K3	O—O
7	R—B1	P—B3
8	Q—B2	P×P
9	B×P	Kt—Q4

A move made popular by Capablanca. It brings about some exchanges, which free Black's crowded position.

10	B×B	Q×B
11	O—O	Kt×Kt
12	Q×Kt	P—QKt3

"This is the key," says Capablanca, "to this system of defense. Having simplified the game considerably by a series of exchanges, Black will now develop his Queen

Bishop along the long diagonal without having created any apparent weakness. The proper development of the Queen Bishop is Black's greatest problem in the Queen's Gambit."

The plan of mobilization (if undisturbed) is for Black to develop his Bishop at Kt2, his Rooks at Q1 and QB1, and his Knight at KB3. Then at the proper time, he attacks the center by ... P—QB4.

13 P—K4	B—Kt2
14 KR—K1	KR—Q1
15 P—Q5	

Marshall proceeds to attack. The immediate threat is *16* P×KP, P×P, and Black is saddled with an isolated Pawn.

15 ...	Kt—B4!

This is an improvement on the passive *15* ... Kt—B1, which Capablanca had played against Kostic in an earlier round of the tournament. Black now threatens either to win a Pawn by *16* ... BP×P *17* P×P, B×P, or to destroy White's Pawn center by *16* ... Kt×P *17* R×Kt, BP×P *18* R—Kt4, P—B4.

16 P×KP	Kt×KP (K3)
17 B×Kt	Q×B

Capablanca was under the impression that White had to lose a move protecting his Queen Rook Pawn, whereupon he could play *18* ... P—QB4 (releasing his Bishop) with a very fine game.

But Marshall disregards the attack on his Pawn, as he has a little surprise prepared!

18 Kt—Q4!

This sets a problem for Capablanca. If *18* ... Q×RP *19* R—R1 wins the Queen instantly. Or if *18* ... Q—K2 *19* Kt×P wins a Pawn. Finally, if *18* ... Q—Q2 (to protect the Queen Bishop Pawn) *19* Kt—B5, P—B3 *20* Q—KKt3 (threatens *21* QR—Q1, Q—KB2 *22* Kt—R6ch, winning the Queen) K—R1 *21* QR—Q1, Q—KB2 *22* P—KR4, with a powerful game for White.

18 ...	Q—K4!

Rather than undergo a Marshall attack (which can be a distressing experience) Capablanca makes this brilliant move, which gives up a Pawn. What he will get in return for the Pawn is not evident at first sight, as Queens will come off the board, and little material will remain with which to work up an attack.

But it was evident to Capablanca, who must have looked deeply into the position!

19 Kt×P	Q×Q
20 R×Q	R—Q7!

The Rook dominates the seventh rank, as part payment for the Pawn.

Marshall should now play for a draw, according to Capablanca, by *21* Kt—K7ch, K—B1 *22* R—B7, R—K1 *23* R×B (best—not *23* Kt—Kt6ch, BP×Kt *24* R×B, R×KP) R×Kt *24* R—Kt8ch, R—K1 *25* R×Rch, K×R, and White should be able to draw (even though he is a Pawn ahead). Black has adequate compensation in the powerful position of his Rook.

21 R—Kt1

A surprisingly passive move, coming from such an aggressive player as Marshall. At this stage, Rooks are supposed to be out in the open, picking up stray Pawns—or at least terrorizing them.

21 ...   R—K1!

This Rook attacks the center, and will soon switch to an attack on the King.

22 P—K5

This is better than defending the Pawn by *22 P—B3*, the reply to which would be *22 ... P—B4*. If then *23 P×P, R(K1)—K7* doubles Rooks on the seventh rank with devastating effect.

This is how things stand, with Black to play:

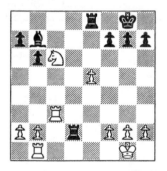

22 ...   P—KKt4!

Masterly play! At one stroke, Capablanca prevents White from supporting his King Pawn by *23 P—B4*, provides a flight square for his King against threats of mate on the last rank, and threatens to win a Pawn by *23 ... B×Kt 24 R×B, R×KP*.

23 P—KR4

Marshall is perfectly willing to return the extra Pawn, if he can thereby disrupt the adverse Pawn position.

23 ...   P×P
24 R—K1

Now he decides to get the Rook back into active play, even if it means losing his Queen-side Pawns.

Had Marshall played *24 P—B4* instead, the sequel would probably have been *24 ... P—R6* (better than *24 ... R—K3 25 R(Kt1)—QB1* followed by *26 P—B5*) *25 P—KKt3* (or *25 P×P, K—R1!*) *P—R7ch 26 K—R1, R—QB1 27 R(Kt1)—QB1, K—B1 28 P—B5, K—K1 29 P—K6* (to prevent *29 ... K—Q2*, attacking the Knight with three pieces) *P×P 30 P×P, R—Q3*, and Black wins the helpless piece.

24 ...   R—K3!

Black does not waste time capturing Pawns. This attack on the Knight forces White to defend it with both Rooks.

25 R(K1)—QB1

The Knight must not budge! For example, if *25 Kt×P, R—Kt3 26 P—KKt3, P—R6* (threatens mate in three by *27 ... P—R7ch 28 K×P, R—R3ch 29 K—Kt1, R—R8 mate*) *27 K—R2, R×Pch 28 K×P, B—Q4! 29 P—KKt4, R—Kt7 30 K—R4, R(Kt3)×Pch 31 K—R3, B—K3*, and mate follows quickly.

25 ...   K—Kt2

A necessary preparation for ... R—Kt3, which played at once, allows *26* Kt—K7ch winning the exchange.

26 P—QKt4   P—Kt4!

To prevent *27* P—Kt5, which would defend the Knight and free White's Rooks for active duty.

27 P—R3   R—Kt3

This is the position, with White to play:

Marshall is running out of moves! For example, if he plays *28* Kt×P, R×Pch *29* K—B1, R(KKt7)×Pch wins quickly. Or if he plays *28* R—B5 (the only move by either Rook which does not lose the Knight!), the reply *28* ... P—R6, striking again at the Knight Pawn, is decisive. Finally, if *28* P—B3 (to cut off the action of the Bishop) R(Kt3)×Pch leads to quick mate.

Marshall can prolong, but not save the game, by *28* P—K6, upon which *28* ... R×KP diverts the Rook for a while from the Knight file.

28 K—B1   R—R7!
29 K—Kt1   P—R6

The isolated doubled Pawn, usually a weakling, suddenly becomes ferocious!

30 P—Kt3   P—QR3

A waiting move. White is all tied up, and any move he makes loses something.

31 P—K6   R×KP

After this, White still may not move his Knight. For instance, if *32* Kt—Q8 (or Kt—Q4) there is a mate in three by *32* ... P—R7ch *33* K×P, R—R3ch *34* K—Kt1, R—R8 mate.

32 P—Kt4   R—R3
33 P—B3

On *33* P—Kt5 instead, there is some pretty play. The continuation would be *33* ... P—R7ch *34* K—R1 (if *34* K—Kt2, P—R8(Q)ch *35* R×Q, B×Ktch *36* R×B, R× R(B3), and Black is a Rook ahead) R×Kt *35* R×R, R×BP *36* P—R4 (trying for stalemate) P×P *37* P—Kt5, P×P *38* P—Kt6, RP×P *39* R(B1)—B2, R—B3, and it's all over.

33 ...   R—Q3!

This is manifestly stronger than *33* ... P—R7ch.

34 Kt—K7   R(Q3)—Q7

A dream position—doubled Rooks on the seventh rank!

35 Kt—B5ch

Hope springs eternal in Marshall's breast. If Black replies *35* ... K—B1 carelessly, then *36* R—B8ch forces mate.

35 ...   K—B3
36 Kt—R4   K—Kt4

Even the King takes a hand. The Knight must be driven off, for the Rook to check at Kt7.

37 Kt—B5   R—Kt7ch
38 K—B1

If *38* K—R1, R—R7ch and mate in two more moves.

38 ...   P—R7

39 P—B4ch

Last chance! If *39* ... K—B3 in reply, *40* R—B6ch, B×R *41* R×B is mate.

39 ...   K×BP
40 Resigns

"An ending worth very careful study," says Capablanca.

The Flash of a Mighty Surprise

F. Olafsson · R. Fischer

Portoroz 1958, QUEEN'S GAMBIT DECLINED

One of the beauties of chess is that it never lacks surprises. Even the greatest masters are caught unawares at times.

Take this game for instance, where Bobby Fischer plays to win a Rook for his Knight. Picture his astonishment to discover that he has been lured into a deeply-hidden trap. In order to win the exchange, Fischer has had to weaken his King-side ever so slightly, and this weakness is exploited by Olafsson through a series of clever moves. For a while it looks as though Fischer will equalize, but Olafsson plays it in fine style, and his position gains quietly in strength. With the creation of two connected passed Pawns, its power becomes irresistible.

Olafsson's play is elegant throughout, and this game of his is a jewel in the treasury of modern chess.

1 P—QB4	Kt—KB3
2 Kt—QB3	P—K3
3 Kt—B3	P—Q4
4 P—Q4	B—Kt5
5 P×P	P×P

Recapturing with the Queen is recommended by the opening theorists.

6 B—Kt5	P—KR3
7 B—R4	P—B4!

This attack on White's center is essential in almost every form of Queen's Pawn openings.

8 P—K3

A strong alternative is *8* R—B1, with which Stahlberg won a fine game against Filip at Helsinki in 1952. The next few moves were: *8* ... P—B5 *9* Kt—Q2! (threatens *10* B×Kt) B—B3 *10* P—K3, O—O *11* B—K2, Kt—B3 *12* O—O, P—R3 *13* P—KB4, Kt—K2 *14* P—KKt4!, and a vigorous King-side attack decided the issue.

8 ...	Kt—B3

An adventurous line is *8* ... P—KKt4 *9* B—Kt3, Q—R4 *10* Q—B2, Kt—K5 *11* R—B1, Q×P. Whether it is worthwhile breaking up the King-side to chase after a Pawn is less a matter of exact analysis than a course to be decided on by a player's style and temperament.

9 R—B1	P—B5

This releases the tension in the center, but Black had to do something about threats against his Queen Pawn by *10 P × P*.

10 B—K2	B—K3
11 O—O	O—O
12 Kt—Q2	B—K2

This unpins the Knight, and makes it possible to reply to *13 P—B4* with *13 ... Kt—Q2*.

13 P—QKt3!

The key to the position! The idea is to break up Black's Pawns and open lines of attack, even at the cost of the exchange.

| 13 ... | P—KKt4 |

This move is necessary, if Black is to go after the Rook. If at once *13 ... B—QR6*, then *14 B × Kt, Q × B 15 R—Kt1, B—KB4 16 Kt × QP* is favorable to White.

| 14 B—Kt3 | B—QR6 |
| 15 R—B2 | Kt—QKt5 |

It seems to me that Black might have won the exchange to better advantage with *15 ... P × P 16 Kt × KtP* (if *16 P × P*, Kt—QKt5 corners the Rook) B—KB4 *17 R—Q2* (or *17 B—Q3*, B × B *18 Q × B*, Kt—QKt5 with an attack on Queen and Rook) B—QKt5 *18 Q—R1*, B × Kt *19 Q × B*, Kt—K5, and the King Knight does the trick this time.

| 16 P × P | Kt × R |
| 17 Q × Kt | P × P |

This is the position, with White to play:

18 Kt—Kt5!

A clever interpolation, far superior to the immediate recapture of the Pawn.

| 18 ... | B—QKt5 |

An attack on the Knight, the purpose of which is to keep White's Queen tied down to its defense.

On *18 ... B—K2* instead, the continuation would be *19 Kt—B7, R—B1 20 Kt × B, P × Kt 21 Q—Kt6ch*, and White starts collecting Pawns.

| 19 Kt—B7 | B × Kt |

The move on which Black depended.

| 20 Kt × B! |

But not *20 Kt × R, B—R4 21 Q—R4, Kt—K5 22 B—K5, Kt—B6 23 Q—B2, Kt × Bch 24 Q × Kt, Q × Kt*, and Black has won a piece.

White's actual move creates weak spots in Black's position on the King-side.

| 20 ... | P × Kt |
| 21 B × P! |

Beautiful play, and probably a surprise to Fischer! He must have expected *21* Q×B, whereupon *21* ... P—Kt4 gave him an approximately even game.

| *21* ... | Q—K1 |

Black has no time to rescue the Bishop, as after *21* ... B—R4 *22* Q—Kt6ch, K—R1 *23* Q×Pch, Kt—R2 (if *23* ... K—Kt1 *24* B×Pch, R—B2 *25* Q—Kt6ch wins for White) *24* B—Q3, R—B2 *25* B—K5ch, K—Kt1 *26* B×Ktch, R×B *27* Q—Kt6ch, K—B1 *28* Q×R, White has an easy win.

| *22* Q×B | Kt—K5 |

In order to get rid of one of the troublesome Bishops.

| *23* Q—Q3 | Kt×B |
| *24* RP×Kt | R—B3 |

To guard against *25* Q—Kt3, winning a Pawn. Apparently Black has equalized, since he has a Rook for a Bishop and Pawn, but appearances are deceptive. For the time being, Black is restricted to defense, his isolated King Pawn especially requiring tender care.

This is the position, with White to play:

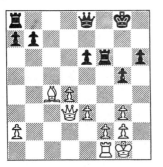

25 Q—K4!

A fine spot for the Queen, who dominates the board from the center.

| *25* ... | R—QB1 |

But not the plausible *25* ... Q—B3, as then *26* P—Q5! would be another unpleasant surprise.

| *26* B—Kt3 | Q—Q2 |
| *27* R—Q1 | |

With this powerful threat: *28* P—Q5, R—K1 (if *28* ... P×P *29* R×P, and Black is threatened with a deadly discovered check) *29* P×P, Q—K2 *30* R—Q7, and Black must give up his Queen or be mated.

| *27* ... | R—K1 |

Anticipating *28* P—Q5, P—K4 *29* P—Q6 dis ch, K—Kt2, and Black is out of the woods (*30* B—R4, P—Kt4).

28 P—B4!

A new menace on the scene! The Pawn threatens to push on to B5, striking another blow at the pinned King Pawn.

| *28* ... | Q—R2 |
| *29* Q—K5 | Q—B4 |

Hoping to ease his difficulties either by forcing an exchange of Queens, or by driving off White's Queen.

30 P—Kt4!

Once again Black gets a rude jolt! He can exchange Queens, but the subsequent position is greatly in White's favor.

30 ...	Q×Q
31 QP×Q	R—B2
32 P—B5	R—B2

Of course not *32 ... P×P*, as *33 R—Q7* in reply is immediately decisive.

33 R—Q6!

Far better than *33 B×Pch*, after which Black might sacrifice the exchange to give his opponent a feeble column of Pawns on the King file.

33 ...	R—B4
34 B×Pch	K—B1
35 B—Kt3	R(B4)×P
36 R×P	R×KP

Black's only hope is to counter-attack. An attempt to save his Knight Pawn instead by *36 ... R(K1)—K2* loses quickly by either of these two pretty continuations:

(1) *37 R—R8ch, K—Kt2 38 R—Kt8ch, K—R3* (if *38 ... K—B3 39 R—Kt6* is an epaulette mate) *39 P—B6, R—K1 40 P—B7*, and the Pawn will become a Queen.

(2) *37 R—R5, R—Kt2 38 P—B6, R—Kt1* (if *38 ... R—KB2 39 R—R8* is mate) *39 R—R7, R—QKt4*

40 R—B7ch, K—K1 41 R—K7ch, K—B1 42 R—K8ch, K×R 43 P—B7ch, and White gets a Queen and wins.

37 R—KKt6!

Better than *37 P—B6, R(K1)—K3*, and Black still needs subduing.

After the move in the text, White obtains two connected passed Pawns—a tangible superiority.

37 ...	R(K1)—K5
38 R×P	R—Kt6
39 R—Kt8ch	K—K2
40 P—Kt5	R—K7
41 B—Q5	

Everything is under control. The King Knight Pawn is protected, and the Pawn roller can advance.

41 ...	K—Q3
42 B—B3	R×RP
43 P—B6	K—K3
44 R—K8ch!	

The *coup de grâce*! If Black replies *44 ... K—B2 45 B—R5* mates neatly, while any other move allows *45 P—B7* followed by Queening the Pawn.

| 44 ... | Resigns |

Symphony of Heavenly Length

L. Evans · Opsahl

Dubrovnik 1950, QUEEN'S GAMBIT DECLINED

To call this game a masterpiece is to do it insufficient justice. It is more than that. It is a symphony played over a chessboard with an orchestra of pieces and Pawns.

It consists of four movements, whose style and tempo may be described as follows:

(1) The Minority Attack—lively and with vigor, (this is the dominant theme of the movement, and determines the play of the entire composition).

(2) The Knight's Tour—lightly and gracefully.

(3) The Rook's Maneuvers—with energy and spirit.

(4) The Pawn Finale—simply and precisely.

You may get the idea from the foregoing that I am wild about this game, and that I wish it lasted more than the 81 moves it does. If you do, then I have conveyed the right impression.

1 P—Q4	Kt—KB3
2 P—QB4	P—K3
3 Kt—QB3	P—Q4
4 B—Kt5	QKt—Q2
5 P—K3	B—K2
6 Q—B2	O—O
7 P×P	P×P

The Exchange Variation, a line of play which has long been a favorite with masters of disparate styles—Marshall, Keres, Reshevsky and Botvinnik. Apparently it has something to offer the tactician as well as the strategist.

The exchange of the center Pawns seems to free Black's game, but certain weaknesses remain in his Queen side Pawn structure. These are susceptible to the so-called Minority Attack. This is a remarkable concept as it involves an assault on three Pawns by only two Pawns! Its purpose is to split up Black's Pawn majority and leave him with an isolated Pawn that is difficult to defend.

| 8 Kt—B3 | P—B3 |

Black supports the center Pawn, and provides an outlet for his Queen.

| 9 B—Q3 | R—K1 |

The Rook moves toward the center, where it will exert pressure on the half-open file. Meanwhile the square KB1 is made available to the Queen Knight, which will help defend the King-side.

| 10 O—O | Kt—B1 |
| 11 QR—Kt1 | |

The beginning of the Minority Attack. The Rook supports the

Queen Knight Pawn, which will advance to Kt4 and Kt5, with the idea of breaking up Black's Queen-side Pawns.

| 11 ... | Kt—K5 |

An attempt to stop the Minority Attack by *11 ... P—QR4* would only be a temporary deterrent, since White could pursue his plan by *12 P—QR3* followed by *13 P—QKt4.*

12 B×B

Of course not *12 Kt×Kt, P×Kt 13 B×B, Q×B,* and Black wins a piece by the Pawn fork.

| 12 ... | Q×B |
| 13 P—QKt4 | P—QR3 |

Ready to meet an eventual P—Kt5 with ... RP×P, opening a file for his Queen Rook.

14 P—QR4	Kt×Kt
15 Q×Kt	B—Kt5
16 Kt—Q2	Q—Kt4

With the transparent threat of *17 ... B—R6,* winning the exchange.

| 17 KR—B1 | R—K3 |

Black plays for a King-side attack, not only because his chances lie in that area, but to divert White from carrying out his designs on the other wing.

18 P—Kt5!

White is not to be dissuaded! He intends to force exchanges which will leave Black with a permanently weak Pawn position on the Queen-side.

| 18 ... | RP×P |
| 19 P×P | |

Now we see one of the likely consequences of the breakthrough. If Black were to play *19 ... P×P,* the recapture would leave him with two weak isolated Pawns—the Queen Knight Pawn and the Queen Pawn. These would make fine objects of attack for White.

| 19 ... | B—R6 |
| 20 P—Kt3 | |

This weakens the white squares and creates holes in the position, but as Nimzovich once said, "We cannot always be happy."

The alternative, *20 B—B1,* would be dangerous, if not fatal, after *20 ... B×P 21 B×B, R—Kt3.*

| 20 ... | QR—K1 |
| 21 P×P | P×P |

This is the position, with White to play:

White has accomplished what he set out to do with the Minority Attack. He has saddled Black with a backward Pawn on an open file—a Pawn which is vulnerable to attack, as it dare not advance, and can be defended only with pieces.

Against this weakling, White will direct his fire.

22 B—B1!

Excellent! White sees to it that his King is properly protected before starting an attack on the weak Pawn. Black must now withdraw his Bishop from its strongly-placed position, or allow its exchange— either of which will be to White's advantage.

Had White been hasty and played 22 R—Kt6 instead, the consequences would have been painful, the continuation being 22 ... R × P! 23 P × R, Q × KPch 24 K—R1, Q—B7 (threatens mate on the move) 25 R—KKt1, R—K8!, and White is faced with four threats of mate on the move!

22 ...	B × B
23 Kt × B	

The exchange of pieces has noticeably strengthened White's position. The Bishops are off the board, but Black's (a troublesome attacking piece) has disappeared, while White's has been replaced by another piece— the Knight.

The Knight, from its modest post at KB1, securely guards the Knight Pawn and the King Pawn, the two vulnerable points in White's King-side position. Any hopes Black had of breaking through by a sacrifice at K6, are now shattered.

Another consideration in White's favor is that any further exchanges of pieces will accentuate the weakness of the unfortunate Queen Bishop Pawn.

23 ...	Kt—Kt3
24 R—Kt6	Kt—K2

All points are safeguarded, but Black is restricted to defensive measures, while his opponent can trouble him with all manner of threats.

25 Q—Kt4	P—R4

Primarily, this is to provide the King with a flight square against threats of mate on the back rank, but Black also has visions of starting an attack by 25 ... P—R5 and 26 ... P × P.

26 R—Kt8

White is of course anxious to bring it to an endgame by exchanging as many pieces as possible.

26 ...	R × R
27 Q × Rch	K—R2
28 Q—B4!	Q × Q
29 KtP × Q	

The disappearance of the Queens puts an end to any possibility of Black's conjuring up a King-side attack, and brings matters to an ending, where White has all the winning chances.

29 ...	P—Kt3
30 Kt—Q2	

The Knight heads for QB5, where it can occupy a fine outpost, and blockade the backward Pawn.

30 ...	R—Q3

Black also seeks to improve his position, by maneuvering the Rook over to an open file.

31 K—B1	K—Kt2

The Kings too move toward the

center, where they can take an active part in the endgame.

32 R—R1

An attempt to seize control of the seventh rank . . .

32 . . .   R—Q2

. . . which is promptly repulsed.

33 Kt—Kt3   R—Kt2
34 Kt—B5   R—Kt7

This offers better chances than the passive *34 . . . R—B2.*

35 R—R7   K—B3
36 R—R6

Evans wastes a few moves here before hitting on the decisive combination, but he may have been in time pressure.

36 . . .   R—Kt8ch
37 K—Kt2   R—Kt7
38 R—R7   R—Kt8
39 R—B7!

Finally getting behind the Pawn. Black is now held in a tight grip, his King and Knight being unable to move without loss of material.

39 . . .   R—QR8
40 Kt—Q3   K—K3

But not *40 . . . R—R7* (to prevent *41 P—B3* followed by *42 P—K4*) as then comes *41 Kt—Kt4, R—Kt7 42 Kt×BP, R—B7* (the pin) *43 Kt×Kt!* (breaks the pin neatly) *R×R 44 Kt×Pch,* and White regains the Rook, winning a piece and the game.

This is the position, with White to play:

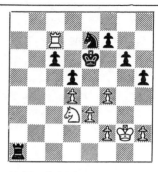

41 Kt—B5ch!

The beginning of a remarkable Knight's tour (reminiscent of the famous Capablanca maneuver against Yates in 1924) which results in White's winning a valuable Pawn.

41 . . .   K—B3

Clearly, not *41 . . . K—Q3 42 R—Q7* mate.

42 Kt—Q7ch   K—K3

Here if *42 . . . K—Kt2 43 Kt—K5, K—B1 44 Kt×QBP, R—QB8 45 R×Kt, R×Kt 46 R—Q7* wins two Pawns.

43 Kt—B8ch   K—B3

The King has no choice. If *43 . . . K—Q3 44 R—Q7* is mate.

44 Kt—R7ch   K—K3

On *44 . . . K—Kt2 45 R×Kt, K×Kt 46 R×Pch* picks up a Pawn and wins.

45 Kt—Kt5ch   K—Q3

Black avoids *45 . . . K—B3,* the reply to which might be *46 P—B3* followed by *47 P—K4* and *48 P—K5ch,* with dangerous consequences.

46 R—Kt7   P—B3

Black misses his chance! He should play *46 ... P—KB4* instead, risky though it looks. If then *47 Kt—R7* (threatens *48 Kt—B8* and *49 R—Q7 mate) K—K3 48 Kt—B8ch, K—B3* (but not *48 ... K—B2* when *49 Kt×P, K×Kt 50 R×Kt* wins a Pawn) and Black holds on to his Pawns for the time being.

47 Kt—R7

A new attack on the Pawn, to which the reply *47 ... P—KB4* would be fatal. There would follow *48 Kt—B8* (threatens mate on the move) P—B4 (forced) *49 P×Pch, K×P 50 R×Kt*, and White has won a piece.

47 ...	K—K3
48 Kt—B8ch!	

Return tour for the Knight!

48 ...	K—B2

The only move to avoid mate or loss of the Knight.

49 Kt×P

Finally winning a Pawn!

49 ...	K×Kt
50 R×Kt	

The position still needs to be won, as Rook and Pawn endings often lead to a draw even with an extra Pawn.

This one is unusually instructive.

50 ...	K—B4
51 R—QB7	R—QB8
52 R—B8	K—Kt3
53 K—Kt3	R—B7
54 P—R4	K—B4
55 R—KR8	K—Kt3
56 P—B5ch	

Forces an exchange favorable to White. The doubled Pawn is dissolved, and he acquires a passed Pawn on the Rook file.

56 ...	K×P
57 R×Pch	K—Kt3
58 R—R8	K—B4
59 R—KKt8	

Cuts off the King from the passed Pawn.

59 ...	R—B8

The Rook tries to get behind the dangerous Pawn.

60 K—Kt2	R—QR8

Foiled in the attempt to get behind the Pawn, the Rook rushes over to head off its advance.

61 P—R5	R—R2
62 R—Kt3	

While this Rook, complying with Tarrasch's precept, prepares to support the Pawn from the rear.

62 ...	R—R2
63 R—R3	K—Kt4
64 K—B3!	

Allows Black to capture the Pawn, since the ensuing ending would be hopeless for him, viz: *64 ... R×P 65 R×Rch, K×R 66 K—B4, K—Kt3 67 K—Kt4, P—B4ch 68 K—B4, K—B3 69 P—B3* (the spare move that assures the win) *K—Kt3 70 K—K5, K—Kt4 71 K—Q6 K—R5 72 K×P, K—Kt 6 73 P—B 4*, and the rest is elementary.

64 ...	R—R3
65 R—R1	K—B4
66 K—Kt3	K—Kt4

Black fights hard. There is no hope in *66* ... K—K5 *67* K—Kt4, P—B4ch *68* K—Kt5, R—R1 *69* R—R4ch, K—B6 *70* R—B4ch followed by *71* P—R6.

| 67 R—R4 | K—B4 |
| 68 R—B4ch | K—Kt4 |

Time for a diagram!

69 R—Kt4ch!

Star move to win! Black must now either capture the Pawn, or allow White's King to reach R4.

69 ...   K—B4

The alternative is *69* ... K × P *70* R—R4ch, K—Kt4 *71* R × R, K × R *72* K—B4, K—Kt3 *73* K—Kt4, and White wins, as shown in an earlier note.

70 K—R4   R—R1

On *70* ... K—K3 instead, *71* R—Kt6 forces the blockader to retreat.

71 R—Kt7

Threatens *72* R—QB7, winning another Pawn.

71 ...   R—R1

The Rook tries once more to get behind the passed Pawn. Defending the Bishop Pawn instead by *71* ... R—QB1 succumbs to *72* P—R6, K—K5 *73* P—R7, R—KR1 (otherwise *74* R—Kt8 wins) *74* K—R5, P—KB4 *75* K—Kt6, and White wins.

72 P—R6	R—R8
73 R—Kt3	R—R8ch
74 R—R3	R—KKt8

Here too, Black must not exchange Rooks: *74* ... R × Rch *75* K × R, K—Kt3 *76* K—Kt4, K × P *77* K—B5, K—Kt2 *78* K—K6, and his Queen-side Pawns will fall.

It is White's turn to move, and if he is hasty, he can ruin everything. If he plays *75* P—R7, which looks as though it wins on the spot, Black rescues himself by *75* ...R—Kt5ch *76* K—R5, R—Kt4ch *77* K—R6, R—Kt3ch *78* K—R5, R—Kt4ch, and forces a draw by perpetual check.

Many masters, making an error of this sort, have killed themselves, or (even worse) given up chess.

75 R—B3ch   K—Kt3

This allows the exchange of Rooks, but on *75* ... K—K3 instead, there follows *76* P—R7, R—R8ch *77* R—R3, and White wins.

76 R—Kt3ch	R × R
77 K × R	K × P
78 K—Kt4	K—Kt3
79 K—B4	K—Kt2

If *79* ... P—B4 *80* K—K5, K—Kt4 *81* P—B3 K—Kt3 *82* P—B4, and Black must abandon his Pawn.

80 K—B5	K—B2
81 P—B3	

Black must now give way, and allow White's King to enter either at K6 or Kt6, with decisive effect.

If *81* ... K—Kt2, White plays *82* K—K6 and then gathers up the Queen-side Pawns. Or if *81* ...

K—K2, there follows *82* K—Kt6, K—K3 *83* P—B4, K—K2 (on *83* ... P—B4 *84* K—Kt5 wins the Pawn) *84* P—B5, and White wins the Pawn and the game.

81 ...	Resigns

A fine game, and one of which Evans can justifiably be proud.

INDEX OF OPENINGS

(The numbers refer to Games)

INDEX OF PLAYERS

(The numbers refer to Games)

A CATALOG OF SELECTED
DOVER BOOKS
IN ALL FIELDS OF INTEREST

A CATALOG OF SELECTED DOVER
BOOKS IN ALL FIELDS OF INTEREST

CONCERNING THE SPIRITUAL IN ART, Wassily Kandinsky. Pioneering work by father of abstract art. Thoughts on color theory, nature of art. Analysis of earlier masters. 12 illustrations. 80pp. of text. 5⅜ × 8½.   23411-8 Pa. $3.95

ANIMALS: 1,419 Copyright-Free Illustrations of Mammals, Birds, Fish, Insects, etc., Jim Harter (ed.). Clear wood engravings present, in extremely lifelike poses, over 1,000 species of animals. One of the most extensive pictorial sourcebooks of its kind. Captions. Index. 284pp. 9 × 12.   23766-4 Pa. $12.95

CELTIC ART: The Methods of Construction, George Bain. Simple geometric techniques for making Celtic interlacements, spirals, Kells-type initials, animals, humans, etc. Over 500 illustrations. 160pp. 9 × 12. (USO)   22923-8 Pa. $9.95

AN ATLAS OF ANATOMY FOR ARTISTS, Fritz Schider. Most thorough reference work on art anatomy in the world. Hundreds of illustrations, including selections from works by Vesalius, Leonardo, Goya, Ingres, Michelangelo, others. 593 illustrations. 192pp. 7⅛ × 10¼.   20241-0 Pa. $9.95

CELTIC HAND STROKE-BY-STROKE (Irish Half-Uncial from "The Book of Kells"): An Arthur Baker Calligraphy Manual, Arthur Baker. Complete guide to creating each letter of the alphabet in distinctive Celtic manner. Covers hand position, strokes, pens, inks, paper, more. Illustrated. 48pp. 8¼ × 11.
      24336-2 Pa. $3.95

EASY ORIGAMI, John Montroll. Charming collection of 32 projects (hat, cup, pelican, piano, swan, many more) specially designed for the novice origami hobbyist. Clearly illustrated easy-to-follow instructions insure that even beginning papercrafters will achieve successful results. 48pp. 8¼ × 11.   27298-2 Pa. $2.95

THE COMPLETE BOOK OF BIRDHOUSE CONSTRUCTION FOR WOOD-WORKERS, Scott D. Campbell. Detailed instructions, illustrations, tables. Also data on bird habitat and instinct patterns. Bibliography. 3 tables. 63 illustrations in 15 figures. 48pp. 5¼ × 8½.   24407-5 Pa. $1.95

BLOOMINGDALE'S ILLUSTRATED 1886 CATALOG: Fashions, Dry Goods and Housewares, Bloomingdale Brothers. Famed merchants' extremely rare catalog depicting about 1,700 products: clothing, housewares, firearms, dry goods, jewelry, more. Invaluable for dating, identifying vintage items. Also, copyright-free graphics for artists, designers. Co-published with Henry Ford Museum & Green-field Village. 160pp. 8¼ × 11.   25780-0 Pa. $9.95

HISTORIC COSTUME IN PICTURES, Braun & Schneider. Over 1,450 costumed figures in clearly detailed engravings—from dawn of civilization to end of 19th century. Captions. Many folk costumes. 256pp. 8⅜ × 11¾.   23150-X Pa. $11.95

ANATOMY: A Complete Guide for Artists, Joseph Sheppard. A master of figure drawing shows artists how to render human anatomy convincingly. Over 460 illustrations. 224pp. 8⅜ × 11¼. 27279-6 Pa. $10.95

MEDIEVAL CALLIGRAPHY: Its History and Technique, Marc Drogin. Spirited history, comprehensive instruction manual covers 13 styles (ca. 4th century thru 15th). Excellent photographs; directions for duplicating medieval techniques with modern tools. 224pp. 8⅜ × 11¼. 26142-5 Pa. $11.95

DRIED FLOWERS: How to Prepare Them, Sarah Whitlock and Martha Rankin. Complete instructions on how to use silica gel, meal and borax, perlite aggregate, sand and borax, glycerine and water to create attractive permanent flower arrangements. 12 illustrations. 32pp. 5⅜ × 8½. 21802-3 Pa. $1.00

EASY-TO-MAKE BIRD FEEDERS FOR WOODWORKERS, Scott D. Campbell. Detailed, simple-to-use guide for designing, constructing, caring for and using feeders. Text, illustrations for 12 classic and contemporary designs. 96pp. 5⅜ × 8½. 25847-5 Pa. $2.95

OLD-TIME CRAFTS AND TRADES, Peter Stockham. An 1807 book created to teach children about crafts and trades open to them as future careers. It describes in detailed, nontechnical terms 24 different occupations, among them coachmaker, gardener, hairdresser, lacemaker, shoemaker, wheelwright, copper-plate printer, milliner, trunkmaker, merchant and brewer. Finely detailed engravings illustrate each occupation. 192pp. 4⅝ × 6. 27398-9 Pa. $4.95

THE HISTORY OF UNDERCLOTHES, C. Willett Cunnington and Phyllis Cunnington. Fascinating, well-documented survey covering six centuries of English undergarments, enhanced with over 100 illustrations: 12th-century laced-up bodice, footed long drawers (1795), 19th-century bustles, 19th-century corsets for men, Victorian "bust improvers," much more. 272pp. 5⅝ × 8¼. 27124-2 Pa. $9.95

ARTS AND CRAFTS FURNITURE: The Complete Brooks Catalog of 1912, Brooks Manufacturing Co. Photos and detailed descriptions of more than 150 now very collectible furniture designs from the Arts and Crafts movement depict davenports, settees, buffets, desks, tables, chairs, bedsteads, dressers and more, all built of solid, quarter-sawed oak. Invaluable for students and enthusiasts of antiques, Americana and the decorative arts. 80pp. 6½ × 9¼. 27471-3 Pa. $7.95

HOW WE INVENTED THE AIRPLANE: An Illustrated History, Orville Wright. Fascinating firsthand account covers early experiments, construction of planes and motors, first flights, much more. Introduction and commentary by Fred C. Kelly. 76 photographs. 96pp. 8¼ × 11. 25662-6 Pa. $8.95

THE ARTS OF THE SAILOR: Knotting, Splicing and Ropework, Hervey Garrett Smith. Indispensable shipboard reference covers tools, basic knots and useful hitches; handsewing and canvas work, more. Over 100 illustrations. Delightful reading for sea lovers. 256pp. 5⅜ × 8½. 26440-8 Pa. $7.95

FRANK LLOYD WRIGHT'S FALLINGWATER: The House and Its History, Second, Revised Edition, Donald Hoffmann. A total revision—both in text and illustrations—of the standard document on Fallingwater, the boldest, most personal architectural statement of Wright's mature years, updated with valuable new material from the recently opened Frank Lloyd Wright Archives. "Fascinating"—*The New York Times*. 116 illustrations. 128pp. 9¼ × 10¾. 27430-6 Pa. $10.95

MY BONDAGE AND MY FREEDOM, Frederick Douglass. Born a slave, Douglass became outspoken force in antislavery movement. The best of Douglass' auto-biographies. Graphic description of slave life. 464pp. 5⅜ × 8½.　22457-0 Pa. $8.95

FOLLOWING THE EQUATOR: A Journey Around the World, Mark Twain. Fascinating humorous account of 1897 voyage to Hawaii, Australia, India, New Zealand, etc. Ironic, bemused reports on peoples, customs, climate, flora and fauna, politics, much more. 197 illustrations. 720pp. 5⅜ × 8½.　26113-1 Pa. $15.95

THE PEOPLE CALLED SHAKERS, Edward D. Andrews. Definitive study of Shakers: origins, beliefs, practices, dances, social organization, furniture and crafts, etc. 33 illustrations. 351pp. 5⅜ × 8½.　21081-2 Pa. $8.95

THE MYTHS OF GREECE AND ROME, H. A. Guerber. A classic of mythology, generously illustrated, long prized for its simple, graphic, accurate retelling of the principal myths of Greece and Rome, and for its commentary on their origins and significance. With 64 illustrations by Michelangelo, Raphael, Titian, Rubens, Canova, Bernini and others. 480pp. 5⅜ × 8½.　27584-1 Pa. $9.95

PSYCHOLOGY OF MUSIC, Carl E. Seashore. Classic work discusses music as a medium from psychological viewpoint. Clear treatment of physical acoustics, auditory apparatus, sound perception, development of musical skills, nature of musical feeling, host of other topics. 88 figures. 408pp. 5⅜ × 8½.　21851-1 Pa. $9.95

THE PHILOSOPHY OF HISTORY, Georg W. Hegel. Great classic of Western thought develops concept that history is not chance but rational process, the evolution of freedom. 457pp. 5⅜ × 8½.　20112-0 Pa. $9.95

THE BOOK OF TEA, Kakuzo Okakura. Minor classic of the Orient: entertaining, charming explanation, interpretation of traditional Japanese culture in terms of tea ceremony. 94pp. 5⅜ × 8½.　20070-1 Pa. $3.95

LIFE IN ANCIENT EGYPT, Adolf Erman. Fullest, most thorough, detailed older account with much not in more recent books, domestic life, religion, magic, medicine, commerce, much more. Many illustrations reproduce tomb paintings, carvings, hieroglyphs, etc. 597pp. 5⅜ × 8½.　22632-8 Pa. $10.95

SUNDIALS, Their Theory and Construction, Albert Waugh. Far and away the best, most thorough coverage of ideas, mathematics concerned, types, construction, adjusting anywhere. Simple, nontechnical treatment allows even children to build several of these dials. Over 100 illustrations. 230pp. 5⅜ × 8½.　22947-5 Pa. $7.95

DYNAMICS OF FLUIDS IN POROUS MEDIA, Jacob Bear. For advanced students of ground water hydrology, soil mechanics and physics, drainage and irrigation engineering, and more. 335 illustrations. Exercises, with answers. 784pp. 6⅛ × 9¼.　65675-6 Pa. $19.95

SONGS OF EXPERIENCE: Facsimile Reproduction with 26 Plates in Full Color, William Blake. 26 full-color plates from a rare 1826 edition. Includes "The Tyger," "London," "Holy Thursday," and other poems. Printed text of poems. 48pp. 5¼ × 7.　24636-1 Pa. $4.95

OLD-TIME VIGNETTES IN FULL COLOR, Carol Belanger Grafton (ed.). Over 390 charming, often sentimental illustrations, selected from archives of Victorian graphics—pretty women posing, children playing, food, flowers, kittens and puppies, smiling cherubs, birds and butterflies, much more. All copyright-free. 48pp. 9¼ × 12¼.　27269-9 Pa. $5.95

THE BEST TALES OF HOFFMANN, E. T. A. Hoffmann. 10 of Hoffmann's most important stories: "Nutcracker and the King of Mice," "The Golden Flowerpot," etc. 458pp. 5⅜ × 8½. 21793-0 Pa. $8.95

FROM FETISH TO GOD IN ANCIENT EGYPT, E. A. Wallis Budge. Rich detailed survey of Egyptian conception of "God" and gods, magic, cult of animals, Osiris, more. Also, superb English translations of hymns and legends. 240 illustrations. 545pp. 5⅜ × 8½. 25803-3 Pa. $11.95

FRENCH STORIES/CONTES FRANÇAIS: A Dual-Language Book, Wallace Fowlie. Ten stories by French masters, Voltaire to Camus: "Micromegas" by Voltaire; "The Atheist's Mass" by Balzac; "Minuet" by de Maupassant; "The Guest" by Camus, six more. Excellent English translations on facing pages. Also French-English vocabulary list, exercises, more. 352pp. 5⅜ × 8½. 26443-2 Pa. $8.95

CHICAGO AT THE TURN OF THE CENTURY IN PHOTOGRAPHS: 122 Historic Views from the Collections of the Chicago Historical Society, Larry A. Viskochil. Rare large-format prints offer detailed views of City Hall, State Street, the Loop, Hull House, Union Station, many other landmarks, circa 1904–1913. Introduction. Captions. Maps. 144pp. 9⅜ × 12¼. 24656-6 Pa. $12.95

OLD BROOKLYN IN EARLY PHOTOGRAPHS, 1865–1929, William Lee Younger. Luna Park, Gravesend race track, construction of Grand Army Plaza, moving of Hotel Brighton, etc. 157 previously unpublished photographs. 165pp. 8⅞ × 11¾. 23587-4 Pa. $13.95

THE MYTHS OF THE NORTH AMERICAN INDIANS, Lewis Spence. Rich anthology of the myths and legends of the Algonquins, Iroquois, Pawnees and Sioux, prefaced by an extensive historical and ethnological commentary. 36 illustrations. 480pp. 5⅜ × 8½. 25967-6 Pa. $8.95

AN ENCYCLOPEDIA OF BATTLES: Accounts of Over 1,560 Battles from 1479 B.C. to the Present, David Eggenberger. Essential details of every major battle in recorded history from the first battle of Megiddo in 1479 B.C. to Grenada in 1984. List of Battle Maps. New Appendix covering the years 1967–1984. Index. 99 illustrations. 544pp. 6½ × 9¼. 24913-1 Pa. $14.95

SAILING ALONE AROUND THE WORLD, Captain Joshua Slocum. First man to sail around the world, alone, in small boat. One of great feats of seamanship told in delightful manner. 67 illustrations. 294pp. 5⅜ × 8½. 20326-3 Pa. $5.95

ANARCHISM AND OTHER ESSAYS, Emma Goldman. Powerful, penetrating, prophetic essays on direct action, role of minorities, prison reform, puritan hypocrisy, violence, etc. 271pp. 5⅜ × 8½. 22484-8 Pa. $5.95

MYTHS OF THE HINDUS AND BUDDHISTS, Ananda K. Coomaraswamy and Sister Nivedita. Great stories of the epics; deeds of Krishna, Shiva, taken from puranas, Vedas, folk tales; etc. 32 illustrations. 400pp. 5⅜ × 8½. 21759-0 Pa. $9.95

BEYOND PSYCHOLOGY, Otto Rank. Fear of death, desire of immortality, nature of sexuality, social organization, creativity, according to Rankian system. 291pp. 5⅜ × 8½. 20485-5 Pa. $8.95

A THEOLOGICO-POLITICAL TREATISE, Benedict Spinoza. Also contains unfinished Political Treatise. Great classic on religious liberty, theory of government on common consent. R. Elwes translation. Total of 421pp. 5⅜ × 8½. 20249-6 Pa. $8.95

FRANK LLOYD WRIGHT'S HOLLYHOCK HOUSE, Donald Hoffmann. Lavishly illustrated, carefully documented study of one of Wright's most controversial residential designs. Over 120 photographs, floor plans, elevations, etc. Detailed perceptive text by noted Wright scholar. Index. 128pp. 9¼ × 10¾.
27133-1 Pa. $11.95

THE MALE AND FEMALE FIGURE IN MOTION: 60 Classic Photographic Sequences, Eadweard Muybridge. 60 true-action photographs of men and women walking, running, climbing, bending, turning, etc., reproduced from rare 19th-century masterpiece. vi + 121pp. 9 × 12. 24745-7 Pa. $10.95

1001 QUESTIONS ANSWERED ABOUT THE SEASHORE, N. J. Berrill and Jacquelyn Berrill. Queries answered about dolphins, sea snails, sponges, starfish, fishes, shore birds, many others. Covers appearance, breeding, growth, feeding, much more. 305pp. 5¼ × 8¼. 23366-9 Pa. $7.95

GUIDE TO OWL WATCHING IN NORTH AMERICA, Donald S. Heintzelman. Superb guide offers complete data and descriptions of 19 species: barn owl, screech owl, snowy owl, many more. Expert coverage of owl-watching equipment, conservation, migrations and invasions, etc. Guide to observing sites. 84 illustrations. xiii + 193pp. 5⅜ × 8½. 27344-X Pa. $8.95

MEDICINAL AND OTHER USES OF NORTH AMERICAN PLANTS: A Historical Survey with Special Reference to the Eastern Indian Tribes, Charlotte Erichsen-Brown. Chronological historical citations document 500 years of usage of plants, trees, shrubs native to eastern Canada, northeastern U.S. Also complete identifying information. 343 illustrations. 544pp. 6½ × 9¼. 25951-X Pa. $12.95

STORYBOOK MAZES, Dave Phillips. 23 stories and mazes on two-page spreads: Wizard of Oz, Treasure Island, Robin Hood, etc. Solutions. 64pp. 8¼ × 11.
23628-5 Pa. $2.95

NEGRO FOLK MUSIC, U.S.A., Harold Courlander. Noted folklorist's scholarly yet readable analysis of rich and varied musical tradition. Includes authentic versions of over 40 folk songs. Valuable bibliography and discography. xi + 324pp. 5⅜ × 8½. 27350-4 Pa. $7.95

MOVIE-STAR PORTRAITS OF THE FORTIES, John Kobal (ed.). 163 glamor, studio photos of 106 stars of the 1940s: Rita Hayworth, Ava Gardner, Marlon Brando, Clark Gable, many more. 176pp. 8⅜ × 11¼. 23546-7 Pa. $11.95

BENCHLEY LOST AND FOUND, Robert Benchley. Finest humor from early 30s, about pet peeves, child psychologists, post office and others. Mostly unavailable elsewhere. 73 illustrations by Peter Arno and others. 183pp. 5⅜ × 8½.
22410-4 Pa. $5.95

YEKL and THE IMPORTED BRIDEGROOM AND OTHER STORIES OF YIDDISH NEW YORK, Abraham Cahan. Film Hester Street based on Yekl (1896). Novel, other stories among first about Jewish immigrants on N.Y.'s East Side. 240pp. 5⅜ × 8½. 22427-9 Pa. $6.95

SELECTED POEMS, Walt Whitman. Generous sampling from *Leaves of Grass*. Twenty-four poems include "I Hear America Singing," "Song of the Open Road," "I Sing the Body Electric," "When Lilacs Last in the Dooryard Bloom'd," "O Captain! My Captain!"—all reprinted from an authoritative edition. Lists of titles and first lines. 128pp. 5$^{3}/_{16}$ × 8¼. 26878-0 Pa. $1.00

THE INFLUENCE OF SEA POWER UPON HISTORY, 1660–1783, A. T. Mahan. Influential classic of naval history and tactics still used as text in war colleges. First paperback edition. 4 maps. 24 battle plans. 640pp. 5⅜ × 8½.
25509-3 Pa. $12.95

THE STORY OF THE TITANIC AS TOLD BY ITS SURVIVORS, Jack Winocour (ed.). What it was really like. Panic, despair, shocking inefficiency, and a little heroism. More thrilling than any fictional account. 26 illustrations. 320pp. 5⅜ × 8½.
20610-6 Pa. $8.95

FAIRY AND FOLK TALES OF THE IRISH PEASANTRY, William Butler Yeats (ed.). Treasury of 64 tales from the twilight world of Celtic myth and legend: "The Soul Cages," "The Kildare Pooka," "King O'Toole and his Goose," many more. Introduction and Notes by W. B. Yeats. 352pp. 5⅜ × 8½.
26941-8 Pa. $8.95

BUDDHIST MAHAYANA TEXTS, E. B. Cowell and Others (eds.). Superb, accurate translations of basic documents in Mahayana Buddhism, highly important in history of religions. The Buddha-karita of Asvaghosha, Larger Sukhavativyuha, more. 448pp. 5⅜ × 8½. ,
25552-2 Pa. $9.95

ONE TWO THREE . . . INFINITY: Facts and Speculations of Science, George Gamow. Great physicist's fascinating, readable overview of contemporary science: number theory, relativity, fourth dimension, entropy, genes, atomic structure, much more. 128 illustrations. Index. 352pp. 5⅜ × 8½.
25664-2 Pa. $8.95

ENGINEERING IN HISTORY, Richard Shelton Kirby, et al. Broad, nontechnical survey of history's major technological advances: birth of Greek science, industrial revolution, electricity and applied science, 20th-century automation, much more. 181 illustrations. ". . . excellent . . ."—Isis. Bibliography. vii + 530pp. 5⅜ × 8¼.
26412-2 Pa. $14.95